Mosaic 1

Reading

Mosaic 1

Reading

4th Edition

Brenda Wegmann

Miki Knezevic

McGraw-Hill Contemporary

McGraw-Hill/Contemporary

A Division of The **McGraw·Hill** Companies

Mosaic 1 Reading, 4th Edition

Published by McGraw-Hill/Contemporary, a business unit of The McGraw-Hill Companies, Inc.,
1221 Avenue of the Americas, New York, NY 10020. Copyright © 2002, 1996, 1990, 1985 by
The McGraw-Hill Companies, Inc. All rights reserved. No part of this publication may be
reproduced or distributed in any form or by any means, or stored in a database or retrieval
system, without the prior written consent of The McGraw-Hill Companies, Inc., including,
but not limited to, in any network or other electronic storage or transmission, or broadcast
for distance learning.

Some ancillaries, including electronic and print components, may not be available to customers
outside the United States.

 This book is printed on recycled, acid-free paper containing 10% postconsumer waste.

3 4 5 6 7 8 9 0 CUS/CUS 0 9 8 7 6 5 4 3

ISBN 0-07-232979-3
ISBN 0-07-118021-4

Editorial director: *Tina B. Carver*
Series editor: *Annie Sullivan*
Developmental editor: *Louis Carrillo*
Director of marketing and sales: *Thomas P. Dare*
Project manager: *Sheila M. Frank*
Production supervisor: *Genevieve Kelley*
Coordinator of freelance design: *David W. Hash*
Interior designer: *Michael Warrell, Design Solutions*
Photo research coordinator: *John C. Leland*
Photo researcher: *Amelia Ames Hill Associates/Amy Bethea*
Compositor: *Point West, Inc.*
Typeface: *10.5/12 Times Roman*
Printer:

The credits section for this book begins on page 247 and is considered an extension of
the copyright page.

INTERNATIONAL EDITION ISBN 0-07-118021-4
Copyright © 2002. Exclusive rights by The McGraw-Hill Companies, Inc., for manufacture and
export. This book cannot be re-exported from the country to which it is sold by McGraw-Hill.
The International Edition is not available in North America.

www.mhcontemporary.com/interactionsmosaic

Mosaic 1
Reading

Mosaic 1 **Reading**

Boost your students' academic success!

Interactions Mosaic, 4th edition is the newly revised five-level, four-skill comprehensive ESL/EFL series designed to prepare students for academic content. The themes are integrated across proficiency levels and the levels are articulated across skill strands. The series combines communicative activities with skill-building exercises to boost students' academic success.

Interactions Mosaic, 4th edition features

- updated content
- five videos of authentic news broadcasts
- expansion opportunities through the Website
- new audio programs for the listening/speaking and reading books
- an appealing fresh design
- user-friendly instructor's manuals with placement tests and chapter quizzes

In This Chapter gives students a preview of the upcoming material.

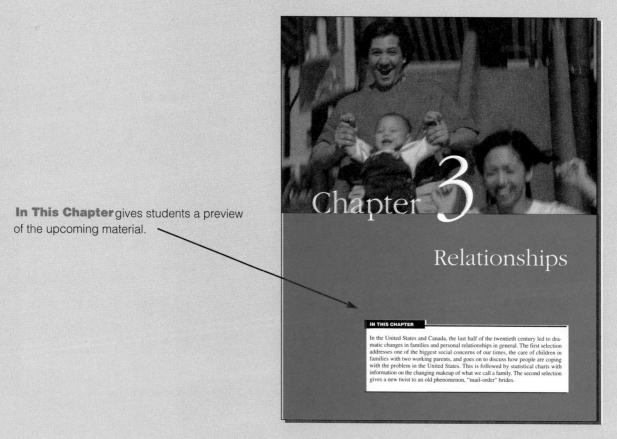

Chapter 3

Relationships

IN THIS CHAPTER

In the United States and Canada, the last half of the twentieth century led to dramatic changes in families and personal relationships in general. The first selection addresses one of the biggest social concerns of our times, the care of children in families with two working parents, and goes on to discuss how people are coping with the problem in the United States. This is followed by statistical charts with information on the changing makeup of what we call a family. The second selection gives a new twist to an old phenomenon, "mail-order" brides.

Timed Reading

Using Clustering for Speed and Comprehension

Did you recognize the three references that Bill Cosby made to literature: Mark Twain, *War and Peace*, and Shakespeare? Learn more about one of them as you practice the technique of clustering described in Cosby's article. (Reread this part if necessary, page 23.)

> This reading is taken from the Encyclopedia Britannica entry for Mark Twain. Read quickly to learn about the early life and works of this great author.

- Force your eyes to cluster the words rather than reading them one at a time
- After you read the selection, do the Comprehension Quiz that follows.
- Try to finish both in eight minutes. (Hint: Look over the quiz first to see what it covers.)

Twain, Mark, was the pen name of Samuel Langhorne Clemens (1835–1910), the United States' most famous humorist and the author of popular and outstanding autobiographical works, travel books, and novels. The first thirty-six years of Clemens' life gave him experiences as a boy in a little town in Missouri, as a steamboat pilot, as a reporter on the far western frontier, and as a traveler abroad—which he thereafter used as materials for his best and most successful writings.

He was born November 30, 1835, the... fifth child of John Marshall and Jane (Lampton) Clemens, both descendants of Virginians. His birthplace was Florida, Missouri, a village to which the family had moved the previous June. The boy's father, a storekeeper and at times a lawyer, had little talent for money-making and failed there as he had elsewhere. The Clemenses therefore moved in the fall of 1839 to Hannibal, Missouri.

Hannibal was the town of Sam Clemens' boyhood, destined to figure importantly in several of his finest books. Almost in the geographical center of the United States, it had the wide Mississippi River rolling past it on the east, and on the other sides were forests, farmlands, and prairie. The river was the route from and to the rest of the nation, bringing as it did all sorts of exciting visitors—river men, (religious) revivalists, circus troupes, ...migrants to points as far westward as California. The steamboats which Sam and his gang of boyhood friends watched wheeling past or docking at the wharf were endlessly fascinating. So, too, were

Photos and illustrations ensure comprehension by supporting the text.

Timed Readings give students specific strategies for improving their reading speed without sacrificing comprehension.

PART 1   ## Ethnocentrism

Before You Read

1   **Skimming for the Main Idea.** *Ethnocentrism* is a term commonly used by anthropologists, but the average English-speaking reader may not be familiar with it. In fact, the purpose of the whole selection is to give you an idea of what this term means and why it is important. Skim the first two paragraphs to find the author's explanation of *ethnocentrism* and write it here.

_____

_____

2   **Scanning for the Development of the Main Idea.** Scan the article to answer the following questions.

1. Like most readings taken from textbooks, this one is written in rather long paragraphs. How many of the seven paragraphs begin with a sentence containing the word *ethnocentrism*?
2. The main idea is the meaning and importance of ethnocentrism. It is developed through examples. Put a check in front of the aspects of human culture that are discussed in the reading as examples of ethnocentrism.
   - ____ choice of clothing
   - ____ food preferences
   - ____ language
   - ____ marriage ceremonies
   - ____ myths and folktales

3   Discuss these questions in small groups.

- What do you imagine when you think of anthropologists?
- Have you ever taken a course in anthropology or read an article about it?
- Why do you think people study this subject?

Read

> The following reading is taken from an anthropology textbook. Anthropology is defined in the dictionary as "the science that deals with the origins, physical and cultural development, racial characteristics, and social customs and beliefs of humankind."

Ethnocentrism

Culture shock can be an excellent lesson in relative values and in understanding human differences. The reason culture shock occurs is that we are not prepared for these differences. Because of the way we are taught our cul

Preliminary activities provide scaffolding to help students understand authentic language.

Introduction to readings builds background knowledge by giving students information on the writer and the source.

Varied genres include formal and informal essays, biographies, speeches, interviews, stories, and poetry.

Making Connections

Alone or with others, do one of the following projects.

- From the library or the Internet find out what different kinds of movies Spielberg makes and what themes he presents in them. Give the titles and a brief description of movies from each type. What themes are common in his work?
- Choose your favorite (or at least one that you like) Steven Spielberg movie. With facts from the Web or the library explain why you like it or show a short scene from the movie on video and tell why you liked that scene.
- Choose a film by Steven Spielberg that you do not like and follow the same procedure as in the previous instruction, except this time explain or show why you do not like it.

Talk It Over

In small groups, discuss the following questions.

1. In your opinion is the position of a child in the family (as oldest, youngest, and so on) important for the child's character? Explain.
2. Did luck play a role in Spielberg's becoming a director?
3. What are "old-fashioned values"? Are they necessary for good films?
4. Do you think there should be more censorship of films to eliminate a lot of the sex and violence? Why or why not?
5. What movie do you consider a creative work of art? Why?

What Do You Think?

Creativity in Men and Women

Margaret Mead, one of the most famous and widely read writers in the field of anthropology, expressed her ideas on creativity in men and women. In the two following paragraphs, she gives her opinion on why men have achieved more than women in almost every field throughout history. Read the selection by Mead and answer the questions that follow it.

Are Men More Creative Than Women?

Throughout history it has been men, for the most part, who have engaged in public life. Men have sought public achievement and recognition, while women have obtained their main satisfactions by bearing and rearing children. In women's eyes, public achievement makes a man more attractive as a marriage partner. But for men the situation is reversed. The more a woman achieves publicly, the less desirable she seems as a wife.

There are three possible positions one can take about male and female creativity. The first is that males are inherently more creative in all fields. The second is that if it were not for the greater appeal of creating

Making Connections and **Around the Globe** suggest research topics related to the chapter theme and give students new perspectives on culture.

Talk It Over and **What Do You Think?** encourage students to evaluate arguments and to do independent research related to the topic of the chapter.

Groupwork maximizes opportunities for discussion and negotiation.

After You Read

3 Selecting the Main Idea. The main idea of a piece of writing (a paragraph, an article, a book) brings together all or most of the different parts of that piece of writing. It does not express the idea of just one part.

Circle the number of the statement that you think best expresses the main idea of Bill Cosby's article. Why is it better than the other two?

1. Moving your eyes fast across each line will give you a general idea of the content of reading material in much less time than it would take to read every word.
2. It is necessary to choose your method of reading according to the kind of material you have to read and the amount of comprehension you need.
3. You should preview long and difficult readings, skim simple ones, and read in groups or clusters when you have to understand most of the material quite well.

4 More Prefixes. Here are three common prefixes used in words from the reading. See page 14 for an explanation of prefixes. Fill in the blanks with definitions of the words in italics.

1. The prefix *pre-* means "before." One of the reading techniques mentioned in the selection is previewing (line 35). What does *to preview* mean? _to look over a piece of writing before reading it._
2. The prefix *re-* means "again." The article talks about reviewing (line 54) material that you've read before. What does *to review* material mean? _____
3. The article also mentions the word *reread*. What does it mean to *reread* a reading selection? _____
4. The prefix *un-* means "not." Author Bill Cosby speaks of getting an overall view of long unfamiliar material (line 47)? What is *unfamiliar* material? _____
5. He also refers to cutting down on unnecessary reading. What is *unnecessary* reading? _____

5 Making New Words by Adding Prefixes. Form words by adding the appropriate prefix (*pre-, re-,* or *un-*) to each italicized word to fit the context.

1. These tickets do not need to be *paid* for now. They have already been _prepaid._
2. Don't *cook* those vegetables. The chef took the time to _____ them this morning.
3. We are looking for a *cooperative* sales clerk. The last one we had was very _____.
4. You didn't *do* the report very well. The boss wants you to _____ it.
5. My niece is too young to go to regular *school*. She goes to _____ every afternoon.
6. In sales you have to be *aware* of people's reactions, but the new man seems _____ that the clients don't like him.
7. They don't *run* new episodes of that TV show in the summer. What you'll see is a _____.

Skill development prepares students for standardized tests through skimming, scanning, main idea, paragraph and essay organization, supporting a position, and so on.

Vocabulary and language-learning strategies for synonyms, antonyms, context clues, and word families give students comprehension and self-assessment tools.

Focus on Testing

Doing the Easy Ones First

Tests include some items that are designed to be easy, some to be moderately difficult, and others to be hard. Usually students do the items in the order given. Sometimes they get stuck on one item and do not finish the test during the time limit. A good strategy is to quickly do the easy items first, skipping the ones that seem hard. Then go back and do the difficult ones.

Skim the following exercise to find the easy items that you can do right away. Which ones are they? Compare the item numbers you wrote with the ones selected by your classmates. Did you all choose the same ones? Now look at the remaining ones. What makes them harder?

Practice picking out hard items quickly and leaving them for later. Use this technique for exercises and tests in the future, and you will learn to "beat the clock."

Take a minute or two to look over your outline of the selection "Migration and Homing." Then test your understanding of the article by selecting the correct answers to complete the following statements.

1. After becoming mature, salmon swim back to spawn _____ .
   a. in the sea.
   b. in the same stream in which they were born
   c. in any one of hundreds of tributaries
2. Salmon are able to find their way back because of their good sense of _____.
   a. sight
   b. taste
   c. smell
3. Each year sooty terns fly from Africa to an island near Florida to nest, probably because _____.
   a. there is no food for birds on the nearby African shores
   b. they are safe there from animals that would eat them
   c. their wing muscles become developed from the flight
4. Caged starlings fly in the direction of their migration route on sunny days but make only nondirectional movements when there is no sun. This experiment suggests that the starlings _____ .
   a. navigate by an inborn compass
   b. fly only when it is warm
   c. use celestial clues for migration
5. Other experiments indicate that indigo buntings and certain other birds that fly at night navigate by _____ .
   a. the position of the stars

Focus on Testing prepares students for standardized tests by analyzing points of contrast, eliminating incorrect choices, reading between the lines, making inferences, and finding implied ideas in passages.

Video Activities: Internet Publishing

Before You Watch.

1. Match the words with their meanings.
   1. online   a. part of a story usually published in chronological order
   2. download   b. on the Internet
   3. installment   c. to move information from the Internet to your computer
2. Do you use the Internet? What do you use it for?

Watch. Circle the correct answers.

1. What kinds of things does William Bass download onto his computer?
   a. music   b. research   c. sports articles   d. pictures
2. What is true about Stephen King's book, *The Plant*?
   a. It was published online.   b. It was free.
   c. It was published in parts.   d. It was a bestseller.
3. According to William Bass, the best thing about books online is that they're _____
   a. cheap   b. convenient   c. easy to read
4. What did Stephen King threaten to do if not enough people paid for his book?
   a. charge more for the rest of the book
   b. not write another book online
   c. not finish rest of the book
5. Gillian McCombs says that electronic books will _____.
   a. help sell regular books
   b. let authors make more money
   c. never replace paper and ink books

Watch Again. Compare answers in small groups.

1. How much did Stephen King charge for *The Plant*? _____
2. What was the minimum percentage of paid downloads would Stephen King accept?
   a. 25%   b. 75%   c. 95%
3. The male publishing expert says that Stephen King's book will _____.
   a. be the death of paper and ink books
   b. not change the publishing industry
   c. not be a success

After You Watch. Find an article in which the writer gives his/her opinion about technology.

Video news broadcasts immerse students in authentic language, complete with scaffolding and follow-up activities to reinforce reading skills.

Don't forget to check out the new *Interactions Mosaic* Website at www.mhcontemporary.com/interactionsmosaic.

- ◼ Traditional practice and interactive activities
- ◼ Links to student and teacher resources
- ◼ Cultural activities
- ◼ Focus on Testing
- ◼ Activities from the Website are also provided on CD-ROM

Language	Critical Thinking Skills/Culture	Focus on Testing	Video Topics
■ Understanding compound words	■ Meeting and greeting ■ Social distance ■ Customs ■ Panhandling	■ Analyzing points of contrast	■ An Exchange Student
■ Understanding informal style ■ Understanding descriptive adjectives	Book censorship	■ Taking an objective test	■ High-Tech Jobs and Low-Tech People
■ Reading a chart	■ Roles in a relationship ■ Cross-cultural marriages ■ Adoption	■ Eliminating the incorrect choices	■ True Love
■ Understanding specialized vocabulary uses ■ Scanning charts	■ Smoking ■ Tourism and development	■ Analyzing compound words	■ Bottled Water
■ Using compound words ■ Writing supporting details ■ Paraphrasing	■ Benefits of technology ■ Traffic congestion	■ Computerized testing	■ Internet Publishing
■ Understanding irony	■ Shopping on the Internet	■ Reading between the lines	■ Welfare Payments
■ Forming related words ■ Comparing and contrasting	■ Leadership	■ Previewing the questions	■ Overcoming Serious Illness
■ Understanding suspense ■ Identifying synonyms from parallel constructions	■ Innovation in architecture ■ Movie censorship ■ Creativity in men and women	■ Making inferences to answer "tricky" questions	■ A Life of Painting

Language	Critical Thinking Skills/Culture	Focus on Testing	Video Topics
■ Understanding figurative language	■ Culture shock ■ Personal responsibility	■ Finding statements and implied ideas in passages	■ People Skills
■ Understanding compound words ■ Analyzing a line of argument ■ Interpreting charts	■ Analyzing the cause of crime ■ The death penalty	■ Judging something true or false	■ Victim Support Groups
■ Imagining historical contexts ■ Understanding poetic prose	■ Spiritual power ■ Experimenting on animals ■ Littering	■ Doing the easy ones first	■ Air Pollution
■ Understanding essays ■ Understanding poetry ■ Understanding speeches ■ Understanding stories	■ Friendship ■ Political goals ■ Future of books	■ Developing analytical, inferential, and critical-thinking skills	■ An Endangered Species

Chapter 1

New Challenges

IN THIS CHAPTER

People from all over the world see "the American lifestyle" represented in Holly-wood movies and television programs. The truth about how Americans live is more complex. The United States has many distinct regions and citizens from diverse backgrounds. The first reading in this chapter gives facts about this huge country and discusses some of the customs and attitudes of its people. The second reading presents facts about Canada, also a large and diverse nation, and offers one view of Canadians and the qualities that make them different from their neighbors to the south.

Living in the U.S.A.

Before You Read

1   **Reading Without Knowing the Meaning of Every Word.** The following article probably contains a number of words you do not know. This is not surprising. Linguists tell
us that, for historical reasons, English has a larger vocabulary than any other known
language. Practice the important skill of reading without knowing the meaning of every
word by following these three steps:

1.   Look over the article quickly, paying attention to the headings of the sections and
trying to get a general idea of the contents of each one.
2.   Read the article for the main ideas. Skip words and phrases you do not understand.
Do not slow yourself down by looking up words in a dictionary. Keep going.
3.   Do the post-reading exercise, Recalling Information. If you have trouble with it,
read the article (or parts of it) again. Two or three quick readings are better for understanding than one slow one. If you can do the exercise, you have read well
enough for your present purpose.

> The following selections are taken from *Living in the U.S.A.*, a book written by
> Alison Raymond Lanier and updated after her death by Charles William Gay.
> What purpose do you think the authors had for writing this book? Perhaps you
> will be surprised by some of the facts given about the United States and its
> people.

Read

Living in the U.S.A.

Size

It is difficult to really experience or "feel" the size of the United States, even
when you know the actual number of miles from coast to coast. To get the full
impact you should realize, for example, that it takes forty-eight hours (two en-
5   tire days and two long nights) to travel by train from Chicago to Los Angeles,
rolling along hour after hour across wheat fields, mountains, and deserts;
Chicago is an overnight train trip from New York.

Another way to think about it is to compare distances in the United States
with others more familiar to you. For example, New York to Washington, D.C.,
10   is about the same as London to Paris or Nairobi to Mombasa or Tokyo to
Kyoto; New York to Los Angeles is farther than Lisbon to Cairo or Moscow to
Montreal or New Delhi to Rome.

Climate

Naturally, with such distances, the climate in the continental United States is
15   also one of great extremes. From New England and New York through

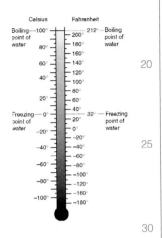

20

25

30

35

40

45

50

55

60

Chicago and much of the Midwest and Northwest, temperatures vary from subzero in winter to the high nineties or over in summer (Fahrenheit).

The South and Southwest have warmer weather, though even these sections have occasional frosts and periods of moderate cold. Generally, summers are likely to range from 70° F to 100° F (21° C to 38° C), and many areas can be quite humid. However, air conditioning is so widespread that you can expect most buildings—even many private homes—to be kept at relatively comfortable temperatures.

Americans in Motion

Americans are a restless people. Most travel whenever they get the chance. They crowd onto trains, buses, and planes. In increasing numbers, they hike with packs on their backs or ride bicycles, heading for the mountains, seashore, or national parks. Highways are jammed with cars, especially on holidays. Americans are joined by millions of tourists from other countries who come to enjoy the people and the culture.

Blunt Speech

Don't think that Americans are being rude if we tend to speak in monosyllables or answer with a mere "O.K.," "Sure," or "Nope" or greet you with "Hi." Our brevity is not a personal insult, though to those accustomed to formal phrases, we seem blunt. American informality has become more desirable than formal expressions of greeting or farewell.

A Do-It-Yourself Society

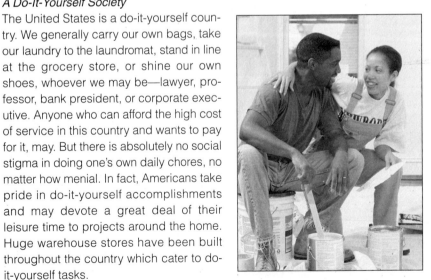

The United States is a do-it-yourself country. We generally carry our own bags, take our laundry to the laundromat, stand in line at the grocery store, or shine our own shoes, whoever we may be—lawyer, professor, bank president, or corporate executive. Anyone who can afford the high cost of service in this country and wants to pay for it, may. But there is absolutely no social stigma in doing one's own daily chores, no matter how menial. In fact, Americans take pride in do-it-yourself accomplishments and may devote a great deal of their leisure time to projects around the home. Huge warehouse stores have been built throughout the country which cater to do-it-yourself tasks.

Many Americans who could afford household help or a driver or a gardener do not employ them. They prefer family privacy, independence, and freedom from responsibility, all of which are at least partially lost when one has help in one's home.

65   Houses interest Americans greatly. They spend much of their time thinking and reading and talking about the design of houses, their decorations,
how to improve them. Many weekend hours are passed in do-it-yourself projects around the house. People also love to look at each other's houses. Since
they would thoroughly enjoy visiting and examining a house in another coun-
70   try, they assume that you will probably have the same desire. Don't be surprised, therefore, if you are shown the entire house from top to bottom,
including bathrooms and closets! Don't make the mistake of refusing: the
whole house may have been cleaned especially for you!

    Because our people have come from so many nationalities, there is a far
75   wider range of what is acceptable than in some countries where the inhabitants have grown up with a common heritage. As a result, no one needs to
feel awkward or uncomfortable in following his or her own customs. Although
Americans are noticeably informal, if you prefer somewhat greater formality,
feel free to act in your own way. This will be acceptable to those around you.
80   You can "do your own thing" and be respected here to a very large extent.

After You Read

2 **Recalling Information.** Mark each of these sentences with a T (for true) or F (for false).
Correct the false statements to make them true.

_____T_____ 1. The United States has a varied geography, including fields, mountains,
and deserts.

_____ 2. Its continental climate is basically one of moderation.

_____ 3. Its people are not very active and spend most of their time watching
television.

_____ 4. They are rude and like to insult others with simple direct words.

_____ 5. Americans are very interested in their homes and love to show them
off, even to people they don't know very well.

_____ 6. Americans spend a lot of time thinking and talking about projects to fix
up their homes.

_____ 7. They send their servants to huge warehouse stores to buy house decorations.

_____ 8. Americans come from many different nationalities.

_____ 9. They generally prefer formality and do not like people to be informal.

3 **Analyzing Topic Sentences.** An important skill for reading is finding the main idea.
Often the main idea of a paragraph is stated directly. The sentence that states the main
idea is called the topic sentence. The topic sentence is usually (but not always) the first
sentence of the paragraph. The other sentences support or develop the paragraph in different ways:

a. by giving examples or details to illustrate the main idea

b. by expanding upon it with related ideas

c. by expressing an emotional reaction to the main idea.

Analyze the topic sentences of the first five paragraphs of the previous reading.

1. The topic sentences of the first five paragraphs are always the first sentence. True or false?

2. The first three paragraphs develop the topic sentence in the same way. Which way is that: a, b, or c?

3. The fourth and fifth paragraphs also use that same way, but finish up with one other way in their last sentence. Which way do they use to finish up: a, b, or c?

4. What punctuation mark indicates an emotional reaction? Look through the rest of the article and find the paragraph that uses method c (expressing an emotional reaction) to finish up. What are the first four words of that paragraph?

4   **Getting the Meaning of Words from Context.** The *context* of something is its surroundings or situation. The context of a word is what goes before it and after it. You can often guess the meaning of a new word by reading past it to the next sentence. If the meaning is still unclear, read the sentence before the word. If necessary, read the whole paragraph. Then go back and try to understand the word again.
Practice this skill by choosing the best definition for each word.

1.	*blunt* (lines 37, 41)	a. loud and rude	b. short and direct	c. personal and formal
2.	*stigma* (line 53)	a. new rule	b. good word	c. negative mark
3.	*leisure* (line 57)	a. not working	b. work	c. family
4.	*chores* (line 53)	a. tasks	b. accounts	c. pastimes
5.	*menial* (line 54)	a. difficult	b. attractive	c. low
6.	*thoroughly* (line 69)	a. somewhat	b. completely	c. possibly
7.	*assume* (line 70)	a. hope	b. believe	c. fear
8.	*refusing* (line 72)	a. saying yes	b. saying no	c. not saying anything
9.	*heritage* (line 76)	a. history and tradition	b. physical appearance	c. economics and class

5   **Six Useful Suffixes.** A suffix is a letter or group of letters put at the end of a word to form a new word. For example, suffixes can make a noun (person, place or thing) out of a verb (action word) or an adjective (a word that describes a noun) out of a noun. Study the meanings of the following suffixes and fill in the second example for each one.

- **-able** The suffix *-able* means relating to the action of a verb. It makes adjectives out of verbs. Something you can love is *loveable*. A house you can afford is an <u>affordable</u> house.

- **-al** The suffix *-al* means relating to some object or thing. It makes adjectives out of nouns. Things that relate to nature are *natural* things. A job you get for only one season of the year is a _____ job.

- **-ant** The suffix *-ant* means a person who does the action of the verb. It makes nouns out of verbs. A person who serves is a *servant*. A person who applies for something is an _____.

- **-er** The suffix *-er* means a person who is capable of doing the action of the verb. It makes nouns out of verbs. A person who can bake is a *baker*. A person who can teach is a _____.

- **-ity** The suffix *-ity* means the state or condition of some quality. It makes a noun out of an adjective. A material that is elastic has *elasticity*. People who are cordial are known for their _____.

- **-less** The suffix *-less* means "without." It makes adjectives out of nouns. A situation without hope is a *hopeless* situation. A person who is causing no harm is a _____ person.

6   **Making New Words by Adding Suffixes.** Form words used in the reading by adding suffixes from the list on page 5. Check your answers by finding the words in the reading. The example is not from the reading.

1. A person who *settles* (comes to live) in a place is a ___settler___.
2. A person who *gardens* (works in a garden) is a _____. (line 61)
3. A person who *drives* is a _____. (line 61)
4. A chair that gives a lot of *comfort* is a _____ chair. (line 24)
5. Some groups of people are *formal*. They are known for their _____. (line 78)
6. Other groups of people are *informal*. They are known for their _____. (line 41)
7. The people who *inhabit* a region are the _____ of that region. (line 75)
8. We *accept* certain ways of acting. Those ways are _____ to us. (line 79)
9. They take that trip only on certain *occasions*. They take an _____ trip. (line 19)
10. A quality we all *desire* to have is a _____ quality. (line 41)
11. Some information relates especially to just one *person*. It is his or her _____ information. (line 40)
12. We are *responsible* for our employees. They are our _____. (line 63)
13. Many Americans participate in numerous activities without much *rest*. They are a _____ people. (line 27).
14. Weather patterns that affect a whole *continent* are _____ weather patterns. (line 14)
15. A speaker sometimes gives a *brief* speech. If we are tired, we appreciate his or her _____. (line 40) (Notice that there is a spelling change in this one.)
16. Part of our identity relates to our *national* origin. We call that our _____. (line 74)

7   **Getting the Meaning of Combination Words.** Some English words are made up of smaller words joined together with hyphens. The reading refers to the *do-it-yourself* projects that Americans love. Guess the meaning of the words in italics by looking at the shorter words inside them and the general context. Write explanations in the blanks.

1. Kim wanted to buy a CD with some *easy-listening* music. _music that is soft and easy to listen to_
2. My friend can't go out until he finishes his *to-do* list. _____
3. The bookstore has a big section of *self-help* books. _____
4. Her brother always helps people out; he's a real *do-gooder*. _____

Other English words are combinations of shorter words without hyphens. These are usually called compound words. The word *bedroom* is an example. It is the room with a bed, the room for sleeping. Guess the meanings of the words in italics taken from the reading and write explanations in the blanks.

1. Chicago is an *overnight* train trip from New York. _____
2. Air conditioning is *widespread*. _____
3. They do not use long formal expressions of greeting or *farewell*. _____
4. People in the U.S. go to the mountains, *seashore*, or national parks to hike. _____
5. Many Americans do not have *household* help. _____

Around the Globe

Working with a classmate, look at the drawings to find out more about customs in the United States and around the world. Take turns reading aloud the descriptions beneath the drawings. Then, follow the directions and answer the questions after each one.

1. Meeting and Greeting

In some cultures people bow to each other when they meet, or fold their hands together in front of their faces and incline their heads. (This is called *namaste* in India and *wai* in Thailand.) In other places, people embrace when they meet or exchange a quick kiss on the cheek. Americans often shake hands, but don't be surprised if they don't. They sometimes just nod and smile. A casual "Hi" or "How ya' doin'?" or "Hello, there" often takes the place of a formal handshake, but it means the same thing. If a person extends her or his hand in greeting, then it is polite to shake hands.

What do you think of these ways of greeting? Which one is similar to the customs in your culture(s)? With your classmates, practice greeting each other American-style and also in some other way.

2. Social Distance

The "comfort zone," or the distance people stand from each other when they talk, varies among different cultures. Asians stand quite far apart when they talk. Greeks, Arabs, and South Americans stand quite close together. Often, they move closer as the conversation heats up. Americans are somewhere in the middle. Studies show that they feel most comfortable in conversation when standing about 21 inches apart from each other.

How far apart do people usually stand when having a conversation in your culture(s)? Stand up and play the role of two people talking about the weather. First pretend you are in Asia, then in Greece and then in the United States. Which distance feels most comfortable to you?

3. Personal Questions

What questions are polite for a first meeting? This varies greatly depending on where you live. Look at the following questions and decide which ones would be polite and which would be impolite for a first meeting in your culture(s).

1.   Where are you from?
2.   How much did you pay for your jacket?
3.   What do you do for a living?
4.   How much do you earn?
5.   Are you married?

6. How old are you?
7. Do you have any children?
8. What is your religion?

How many of these questions are impolite in your culture(s)? Half of them are generally considered impolite in American culture. Can you guess which ones? (Answers on page 17.)

8 **Talking About Preferences.** "Living in the U.S.A." describes some American customs and attitudes. Of course, these would not apply to all Americans. There are cultural preferences and personal preferences. In small groups, talk about the following U.S. customs and attitudes. Which do you each agree with personally, and why?

1. the use of air conditioning in homes and public buildings
2. hiking with backpacks in the mountains
3. blunt speech
4. informal dinners in private homes
5. informality in the workplace
6. doing things for yourself and not having live-in servants in your home

Talk It Over

1. What American customs seem strange to you?
2. What customs in your own country might seem strange to visitors from the United States?
3. Do you agree with the common proverb about travel: "When in Rome, do as the Romans do"? Why or why not?

"Oddly enough, language has proved no problem."

Punch/London

Cartoon by Ken Mahood. Reproduced by permission of Punch, from *Best Cartoons of the World II Atlas.*

PART 2

My Country

Before You Read

1 **Getting the Meaning of Words from Context and Structure.** Use the context (Activity 4, page 5) to choose the correct definition for each italicized word or phrase taken from the reading. Some of the words are combination words (Activity 7, page 6), and some contain a suffix (Activity 5, page 5). Underline the correct definition.

1. Berton says that to a stranger the land must seem *endless*. (line 1) *Endless* means (full of variety/<u>stretching out in all directions</u>).

2. It is the *vastness* of Canada that surprises people. (line 3) *Vastness* means (beauty/large size).

3. The *observant* visitor will note some differences. (line 7) This means the visitor who (looks around/asks questions).

4. The national *makeup* (line 8) refers to the Canadian (economy/character).

5. Berton talks about the American *melting pot*. (line 9) This means a society of people who become very (similar/different).

6. In July and August, eastern Canadians suffer in the heat and *humidity*. (line 15) *Humidity* means (wetness/dryness).

7. A *newcomer* (line 9) is someone who (wants to arrive/has just arrived).

8. Canada did not have a Civil War, but it did have some *uprisings*. (line 29) Uprisings are (big revolutions/small battles).

9. The *lawmen* (line 34) are (robbers and murderers/sheriffs and policemen).

10. The author says that Americans are more *outgoing* than Canadians. (line 44) This means they are not as (shy/loud) as Canadians.

11. The *French-style* cooking of Quebec (line 64) means food prepared (for French people/in the French way).

12. If I talk about my *countrymen* (line 77), I mean people (who do not live in the city/who have the same nationality as I do).

Read

2 **Finding Implied Main Ideas.** Sometimes the main idea of a paragraph is not stated directly. There is no topic sentence. The main idea is implied (suggested by the facts and ideas). A main idea brings together all or most of the different parts of the paragraph. It does not express just one part.

> The following selection by Pierre Berton, one of Canada's leading writers, is a good example of paragraphs with implied main ideas. Most of its paragraphs do not have topic sentences. The main ideas are implied. Practice the skill of finding implied main ideas by analyzing the first five paragraphs of this selection.

Read each paragraph and the three phrases that follow it. Choose the letter of the one that best expresses the main idea. Write its letter in the blank.

My Country (excerpts)

To a stranger, the land must seem endless. A herring gull, winging its way from St. John's, Newfoundland, to Victoria on the southern tip of Vancouver Island, will travel as far as the distance from London to Baghdad. It is the vastness that startles the imagination of all who visit my country.

1. __b__

   a.   Canada is strange and surprising.

   b.   Canada is very, very big.

   c.   Canada is hard to know.

5   Contrary to common belief, we do not live in snow-covered cabins far from civilization. Most of us inhabit cities that do not seem to differ greatly from those to the south of us. The observant visitor, however, will note some differences. The variety of our national makeup is, I believe, more pronounced than it is in the American melting pot. A newcomer in the United States quickly

10   learns to cover up his or her origins and become an American. A newcomer to Canada manages to keep something of the culture and customs of his or her ethnic background.

2. _____

    a. Canadians appear to others as simple people who inhabit snow-covered cabins in the woods.

    b. Canadians live in almost exactly the same way as Americans live but really there are differences.

    c. All Canadians seem alike but they have more variety in their customs and culture than Americans.

15 | Traditionally, the stranger has thought of Canada as a mountainous, snow-swept land. Certainly it can get very cold in Canada. Few non-Canadians understand that it can also get very hot. The eastern cities suffer in the humidity of July and August, and people actually die each year from the heat. In Victoria, roses bloom on Christmas Day.

3. _____

    a. It can get very cold in Canada.

    b. It can get very hot in Canada.

    c. Roses can bloom on Christmas day.

20 | Where temperature is concerned we are a country of extremes; and yet, as a people, we tend toward moderation and even conservatism. Non-Canadians think we are the same as our American neighbors, but we are not really like the Americans. Our temperament, our social attitudes, our environment, and our history make us a different kind of North American.

4. _____

    a. People think Canadians are like Americans, but they are really more conservative and moderate.

    b. Canada is a country of extremes, both in its temperatures and in the character of its people.

    c. The Canadian temperament is like the American one because of social attitudes, environment, and history.

25 | First, there is the matter of our history. It has been called dull because it is not very bloody. We are, after all, the only people in all the Americas who did not separate violently from Europe. We have had three or four small uprisings but no

30 | revolution or civil war.

5. _____

    a. Canadian history is dull.

    b. Canadian history is bloody.

    c. Canadian history is not violent.

We were slow to give up our colonial ties to England. While the Americans chose freedom, we chose order. Our lawmen are ap-

35 pointed from above, not elected from below. The idea of choosing town marshals and county sheriffs by vote to keep the peace with guns never fitted into the Canadian scheme of things. Instead, we invented the North West Mounted Police. The Canadian symbol of the Mountie, neat and clean in his scarlet coat, contrasts with the American symbol of the lawman in his open shirt and

40 gun-belt. The two differing social attitudes persist to this day. In the United States the settlers moved across the continent before law—hence the "wild" west. In Canada the law came first; settlement followed.

Outward displays of emotion are not part of the Canadian style. We are after all a northern people. The Americans are far more outgoing than we are.

45 One reason for this, I think, is the very real presence of nature in our lives. Most of us live within a few hours' drive of the wilderness. No Canadian city is far removed from those mysterious and silent places which can have such an effect on the human soul.

There is another

50 aspect of my country that makes it unique in the Americas, and that is our bilingual and bicultural makeup.

55 (Canada has two official languages, English and French, and in its largest province a majority of the inhabi-

60 tants speak French almost exclusively.) It gives us a picturesque

quality, of course, and that certainly helps tourism: Visitors are attracted to the "foreignness" of Quebec City, with its twisting streets and its French-style

65 cooking. But there is also a disturbing regional tension. Quebec has become a nation within a nation, and the separatist movement is powerful there.

Canadians are not anti-American. We watch American television programs. We tend to prefer American-made cars over the European and Asian products. We welcome hundreds of thousands of American tourists to our

70 country every year and don't complain much when they tell us that we're exactly the same as they are.

Of course, we're not the same. But the visitor may be pardoned for thinking so when he or she first crosses the border. The buildings in our cities are designed in the international styles. The brand names in the supermarkets are

75 all familiar. It is only after several days that the newcomer begins to sense a difference. He cannot put his finger on that difference, but then, neither can many of my countrymen. The only thing we are really sure of is that we are not Americans.

After You Read

3 **Comprehending the Reading.** Mark the following statements T (true) or F (false), according to Pierre Berton. Correct the false statements to make them true.

_____ 1. Most Canadians live in snow-covered cabins far from civilization.

_____ 2. In Canada, newcomers keep more of their original country's customs and culture than do newcomers in the United States.

_____ 3. Canada is a very cold country, even in the summertime.

_____ 4. The history of Canada is more bloody and violent than the history of the United States.

_____ 5. Generally speaking, Canadians are more conservative than Americans.

_____ 6. The "wild west," with its guns and sheriffs with open shirts, was an important part of American and Canadian history.

_____ 7. Canadians express their emotions more openly than Americans do.

_____ 8. The United States has only one official language, but Canada has two.

_____ 9. In general, Canadians are anti-American, and Americans are anti-Canadian.

_____ 10. Canadian buildings, food, and businesses look very different from those in the United States.

4 **Words With the Prefixes *anti-* and *non-*.** A prefix is a group of letters at the beginning of a word that changes its meaning.

In "My Country," there are two words with hyphens that have the prefixes *non-* and *anti-* in them: *non-Canadians* and *anti-American*. (These prefixes are also used at times without hyphens.)

The prefix *non-* means "not." So *non-Canadians* are "people who are not Canadians."

The prefix *anti-* means "against" So being *anti-American* means being "against Americans or things associated with Americans."

Using these examples as models, write definitions for the following words:

1. nonresidents _____ *people who are not residents* _____
2. anti-anxiety pills _____ *pills that work against anxiety* _____
3. an antiwar protest _____
4. a nonviolent group _____
5. non-Germans _____
6. non-Mexicans _____
7. an anticommunist _____
8. nonvoters _____
9. antimonopoly laws _____
10. nonpayment _____

5   **Four More Suffixes.** Here are more common suffixes to add to your knowledge of English words. Study them and fill in the second example for each one. If necessary, review the explanation of suffixes on page 5.

1. The suffix *-ation* means the "process or condition of some action or quality." If a couple is in the process of separating, they are going through a <u>separation</u> . If you are in the process of decorating, you are involved in _____.

2. The suffix *-ful* means "full of or characterized by a certain quality." It makes adjectives out of nouns. Something full of beauty is <u>beautiful</u>. Something that can cause a lot of harm is _____.

3. The suffix *-ment* means "something that results from the action of a verb." It makes nouns out of verbs. The things that people accomplish are <u>accomplishments</u>. The group of people who govern are members of the _____.

4. The suffix *-ous* means "having or being full of some quality." People who are full of fury become <u>furious</u>. A moment that is full of glory is a _____ moment.

6   **Making New Words by Adding Suffixes.** Form words used in the reading by adding suffixes from the previous activity. Check your answers by finding the words in the reading. Line numbers are given in parentheses.

1. Our surroundings are our environs. Everything that is around us is our _____*environment*_____. (line 21)

2. Some countries are hard to imagine. It is difficult to see them in our _____. (line 4)

3. The head of that corporation has a lot of power, and he also has many _____ friends. (line 66)

4. Some people are moderate. They show _____ in their reactions. (line 19)

5. The place that settlers come to live is a _____. (line 42)

6. North America is filled with mountains, and its _____ regions attract many tourists. (line 13)

7. Many of the people who want to separate from their nation are on the move, and hope to build a strong separatist _____. (line 66)

8. Certain natural spots seem full of mystery and their _____ atmosphere can have a strong effect on the human soul. (line 47)

Talk It Over

1. What countries in the Americas did not separate violently from a European colonial power? What effect did this have on the national character of the people?

2. What is special about Quebec, the biggest of the ten provinces of Canada?

3. How many official languages does Canada have? In your opinion, does it make a country weak or strong to have more than one official language?

4. Does a newcomer to your native culture have to cover up his or her origins? Do different groups keep some of their own culture or customs?

5. In your opinion, is there a connection between climate or geography and national character? Do these connections exist in your native country?

Focus on Testing

Analyzing Points of Contrast

When you take a standardized test, you may be asked to analyze points of contrast. A contrast means showing the differences between two things (people, places, objects, or ideas). The differences are the points of contrast.

To Analyze Points of Contrast

- Fix firmly in your mind the two things that are being contrasted.
- Look carefully for the points of contrast, the ways in which the two are different.
- Ask yourself for each point, how exactly they differ.
- Try to see what the overall idea of the contrast is.

Practice this skill by analyzing the points of contrast shown in the following paragraph from the essay "My Country" by Pierre Berton. Read the paragraph. Then mark an X to indicate whether each point refers to Canadian or American society.

> We were slow to give up our colonial ties to England. While the Americans chose freedom, we chose order. Our lawmen are appointed from above, not elected from below. The idea of choosing town marshals and county sheriffs by vote to keep the peace with guns never fitted into the Canadian scheme of things. Instead, we invented the North West Mounted Police. The Canadian symbol of the Mountie, neat and clean in his scarlet coat, contrasts with the American symbol of the lawman in his open shirt and gun-belt. The two differing social attitudes persist to this day. In the United States the settlers moved across the continent before law—hence the "wild" west. In Canada the law came first; settlement followed.

		Canadian	American
1.	freedom rather than order	_____	_____
2.	the neat and clean Mountie	_____	_____
3.	order instead of freedom	_____	_____
4.	sheriffs elected by vote	_____	_____
5.	keeping the peace with guns	_____	_____
6.	lawmen appointed from above	_____	_____
7.	settlement before law	_____	_____
8.	law before settlement	_____	_____
9.	lawmen in scarlet coats	_____	_____
10.	the "wild" west	_____	_____

Now that you have examined some points of contrast, circle the number of the statement that best expresses the main or overall idea of the contrast. If needed, review the steps for finding the main idea, page 4.

1. Canadians and Americans have two different attitudes that persist to this day because in Canada settlement came first and was followed by the law, but in the United States the law came before the settlers.
2. The image of the neat and clean Mountie in his scarlet coat appears in direct contrast to the American symbol of the town marshal or sheriff in his open shirt, who keeps the peace with guns.
3. The relatively nonviolent history of Canada and the rough gun-carrying tradition of the U.S. west are responsible for great differences in thinking and acting between the two societies.

What Do You Think?

Panhandling

Visitors to the United States and certain parts of Canada are often shocked to see individuals on the sidewalks with hands outstretched asking for money. Some of these panhandlers (people begging for money in public places) are just lazy and don't want to work, but most of them are homeless or mentally ill. Many people blame the lack of affordable housing and say that it is a disgrace in such rich countries to have so many people with nowhere to live.

Although there is some sympathy for these people, there's a concern that public spaces are being taken over by homeless beggars. In many big cities, people who live and work in these areas say they will contribute to charities to help the homeless but do not want to be bothered on the street. They want laws to prevent panhandling. What do you think? Should there be laws against begging in public places? Why or why not? Who should help these homeless people?

Answers to Around the Globe, no. 3 (page 8): Questions no. 2, 4, 6, and 8 are generally considered impolite in American culture.

Video Activities: An Exchange Student

Before You Watch. Discuss these questions in small groups.

1. What is an exchange student?
2. What problems do you think exchange students might have?

Watch. Circle the correct answers.

1. Where is Adáh from?
    a. the United States   b. Switzerland   c. Turkey
2. Circle the kinds of problems that exchange students and their families sometimes have.
    a. money   b. chores   c. studying   d. cultural/language problems
3. What kind of problem did Adáh have?
    a. Her homestay sister was jealous of her.
    b. She had to share the computer.
    c. She didn't have a good social life.
4. Who was Adáh's best friend?
    a. Jeli   b. Corey   c. her date
5. What happened to Adáh's best friend?
    a. She got sick.   b. She had a car accident.   c. She went home.

Watch Again. Compare answers in small groups.

1. How old is Adáh? _____
2. What are the initials of the exchange student organization?
    a. EVS   b. AFS   c. ALS
3. Look at Adáh's report card and answer these questions.
    a. What languages is she studying?
    b. What science class is she taking?
    c. What is her average grade?
4. What percentage of exchange students go home early or change families?
    a. 2%   b. 12%   c. 20%
5. Look at the chart that Adáh made of her "highs and lows." In which month did she feel the best?
    a. August   b. September   c. October

After You Watch. Find an article about American culture (or another culture) in a magazine, a newspaper, or online. Make a list of the words that contain these suffixes.

-able	-al	-ant	-er	-ity	-less	-ation	-ful	-ment	-ous

Try to guess the meanings of the words in context. Bring your list to class and share it with your classmates. Who found the most words?

Chapter 2

Looking at Learning

The first selection explains three ways to read faster and comprehend more of what you read. This is followed by a timed reading that gives you an opportunity to try out those methods. The second selection presents techniques for taking tests that improve your scores, even though your knowledge of the subject stays the same. Next is a sample test in which you can practice these techniques and analyze the results.

PART 1

How to Read Faster

Before You Read

1   **Scanning for Slang Words and Expressions.** You can tell that this article is written in informal style by its use of slang. Slang refers to words and phrases that are not accepted in standard usage but are common in conversation and popular writing.

Scanning is reading quickly to find particular bits of information. To scan, follow these steps.

- Think of what you are looking for.
- Move your eyes quickly until you find it. Do not pay attention to anything else.
- Stop and record the information.

Scan lines 1–70 of the reading for the following slang words and write them in the blanks. The words are in the order of their occurrence.

1.   a three-letter word in the first sentence meaning "child" _____
2.   a verb starting with *z* that means "went very fast" _____
3.   the slang way of saying "a very easy job" _____
4.   a humorous expression for *eyes* _____
5.   the name of an animal that is used in slang to mean "afraid" _____
6.   the two words the dad uses to tell the monsters to go away _____
_____

> The following article was written by the well-known African-American comedian and TV star Bill Cosby. He grew up in poor circumstances at a time when opportunities for African-Americans in the United States were very limited. (This situation improved after the Civil Rights movement of the 1960s.) Despite these limitations, Mr. Cosby was successful. After becoming well known, he returned to college and earned a doctorate in education. Over the years, he has been awarded over 100 honorary degrees by universities in recognition of his cultural contributions and service. He is the holder of the second highest number of honorary degrees in the United States. He and his wife suffered a horrifying and public tragedy in 1997 when their son was robbed and murdered on a freeway in Los Angeles. In spite of this terrible loss, they have moved forward, and Bill launched a new TV show characterized by his unique humor. From what you now know about the author's background, why do you think he chose an informal style to present his information?

2   **Characteristics of Informal Style.** Besides the use of slang, informal style has other characteristics. Use this article as an example and answer the following questions.

1.   Which kinds of paragraphs—long or short—seem more characteristic of informal style?

2. What about the length of sentences? Are they long or short?

3. Of these, what kinds of sentences are used most?

   a. simple, those with one clause

   b. compound, those with clauses connected by and, or, or but

   c. complex, those with clauses connected by words like *while, when, since, so that, because*, and so on

4. Can you find some sentence fragments (groups of words written as sentences but without a main subject or a main verb or both)? Learn to recognize sentence fragments, but do not use them for academic work.

5. Is the style personal or impersonal? Explain.

Read

How to Read Faster

When I was a kid in Philadelphia, I must have read every comic book ever published. (There were fewer of them then than there are now.)

5   I zipped through all of them in a couple of days, then reread the good ones until the next issues arrived.

Yes, indeed, when I was a kid,
10 the reading game was a snap.

But as I got older, my eyeballs must have slowed down or something! I mean, comic books started to pile up faster than my brother
15 Russell and I could read them!

It wasn't until much later, when I was getting my doctorate, I realized it wasn't my eyeballs that were to blame. Thank goodness. They're still moving as well as ever.

The problem is, there's too much to read these days, and too little time to
20 read every word of it.

Now, mind you, I still read comic books. In addition to contracts, novels, and newspapers; screenplays, tax returns, and correspondence. Even textbooks about how people read. And which techniques help people read more in less time.

25 I'll let you in on a little secret. There are hundreds of techniques you could learn to help you read faster. But I know of three that are especially good.

And if I can learn them, so can you—and you can put them to use *immediately.*

They are commonsense, practical ways to get the meaning from printed
30 words quickly and efficiently. So you'll have time to enjoy your comic books, have a good laugh with Mark Twain, or a good cry with *War and Peace*. Ready?

They'll give you the *overall meaning* of what you're reading. And let you cut out an awful lot of *unnecessary reading*.

1. Preview—If It's Long and Hard

Previewing is especially useful for getting a general idea of heavy reading like long magazine or newspaper articles, business reports, and nonfiction books.

It can give you as much as half the comprehension in as little as one-tenth the time. For example, you should be able to preview eight or ten 100-page reports in an hour. After previewing, you'll be able to decide which reports (or which parts of which reports) are worth a closer look.

Here's how to preview: Read the entire first two paragraphs of whatever you've chosen. Next read only the first sentence of each successive paragraph. Then read the entire last two paragraphs.

Previewing doesn't give you all the details. But it does keep you from spending time on things you don't really want—or need—to read. Notice that previewing gives you a quick, overall view of long, unfamiliar material. For short, light reading, there's a better technique.

2. Skim—If It's Short and Simple

Skimming is a good way to get a general idea of light reading—like popular magazines or the sports and entertainment sections of the paper.

You should be able to skim a weekly popular magazine or the second section of your daily paper in less than half the time it takes you to read it now.

Skimming is also a great way to review material you've read before.

Here's how to skim: Think of your eyes as magnets. Force them to move fast. Sweep them across each and every line of type. Pick up only a few key words in each line.

Everybody skims differently.

You and I may not pick up exactly the same words when we skim the same piece, but we'll both get a pretty similar idea of what it's all about.

To show you how it works, I circled the words I picked out when I skimmed the following story. Try it. It shouldn't take you more than ten seconds.

My brother Russell thinks monsters live in our bedroom closet at night. But I told him he is crazy.

"Go and check then," he said.

I didn't want to. Russell said I was chicken.

"Am not," I said.

"Are so," he said.

So I told him the monsters were going to eat him at midnight. He started to cry. My Dad came in and told the monsters to beat it. Then he told us to go to sleep.

"If I hear any more about monsters," he said, "I'll spank you." We went to sleep fast. And you know something?

They never did come back.

Skimming can give you a very good idea of this story in about half the words—and in less than half the time it'd take to read every word.

So far, you've seen that previewing and skimming can give you a general idea about content—fast. But neither technique can promise more than 50 percent comprehension, because you aren't reading all the words. (Nobody gets something for nothing in the reading game.)

To read faster and understand most—if not all—of what you read, you need to know a third technique.

3. Cluster—To Increase Speed and Comprehension

85 Most of us learned to read by looking at each word in a sentence—one at a time.

Like this:

My—brother—Russell—thinks—monsters…

You probably still read this way sometimes, especially when the words
90 are difficult. Or when the words have an extra-special meaning—in a poem, a Shakespearean play, or a contract. And that's O.K.

But word-by-word reading is a rotten way to read faster. It actually cuts down on your speed.

Clustering trains you to look at groups of words instead of one at a time—
95 to increase your speed enormously. For most of us, clustering is a totally dif-ferent way of seeing what we read.

Here's how to cluster: Train your eyes to see all the words in clusters of up to three or four words at a glance.

Here's how I'd cluster the story we just skimmed:

100 (My brother Russell) (thinks monsters) (live in) (our bedroom closet)
(at night.) (But I told him) (he is crazy.)
("Go and) (check then,") (he said.)
(I didn't want to.) (Russell said) (I was chicken.)
105 ("Am not,") (I said.)
("Are so,") (he said.)
(So I told him) (the monsters) (were going to) (eat him) (at midnight.)
(He started to cry.) (My Dad came in) (and told the monsters) (to beat it.)
(Then he told us) (to go) (to sleep.)
110 ("If I hear) (any more about) (monsters," he said,) ("I'll spank you.")
(We went) (to sleep fast.) (And you) (know something?)
(They never did) (come back.)

Learning to read clusters is not something your eyes do naturally. It takes
115 constant practice.

Here's how to go about it. Pick something light to read. Read it as fast as you can. Concentrate on seeing three or four words at once rather than one word at a time. Then reread the piece at your normal speed to see what you missed the first time.

120 Try a second piece. First cluster, then reread to see what you missed in this one.

When you can read in clusters without missing much the first time, your speed has increased. Practice fifteen minutes every day and you might pick up the technique in a week or so. (But don't be disappointed if it takes longer.
125 Clustering everything takes time and practice.)

So now you have three ways to help you read faster. Preview to cut down on unnecessary heavy reading. Skim to get a quick, general idea of light read-ing. And cluster to increase your speed and comprehension.

With enough practice, you'll be able to handle more reading at school or
130 work—and at home—in less time. You should even have enough time to read your favorite comic books and *War and Peace*!

After You Read

3   **Selecting the Main Idea.** The main idea of a piece of writing (a paragraph, an article, a book) brings together all or most of the different parts of that piece of writing. It does not express the idea of just one part.

Circle the number of the statement that you think best expresses the main idea of Bill Cosby's article. Why is it better than the other two?

1. Moving your eyes fast across each line will give you a general idea of the content of reading material in much less time than it would take to read every word.

2. It is necessary to choose your method of reading according to the kind of material you have to read and the amount of comprehension you need.

3. You should preview long and difficult readings, skim simple ones, and read in groups or clusters when you have to understand most of the material quite well.

4   **More Prefixes.** Here are three common prefixes used in words from the reading. See page 14 for an explanation of prefixes. Fill in the blanks with definitions of the words in italics.

1. The prefix *pre-* means "before." One of the reading techniques mentioned in the selection is previewing (line 35). What does *to preview* mean? _to look over a piece of writing before reading it._

2. The prefix *re-* means "again." The article talks about reviewing (line 54) material that you've read before. What does *to review* material mean? _____

3. The article also mentions the word *reread*. What does it mean to *reread* a reading selection? _____

4. The prefix *un-* means "not." Author Bill Cosby speaks of getting an overall view of long unfamiliar material (line 47)? What is *unfamiliar* material? _____

5. He also refers to cutting down on unnecessary reading. What is *unnecessary* reading? _____

5   **Making New Words by Adding Prefixes.** Form words by adding the appropriate prefix (*pre-, re-,* or *un-*) to each italicized word to fit the context.

1. These tickets do not need to be *paid* for now. They have already been _prepaid._

2. Don't *cook* those vegetables. The chef took the time to _____ them this morning.

3. We are looking for a *cooperative* sales clerk. The last one we had was very _____.

4. You didn't *do* the report very well. The boss wants you to _____ it.

5. My niece is too young to go to regular *school*. She goes to _____ every afternoon.

6. In sales you have to be *aware* of people's reactions, but the new man seems _____ that the clients don't like him.

7. They don't *run* new episodes of that TV show in the summer. What you'll see is a _____.

8. The big *game* is tonight and there's a _____ party at Carla's house.

9. Young people should be *appreciative* of all that their relatives do for them, but this group is totally _____.

Talk It Over

Answer the following questions about the article.

1. Is previewing a useful technique for all kinds of reading? Why or why not?
2. How many 100-page reports should you be able to preview in an hour?
3. Exactly how do you preview?
4. When is it better to skim rather than preview?
5. How do you skim?
6. Why is it better at times to use clustering instead of previewing or skimming?
7. How do you cluster?
8. What do you think the author means by "heavy" reading and "light" reading? Can you give examples of each of these?

---

6 **Adjectives That Describe a Person.** When an author uses an informal style, he or she often "opens up" to the reader, giving information about his or her personal life or feelings. After reading the article, what description can you give of Bill Cosby as a person? Work with a partner on the following list of adjectives and mark Y for yes after those you consider appropriate for describing him, N for no after those you do not consider appropriate and ? after those that you are uncertain of. Compare your results with those of the rest of the class.

arrogant	competent
effective	good-natured
humorous	negative
serious	snobbish
unpleasant	well-educated

7 Working in small groups, each person should take a turn talking in an informal manner about one of the following topics. The speaker can mention previewing, skimming or clustering, and ideas from his or her own experience. The other members of the group should ask the speaker questions.

1. The best way to read a newspaper
2. How to read a long book the night before a test
3. How to find out if a magazine is worth reading
4. How to reread a lot of material the night before a test
5. A good book I have read in English and how I read it

Timed Reading

Using Clustering for Speed and Comprehension

Did you recognize the three references that Bill Cosby made to literature: Mark Twain, *War and Peace*, and Shakespeare? Learn more about one of them as you practice the technique of clustering described in Cosby's article. (Reread this part if necessary, page 23.)

> This reading is taken from the Encyclopedia Britannica entry for Mark Twain. Read quickly to learn about the early life and works of this great author.

- Force your eyes to cluster the words rather than reading them one at a time
- After you read the selection, do the Comprehension Quiz that follows.
- Try to finish both in eight minutes. (Hint: Look over the quiz first to see what it covers.)

Twain, Mark, was the pen name of Samuel Langhorne Clemens (1835–1910), the United States' most famous humorist and the author of popular and outstanding autobiographical works, travel books, and novels. The first thirty-six years of Clemens' life gave him experiences as a boy in a little town in Missouri, as a steamboat pilot, as a reporter on the far western frontier, and as a traveler abroad—which he thereafter used as materials for his best and most successful writings.

He was born November 30, 1835, the… fifth child of John Marshall and Jane (Lampton) Clemens, both descendants of Virginians. His birthplace was Florida, Missouri, a village to which the family had moved the previous June. The boy's father, a storekeeper and at times a lawyer, had little talent for money-making and failed there as he had elsewhere. The Clemenses therefore moved in the fall of 1839 to Hannibal, Missouri.

Hannibal was the town of Sam Clemens' boyhood, destined to figure importantly in several of his finest books. Almost in the geographical center of the United States, it had the wide Mississippi River rolling past it on the east, and on the other sides were forests, farmlands, and prairie. The river was the route from and to the rest of the nation, bringing as it did all sorts of exciting visitors—river men, (religious) revivalists, circus troupes, …migrants to points as far westward as California. The steamboats which Sam and his gang of boyhood friends watched wheeling past or docking at the wharf were endlessly fascinating. So, too, were the steamboat men and the townspeople, many of whom were prototypes of characters in Twain's books. The river, an island nearby, and the woods around the town were wonderful places for boys to play. In the summer Sam ordinarily paid a vacation visit to the farm of his uncle John Quarles, near Florida. Some of his happiest and most vivid memories were to be of his play around Hannibal and of his visits to the farm....

The Adventures of Tom Sawyer (1876) was one of Twain's best books, certainly his best for a juvenile audience. The setting was St. Petersburg, which was Hannibal made idyllic by the passage of time; the characters were the grownups and the children of the town in the 1830s, also for the most part viewed sympathetically. Twain once characterized the book as "simply a hymn put into prose form to give it a worldly air."

The nostalgic attitude was typical of the period when in every section of the country writers such as Edward Eggleston, Harriet Beecher Stowe, and George Washington Cable were writing local-color stories wistfully re-creating pre-Civil War life. The happenings were shaped by American humor, which for some time had been making fun of the Sunday-school story—its prematurely moral children who were rewarded and its prematurely immoral children who came to grief. Tom, says the first chapter, "was not the Model Boy of the village. He knew the model boy very well though—and hated him." Tom was by contrast "the normal boy," the book implied, mischievous and irresponsible but goodhearted; and the subplots in which he figured showed him again and again winning triumphs. These happy endings endear the book to children; the lifelike picture of a boy and his friends is enjoyed by both young and old....

Comprehension Quiz

Circle the correct answer to finish each of the following statements about Mark Twain's life and his most famous book.

1. Mark Twain's real name was ____ .
    a. John Marshall
    b. Sam Clemens
    c. Tom Sawyer

2. He lived about ____ .
    a. 50 years ago
    b. 100 years ago
    c. 300 years ago

3. Twain spent his boyhood in the state of ___ .
    a. Missouri
    b. Virginia
    c. Pennsylvania

4. His early life could be characterized as ___ .
    a. quiet and scholarly
    b. active and adventurous
    c. sad and difficult

5. Twain based most of his successful writings on ___ .
    a. pure fantasy
    b. facts he learned from school
    c. true-life experience

6. An important element in this author's childhood was the ___ .
    a. Mississippi River
    b. Boston Art Museum
    c. Pacific Ocean

7. As a child, he had a great deal of contact with ___ .
    a. wealthy people
    b. music
    c. nature

8. His famous book *The Adventures of Tom Sawyer* contains ___ .
    a. religious hymns and prayers
    b. accounts of the Civil War
    c. happenings from small-town life

9. The general tone of the book is ___ .
    a. humorous
    b. tragic
    c. critical

10. The book tells the story of a boy who was a ___ .
    a. prematurely immoral child
    b. model of kindness and virtue
    c. normal mixture of good and bad

What Do You Think?

In the United States and Canada, some groups of parents and religious and community leaders are trying to remove books from schools and libraries. They object to certain books because of a negative presentation of women or minority groups. They object to the books because of the violence, bad language, or sexual scenes that are included. In some places, a number of classics have been challenged and sometimes prohibited. Examples of books that have been prohibited for students are *Huckleberry Finn* by Mark Twain, *Romeo and Juliet* by William Shakespeare, and even the traditional fairy tale "Snow White and the Seven Dwarfs."

What do you think? Is it good to censor the books used in libraries and schools? Why or why not?

PART 2

How to Take Tests

Before You Read

1 **Getting the Meaning of Words from Context.** Nine words or expressions that will be important for your understanding of the next reading selection are presented here in contexts designed to help you guess their meaning. Circle the letter of the one word or phrase that best expresses the meaning of the underlined word or phrase.

1. Words and phrases such as *often, usually, sometimes, in part,* or *on occasion* are <u>qualifiers</u> that change or limit the meaning of a sentence.
   a. synonyms
   b. prepositions
   c. objects
   d. modifiers

2. Of all the candidates, Jack is <u>the least likely to win</u> because he does not know many voters.
   a. one who will probably win
   b. one who will probably not win
   c. one who would like to win
   d. one who would not like to win

3. A teacher sometimes will <u>give a hint</u> to aid students with a difficult exam question.
   a. tell the answer
   b. explain the reason
   c. make a suggestion
   d. offer comfort

4. The students <u>assembled</u> their notes from the whole semester before beginning their study session for the final exam.
    a. brought together
    b. took apart
    c. questioned
    d. memorized

5. Her essay was excellent because she presented her <u>thesis</u> very clearly and gave so much evidence that any reader would have to be convinced.
    a. fact
    b. description of events
    c. expression of personal feelings
    d. main idea

6. From the sad expression on Sheila's face, the teacher could see that she <u>was totally stumped by</u> the question.
    a. was pleased about
    b. was trying to comprehend
    c. had finally seen
    d. did not understand

7. The flood itself was terrible, but the next day we saw the <u>aftermath</u>, which was even worse.
    a. resulting situation
    b. news story
    c. number of problems
    d. earlier condition

8. When he saw that half of the test was on word definitions, he knew he would <u>cash in on</u> the many hours he had spent studying vocabulary.
    a. get money for
    b. receive benefit from
    c. forget completely
    d. totally explain

9. Your clear knowledge of math <u>paid off</u> when you were interviewed for the book-keeping job.
    a. was worthwhile
    b. was useless
    c. gave you confidence
    d. caused you to fail

Read

What are objective tests? Which words often indicate a true answer in true/false tests? Which words can indicate a false answer? What should you do before answering multiple-choice questions?

The answers to these and other practical questions concerning tests are in the following selection from Eric Jensen's book *You Can Succeed*. This book belongs to a genre (kind) that is popular with Americans, the "how-to" book. In it, Mr. Jensen explains test-taking techniques that he has taught successfully to more than 3000 students. As you read, pay attention to the headings (titles of sections) and try to remember the suggestions that could help you do well on each type of test.

How to Take Tests: Scoring What You're Worth

Taking Objective Tests

Objective tests are those that include questions in a true/false, multiple-choice, matching, or fill-in format. Usually the answer is provided but the student must decide among several possibilities.

1. True/False Questions

True/false questions are the easiest test questions for the obvious reason that you have at least a fifty-fifty chance of getting the right answer. First, be sure you have read the question correctly. Look for words such as *always* or *never*; these words often indicate a false answer. Words such as *often, usually, rarely*, or *sometimes* can indicate a true answer. Decide if the statement is totally true before you mark it true. Answer what the tester intended, not what you read into the question. For example, the statement "General Motors produces compact cars" is true. If the question had read "General Motors alone produces compact cars," then it would be false. On true/false questions, stick with your first impression. Studies have shown over and over that your first impression is usually right, so be slow to change your answer, if you change it at all. A statement is more likely to be true if it is a fairly long statement; it takes more qualifiers to make a true statement than a false one.

2. Multiple-Choice Questions

An important rule to remember when answering multiple-choice questions is to read the answers first. This way, you'll view each answer separately and equally, without "jumping" on the first and easiest one. Look for an answer that not only seems right on its own but completes the question smoothly. If the question asks why something occurs, then your answer must be a cause. Try to eliminate any obviously poor answers. Suspect as a possible right answer phrases such as "all of the above," "none of the above," or "two of the above." Check the wording of questions to notice qualifying phrases such as "all of the following are true except…" or "which two of the below are not…" Statistically, the least likely correct answer on a multiple-choice question is the first choice. When in doubt, pick the longer of two answers. But, just as in true/false sections, always put something down. Even an educated guess is better than leaving the question blank and getting it wrong for sure.

3. Sentence Completion or Fill-In Questions

These generally ask for an exact word from memory. They don't allow for much error, so make sure your answer is a logical part of the sentence as a whole. Use the length and number of blanks given as a hint. Make sure the grammar is consistent. When in doubt, guess. Even if it's a generalized guess, you may get partial credit. If you are unsure of two possibilities, include both and hope for half credit.

Taking Essay Tests

When answering questions on an essay test, begin by making an outline on a piece of scratch paper. Assemble and organize the main points. Check the wording of the question to make sure you are interpreting the question correctly. For example, if the question asks you to compare and contrast, do not give a description or a discussion. Begin your essay by using the same words in your answer that are in the question. Keep your answer to the point. Always write something in answer to a question, even if you don't have much to say. Think and write by using this format:

1. Introduction. Introduce your topic.
2. Background. Give historical or philosophical background data to orient the reader to the topic.
3. Thesis and arguments. State the main points, including causes and effects, methods used, dates, places, results.
4. Conclusion. Include the significance of each event, and finish up with a summary.

When totally stumped for an answer on an essay, think about book titles, famous names, places, dates, wars, economics, and politics. Usually something will trigger some ideas. If you know nothing about the essay question, invent your own question on the subject and answer it. You'll usually get at least partial credit. That's better than nothing.

The Aftermath

When you complete a test, be sure to reread all your answers. Check the wording of the questions again. Eliminate careless errors, and you can save a lot of disappointment later. This is the time when you can cash in on your brief encounters with your professor. Write your name in large, visible letters. If you have made a positive impression on your professor from personal contact, it will pay off now. Sometimes just a good impression can give you the higher grade in a borderline situation. Take as much time as you need. When you think you have finished the test, turn it upside down on your desk. Think about it for a few minutes, giving your mind some time to relax and come up with some answers. If you still agree with what you have written, then turn it in. But sometimes those few moments spent just thinking about the questions will bring back the answer that gives the A.

Once your corrected test is returned, look it over. Check your errors and find out not what they were but what kind of errors they were. Was it from answering questions too quickly, poor organization, a missed assignment, or incorrect notes? Understand why you made errors and avoid the problem on the next test.

After You Read

2 **Scanning for Specific Information.** Fill in the blanks with the correct information from the article. If you do not remember a specific point, find the appropriate heading and scan that section for the answer.

1. The two main kinds of tests are _____ tests and essay tests.

2. On true/false tests, words such as *often* _____ , _____ , or _____ can indicate a true statement.

3. On true/false tests, a fairly long statement is more likely to be _____ because it takes more qualifiers to make a true statement than a false one.

4. Before answering multiple-choice questions, you should _____ .

5. Phrases such as *all of the above*, _____ , or _____ should be suspected as possible answers on multiple-choice tests.

6. According to statistics, the least likely correct answer on a multiple-choice test is the _____ one.

7. On completion, or fill-in, tests, use the _____ and _____ of blanks as a hint if you are unsure of two possibilities.

8. When answering questions on an essay test, begin by making an _____ on a piece of scratch paper.

9. When writing the answer to an essay question, use the following format: (1) Introduction, (2) _____ , (3) Thesis and Arguments, and (4) _____ .

10. If you know nothing about the essay question, _____ on the subject and answer it in order to get partial credit.

PEANUTS, United Feature Syndicate, Inc.

Talk It Over

In small groups, discuss the following questions.

1. The author suggests that it is better to make an "educated guess" than to leave a question blank. What do you think he means by an educated guess?

2. When is it *not* a good idea to guess on a test?

3. Do you find it hard to answer multiple-choice questions with qualifying phrases such as "all the following are true *except*…" or "which of the below is *not*…?" Will the correct answer to such a question be true or false?

4. How do you prepare for an objective test? How do you prepare for an essay test? Explain your answers.

5. What type of test do you find the most difficult? Why?

6. Which pieces of advice in the article do you think are the most helpful?

7. What do you do the night before an important exam? Do you go to sleep early, or do you stay up late cramming? What can you do to avoid getting nervous?

8. When is it correct to ask a teacher to give you a hint about the type of exam that he or she is going to give? How can you do this in a polite way?

Focus on Testing

Taking an Objective Test

The following sample includes two sections from a test on reading comprehension. They are similar to sections on standardized exams given at many universities. Your teacher may ask you to work on this test by yourself or in a small group. You may find this test tricky. Most people can improve their scores on this kind of exam through practice.

Before beginning, review in your mind or with your classmates the suggestions from the article about taking multiple-choice tests (page 31). Then, apply these suggestions to the exam. After finishing, correct your work. Try to understand why you made the mistakes that you did.

Sample Test of Reading Comprehension

(10 questions)

Section 1 (Questions 1–7)   Directions: The questions in this part are based on two paragraphs about historical events. Choose the one best answer, either A, B, C, or D, and fill in the correct circle. Answer all questions according to what is stated directly or implied in the paragraph.

Paragraph 1: An Augustinian monk named Gregor Mendel was the first person to make precise observations about the biological mechanism of inheritance. This happened a little over 100 years ago in an Austrian monastery, where Mendel spent his leisure hours performing experiments with pea plants of different types. He crossed them carefully and took notes about the appearance of various traits, or characteristics, in succeeding generations. From his observations, Mendel formed a set of rules, now known as the Mendelian Laws of Inheritance, which were found to apply not only to plants but to animals and human beings as well. This was the beginning of the modern science of genetics.

1. The importance of Gregor Mendel is that he was the first person to
   (A) imagine that there existed a precise mechanism for inheritance.
   (B) approach the problem of inheritance scientifically.
   (C) think about why animals and plants inherit certain characteristics
   (D) invent the word genetics.
   Answer: (A)   (B)   (C)   (D)

2. When did Mendel perform his experiments?
   (A) in ancient times   (C) in the 1860s
   (B) in the 1680s   (D) at the beginning of this century
   Answer: (A)   (B)   (C)   (D)

3. Why did Mendel do this work?
   (A) He formed a set of rules.   (C) He lived in Austria.
   (B) He enjoyed it.   (D) He was paid for it.
   Answer: (A)   (B)   (C)   (D)

4. The Mendelian Laws of Inheritance describe the transmission of biological traits in

(A) plants.   (C) human beings.

(B) animals.   (D) all of the above.

Answer: (A)   (B)   (C)   (D)

Paragraph 2: The magnificent warship Wasa, which sank after a maiden "voyage" of some 1,500 yards, was salvaged and restored, after lying at the bottom of Stockholm's harbor for over 330 years. The ship now rests in the National Maritime Museum of that city.

5. The Wasa sank around the year

(A) 1330.   (C) 1650.

(B) 1500.   (D) 1960.

Answer: (A)   (B)   (C)   (D)

6. Which of the following statements about the Wasa is probably not true?

(A) It met with a catastrophe shortly after being built.

(B) It carried many soldiers and cannons.

(C) It was a veteran of many hard-fought battles.

(D) It was raised by modern salvaging techniques.

Answer: (A)   (B)   (C)   (D)

7. The Wasa ship appears to be

(A) Swedish.   (C) American.

(B) Dutch.   (D) British.

Answer: (A)   (B)   (C)   (D)

Section 1 Answers

#	A	B	C	D
1.	●			
2.			●	
3.		●		
4.				●
5.			●	
6.			●	
7.	●			

Section 2 (Questions 8–10)   Directions: In questions 8–10, choose the answer that is closest in meaning to the original sentence. Notice that several of the choices may be factually correct, but you should choose the one answer that is the closest restatement of the given sentence. Fill in the correct circle: A, B, C, or D.

8. No hour is too early or too late to call Jenkins Plumbing Company.
    (A) Jenkins Plumbing Company does not answer calls that are too early or too late.
    (B) Jenkins Plumbing Company accepts calls at any hour of the day or night.
    (C) Whether you call early or late, Jenkins Plumbing Company will come in one hour.
    (D) If you call at an early hour, Jenkins Plumbing Company will never be late.

    Answer: Ⓐ Ⓑ Ⓒ Ⓓ

9. When TV first became available to large numbers of Americans in the 1950s and 1960s, most producers ignored its possibilities as a tool for education.
    (A) In the 1950s and 1960s, there were not many educational programs on American TV.
    (B) Until the 1950s and 1960s, most of the TV programs in the United States were tools for education.
    (C) After the 1950s and 1960s, most American producers did not see the educational possibilities of TV.
    (D) During the 1950s and 1960s, educational programs first became available to Americans.

    Answer: Ⓐ Ⓑ Ⓒ Ⓓ

10. In spite of the high interest rates on home loans, the couple did not change their plans to buy a new house.
    (A) High interest rates caused the couple to change their plans about buying a house.
    (B) The couple did not buy the house because of the high interest rates.
    (C) Since interest rates were no longer high, the couple bought the house.
    (D) Although the interest rates were high, the house was bought by the couple.

    Answer: Ⓐ Ⓑ Ⓒ Ⓓ

Section 2 Answers

Video Activities: High-Tech Jobs and Low-Tech People

Before You Watch.   Discuss these questions in small groups.

1.   Which two of these are high-tech jobs?
    a.   telephone repairperson   b.   computer programmer
    c.   television camera operator   d.   biochemist
2.   What subjects do people usually study in order to get high-tech jobs?
    a.   liberal arts   b.   engineering   c.   mathematics   d.   social sciences

Watch.   Circle the correct answers.

1.   What is surprising about Mark Riley's work?
    a.   He enjoys programming computers.
    b.   He doesn't have a college degree.
    c.   Programming computers used to be his hobby.
2.   What problem do high-tech companies have?
    a.   not enough work   b. not enough high-paying jobs
    c.   not enough qualified job applicants
3.   What kind of people did high-tech companies used to look for?
    a.   college graduates   b.   liberal arts graduates
    c.   engineering graduates
4.   According to an official at Play, Inc., what kind of people are high-tech
     companies looking for now?
    a.   healthy   b.   smart   c.   loyal   d.   creative   e.   driven

Watch Again.   Compare answers in small groups.

1.   What companies are mentioned in the video?
    a.   Play, Inc.   b.   Manpower   c.   Go High Tech
2.   Which company helps people find jobs?
3.   Complete these quotations:
    1.   A job has to offer more than _____.
    2.   It's not so important to Play whether or not you have a _____.
         It's more important that you want _____.

After You Watch.   Find an article about education and/or careers in a newspaper
or a magazine. Use the article to practice improving your reading time. First estimate the number of words in the reading by counting the number of words in two
or three lines, taking the average and then multiplying the average by the number of
lines in the text. Then write down the time and begin reading. Remember to use
clustering to increase your speed. When you are finished, figure out the number of
words per minute. This is your reading speed. Finally, read the article again more
slowly. How many important ideas did you miss? If you missed a lot, then you
should try to read more slowly.

Chapter 3

Relationships

IN THIS CHAPTER

In the United States and Canada, the last half of the twentieth century led to dramatic changes in families and personal relationships in general. The first selection addresses one of the biggest social concerns of our times, the care of children in families with two working parents, and goes on to discuss how people are coping with the problem in the United States. This is followed by statistical charts with information on the changing makeup of what we call a family. The second selection gives a new twist to an old phenomenon, "mail-order" brides.

PART 1   Who's Taking Care of the Children?

Before You Read

1   **Skimming for the General Idea.** Follow these steps to find the general idea of a reading selection quickly.

1.   Move your eyes quickly over the whole piece.
2.   Look at just a few key words in each line, the ones that seem to carry the message, then go on.
3.   Try to express the overall idea in two or three sentences.

Skim the following article to get a general idea of what it is about. (To review what Bill Cosby says about skimming, see page 22.) Circle the number of the summary that best expresses the overall idea of the reading. Why is it better than the other two?

1.   In the United States most women want to be professionals and work as doctors, lawyers, or executives, or in sales or education. They depend on their families to help them with child care. The husband is no longer the only breadwinner.

2.   In the United States most mothers need to find day-care centers, nannies, or other individuals to watch their children while they work outside of the home. Times have changed, and the definition of *family* has expanded. Fathers increasingly help care for children.

3.   In the United States most couples are influenced by monetary factors and are employed full-time, part-time, or in job-sharing positions. Many husbands and wives share working, doing household chores, and staying at home with the children.

Read

2   Now that you know the general idea, read to find out more about the big changes that have occurred in American family life in the last several decades. As you read, try to decide where else these changes have occurred and what the effects of those changes are.

Who's Taking Care of the Children?

Around the world, more and more women are working outside the home. In the United States, over 70 percent of
5   women with children under 18 have another job besides that of mother and homemaker. Most are employed in traditional fields for females, such as
10   clerical, sales, education, and service. However, a growing

number choose a career that necessitates spending many hours away from home. These women are engineers, politicians, doctors, lawyers, and scientists, and a few have begun to occupy executive positions in business, government, and banking, breaking through the so-called glass ceiling.

Monetary factors influence women to work. Some are employed full-time, some part-time, and some seek creative solutions such as flex-time work schedules and job sharing. Many are single mothers raising children by themselves. But in most cases, one income in the household is simply not enough, so both parents must work to support the family.

A backward glance from this side of the new millennium reveals that the role of married women in the U.S. has changed radically since the 1950s and 1960s, when it was taken for granted that they would stay home and raise the children. This is still the image so often portrayed in American movies and advertising. In fact, the traditional combination of the husband as exclusive breadwinner and the wife as a stay-at-home mom caring for one or two children today accounts for only 7 percent of the population in the United States.

Who, then, is taking care of the children?

When extended families—children, parents, grandparents, aunts, and uncles—lived in the same town and sometimes in the same house, a relative of the working parents took care of the children. But beginning with the Industrial Revolution, people moved away from farms and small towns to find better job opportunities in larger cities. Now, most often, the family is just the immediate family—mother, father, and children. Or, it could be a single-parent family, with either the mother or the father living with the children. Another variation is the blended family, the result of a marriage between a previously married man and woman who combine the children from their former marriages into a new family.

So who watches the children while the parents work? Answers to this question are varied.

1. Some parents put children in day-care facilities.
2. Some parents put children in informal day-care centers in private homes.
3. Companies and hospitals are realizing that providing day care at the workplace makes for happier and more productive employees.
4. Individuals or couples that are wealthy enough have a nanny, a woman who comes to care for the children in their own home. Many of these child-care workers are from other countries, e.g., England, Jamaica, Poland, or the Philippines.

A trend that has emerged recently is the sharing of child-care responsibilities between husband and wife. Young couples will try to arrange their work schedules so that they work opposite hours or shifts in order that one parent is always home with the children. Since child care is expensive, this saves money for the young couple trying to establish themselves and provide a secure environment for the family. Husband and wife may also share household chores. Some fathers are just as capable as mothers at cooking dinner, changing and bathing the baby, and doing the laundry.

In some cases, the woman's salary is adequate for family expenses, and the father becomes the "househusband." These cases are still fairly rare. One positive trend, however, is that fathers seem to be spending more time with their children. In a recent survey, 41% of the children sampled said they spend

equal time with their mothers and fathers. "This is one of our most significant
cultural changes," says Dr. Leon Hoffman, who co-directs the Parent Child
Center at the New York Psychoanalytic Society. In practice for 30 years, Hoffman has found a "very dramatic difference in the involvement of the father—
65 | in everything from care taking to general decision making around kids' lives."

Miki Knezevic

After You Read

3   **Matching Words to Their Definitions.** Match each of the numbered words taken from
the reading to its definition in the second column. In some cases you may wish to find
the word in the reading and use its context to help you.

_____c_____   1. glass ceiling   a. all that is needed, sufficient

_____   2. flex-time   b. person who earns the money for a family

_____   3. job sharing   c. invisible barrier to the promotion of women

_____   4. radically   d. man who stays at home and cares for his children

_____   5. adequate   e. two people who each work part-time at one job

_____   6. portrayed   f. tendency or movement in the course of events

_____   7. breadwinner   g. to a great degree, completely

_____   8. extended family   h. shown or represented in a pictorial way

_____   9. nuclear family   i. varying arrival and departure times at work

_____   10. blended family   j. children, parents, grandparents, and other relatives

_____   11. trend   k. children and parent(s)

_____   12. "househusband"   l. parents and children from different marriages

4   **Recalling Information.** Underline the correct word or phrase to complete the following sentences about the article.

1. About (30, 50, 70) percent of American mothers with children under 18 work outside of the home.

2. In the 1950s and 1960s it was taken for granted that a woman would be a (single
mother, breadwinner, stay-at-home mom).

3. In the United States today, the most common type of family is the (nuclear, blended, extended) family.

4. Beginning with the Industrial Revolution, many people moved to (farms, small
towns, larger cities) far away from their relatives.

5. A recent trend is that American fathers seem to be spending (more, less) time with
their children.

5   **Reading a Statistical Chart.** This chart gives you an idea of some changes that occurred in the American family from 1970 to 1998. A chart presents information to us in a clear and compact way. Often, however, a chart contains much more information than we need. This can make it hard to understand. When reading a chart for information, follow these three steps.

1. Skim for a general idea of what the chart shows.
2. Focus clearly on each question you want to answer.
3. Scan the chart for the information.

Find the following information on the chart. Look for the answers to the questions by following the three steps mentioned in Chapter 2:

- Think of what you are looking for.
- Move your eyes quickly until you find it. Do not pay attention to anything else.
- Stop and record the information.

1. In general, what kinds of changes does the chart show?
2. Did the percentage of two-parent households in the United States go up or down between 1970 and 1998?
3. In what year was there the biggest change?

4. Which years showed no change at all?

5. Did the percentage of mother-only households go up or down between 1970 and 1998?

6. Did the percentage of father-only households go up or down in those years?

7. In general, how would you describe the change in the American family shown by this chart?

Families by Type, 1970–1998
(with children under age 18, for selected years 1970–1998)

Family type	1970	1980	1990	1991	1992	1993	1994	1995	1996	1997	1998
Total											
Two parents[1]	85%	77%	73%	72%	71%	71%	69%	69%	68%	68%	68%
Mother only[1]	11	18	22	22	23	23	23	23	24	24	23
Father only[2]	1	2	3	3	3	3	3	4	4	4	4
No parent	3	4	3	3	3	3	4	4	4	4	4
White											
Two parents[1]	90	83	79	78	77	77	76	76	75	75	74
Mother only[1]	8	14	16	17	18	17	10	18	18	18	18
Father only[2]	1	2	3	3	3	3	3	3	4	4	5
No parent	2	2	2	2	2	2	3	3	3	3	3
Black											
Two parents[1]	58	42	38	36	36	36	33	33	33	35	36
Mother only[1]	30	44	51	54	54	54	53	52	53	52	51
Father only[2]	2	2	4	4	3	3	4	4	4	5	4
No parent	10	12	8	7	7	7	10	11	9	8	9
Hispanic[3]											
Two parents[1]	78	75	67	66	65	65	63	63	62	64	64
Mother only[1]	—	20	27	27	28	28	28	28	29	27	27
Father only[2]	—	2	3	3	4	4	4	4	4	4	4
No parent	—	3	3	4	3	4	5	4	5	5	5

1. Excludes families where parents are not living as a married couple. 2. Includes some families where both parents are present in the house hold, but living as unmarried partners. 3. Persons of Hispanic origin may be of any race. NOTE: Data applies to U.S. families.
Source: U.S. Bureau of the Census, *Current Population Reports.*

Talk It Over

In small groups, discuss the following questions.

1. When is it good for the mother of small children to work outside of the home?

2. What do you think of flex-time and job sharing? Would you consider working like that? Why or why not?

3. Would you like to have a nanny from a different country take care of your children? Why or why not?

4. What advantages are there for a child in going to a day-care center? What disadvantages are there?

5. What's your opinion of the following "rules for a successful marriage"?
    a. A wife should be younger than her husband.
    b. A husband should earn more money than his wife.
    c. The families of the husband and the wife should get along well with each other.
    d. A couple should live together for at least a year before marrying.

6. What do you think of the new trends in the United States for the husband and wife to share household chores? What do you think of a "househusband"?

7. What changes in the makeup of the family have occurred in other countries?

| PART 2 | # 70 Brides for 7 Foreigners |

Before You Read

1 **Scanning for Facts.** Scan for the following information in the article "70 Brides for 7 Foreigners," and write the answers on the lines. (If needed, review the rules for scanning given on page 43.) Items are listed in order of their appearance. The first one is done as an example.

1. The percentage of Russian mothers wanting their daughters to marry foreigners: 23 percent

2. The name of the Russian prince whose daughter became queen of France: _____

3. The number of phone calls an Australian man received within two days of placing his personal ad: _____

4. The number of Russian women who go each day to the Alliance dating agency in Moscow: _____

5. The percentage of Russian women from the agency's files who actually get married: _____

6. The three countries of origin of most of the foreign men applying for Russian wives: _____, _____, _____

7. The number of marriages involving a foreigner that are registered in Moscow each year: _____

> Many years ago, there was a popular American musical called *Seven Brides for Seven Brothers*. The title of the following article contains an "echo" of that earlier title, but the numbers are different. The article is about Russian women who marry foreign men. Why do you think they want to do that? Why do you think some men from other countries want to marry Russian women?

Read

70 Brides for 7 Foreigners

Russia seems to be turning into a major exporter of brides. Almost 1,500 marriages with foreigners are registered in Moscow every year. Another 10,000 women go to the international marriage agency Alliance each year, according to a poll, and 23 percent of Russian mothers would like their daughters to
5   marry foreign citizens. Russian brides have always been prized by foreigners—ever since the time of Yaroslav the Wise [an eleventh-century grand prince of Kiev], whose daughter became the queen of France. But during Joseph Stalin's time, the attitude toward marriages to foreigners was intolerant.
     In the 1960s, the registration of foreign marriages was resumed, and since
10 then the trickle of Russian brides abroad has turned into a powerful torrent. Tens of thousands of Russian women dream of an advantageous

marriage and look for foreign husbands. How? One way is through personal ads in newspapers. One ad read: "Man from Australia (37, 5 feet 5, 132 pounds) seeks short (5 feet 1 to 5 feet 5), slender woman 22–29 for marriage." The man is from Sydney. His mother advised him to marry a Russian woman because Australian women are very liberated, change men like gloves, and do not do housework. Russian women, in the opinion of the placer of the ad, love to clean, cook, stay home, and have children. In two days, he got 100 calls.

Many women are not shy about going to dating agencies. Alliance is one of the largest in Moscow, with branches in Russia's large cities and abroad. It has been flourishing for more than five years. The director, Tamara Alekseyevna Shkunova, is an academician and director of the Russian Institute of the Family at the International Academy of Information Systems and editor in chief of *Moskovskaya Brachnaya Gazeta* (the *Moscow Marriage Gazette*).

Each day about 10 women go to the agency, but only two to three of them are put in the files. There are criteria for selection. First, you must be successful in your professional milieu. Second, you must know a foreign language. And third, you must meet a standard of "European looks": blond with blue eyes, slender with long legs. Of the 2,000 women a year who get into the files, only 5 percent get married. Of the 200 who have married recently, one was lucky enough to become the wife of a millionaire.

For a 25-year-old woman without children, the service costs $5.30; for 30- to 40-year-old women with children, the service costs $8.00.

There are 700 foreign men in the files, mostly from the United States, Germany, and Britain. Up to 300 men apply annually. They must meet only one requirement—that they be well-to-do. The information on the man's passport is checked, and a call is made to his place of work.

Once a husband is found, the next stop is Wedding Palace Number 4, the only place in Moscow that registers marriages to foreigners. Each year,

40   1,200 couples get married there. In 1992, the bridegrooms came from 96 countries. The greatest number came from the United States; in second place was Israel, followed by Turkey and Bulgaria.

Registration requires a passport and a guarantee from the groom's embassy that there are no obstacles to his getting married. The French Embassy,
45   for example, takes a very serious attitude toward marriages to foreign women. It requires that the French groom obtain certification of his "legal capacity for marriage." If an embassy official registers a couple that has not passed the requisite medical tests, the official is fined. Stiff requirements are also imposed by Germany.

50   The Wedding Palace requires confirmation that, in the given country, a marriage to a citizen of another state is valid. After all, in a number of countries a foreign wife and her children could find that they have no property rights. In Syria, for example, marriage to a foreigner is considered invalid without special permission.

55   Many countries are trying to erect barriers to the marital migration from Russia. For example, one Moscow woman tried for nine months to get permission to go to the United States, where her fiancé was waiting for her.

Another couple wanted to get registered in Canada. The fiancé was called to the Canadian Embassy for an interview, but an entry visa was never
60   granted. "Prove that this isn't a fictitious marriage," they said.

Many Russian women who marry foreigners quickly get divorced and come back. The reasons are well known: a sense of second-class status, a language barrier, financial difficulties. Deceptions are frequent: One "sweetheart" described his home as a palace with a fountain, but, in reality, it turned
65   out that he lived in a small cottage without a bathtub.

S. Kuzina

After You Read

2 **Identifying General and Specific Statements.** Which one of the following two columns contains general statements related to the article and which contains specific examples? Match each general statement to the specific example that illustrates or supports it.

1. About 10,000 women go to the international marriage agency in Moscow every year.

2. One husband described his home as a palace with a fountain, but it was really a cottage without even a bathtub.

3. The Russian fiancée of a Canadian man was told at the Canadian embassy to "prove that this isn't a fictitious marriage."

4. An Australian man said that his mother advised him to marry a Russian woman because they love to clean, cook, stay home, and have children.

5. Each day about ten women go to the agency, but only two or three of them are selected.

a. Certain countries are trying to stop or slow down the influx of brides from Russia.

b. Many Russian women are looking for foreign husbands.

c.. It is not easy in Moscow for a woman to get in the files of a dating agency.

d. Traditionally, Russian women have the reputation of being good wives.

e. Many Russian women who marry foreigners get disappointed and come back to their homeland.

3 **Selecting the Main Idea.** The article uses both general and specific information to present one main idea. Circle the number of the statement that you think best expresses the main idea of the article. Why is it better than the other two?

1. Each year 1200 couples get married at Wedding Palace Number 4, the only place in Moscow that registers marriages to foreigners; in 1992, the bridegrooms came from 96 different countries.

2. Following an old tradition, a large number of Russian women are marrying foreign men, and, despite some obstacles and disappointments, this seems to be a trend that will continue.

3. Many foreign embassies take a very serious attitude toward the increasing number of brides who are leaving Russia to marry citizens from other nations.

Talk It Over

In small groups, discuss the following questions.

1. What does the mother of the man from Sydney think about Australian women? Why do you think she feels this way?

2. In your opinion, are women from certain cultures generally better wives than the women from other cultures? Why or why not?

3. In your opinion, do men from some cultures make better husbands than those from other cultures? Why or why not?

4. What do you think about the criteria for selection of the dating agencies? Are they fair? Explain.

5. Would you consider marrying someone from a different culture? What advantages and disadvantages are there to such a marriage?

6. Nowadays, some people choose not to marry at all. What do you think about that idea?

4 **Real-Life Reading.** Find some ads from the Personals section of a newspaper or magazine and bring them to class. In small groups, discuss the following questions.

1. What is your opinion of these personal ads as a way to find a marriage partner?

2. Would meeting people this way be safe and effective?

3. Would it be better to go to an agency that uses computers to match possible partners?

Now compare your ads and write a group opinion to read to the class about this topic.

What Do You Think?

Adoption

In the foster care system (where people take care of children who are not their own) in the United States, over 100,000 children are waiting to be adopted. In the past, there have been rigid requirements of race, marital status, and age for those planning to adopt children. Now people who have been prevented from adopting children in the past are petitioning the courts for the right to adopt. This group includes single people, gay couples, people of a race different from that of the child, and older couples.

• Who do you think should be allowed to adopt children?
• What qualifications would you require in adoptive people if you were running an adoption agency?

Focus on Testing

Eliminating the Incorrect Choices

As you know, the vocabulary section of many standardized English tests uses a multiple-choice format; that means that you are given four possible answers and asked to choose the best one. The four items in multiple-choice vocabulary questions often follow a pattern. One of the words is completely wrong and may even have the opposite meaning. One is a sort of "decoy," similar in form but different in meaning; and one is close in meaning but not quite right. Then there is the correct answer.

Example: Ten thousand women go to the international marriage agency Alliance each year, according to a <u>poll</u>.

(a) custom   (b) policy   (c) survey   (d) list

Each sentence has an underlined word or phrase. Below each sentence are four other words or phrases. You are to circle the one word or phrase that best keeps the meaning of the original sentence if it is substituted for the underlined word or phrase. Do the exercise with the pattern described above in mind. What examples do you find that fit these descriptions? The words and phrases all come from the reading selection "70 Brides for 7 Foreigners."

1. During Joseph Stalin's time, the attitude toward marriages to foreigners was <u>intolerant</u>.
    (a) close-minded   (b) indifferent   (c) generous   (d) open

2. Tens of thousands of Russian women dream of an <u>advantageous</u> marriage.
    (a) beneficial   (b) distressful   (c) costly   (d) outrageous

3. In the 1960s, the registration of foreign marriages was resumed, and since then the <u>trickle</u> of Russian brides abroad has turned into a powerful torrent.
    (a) large number   (b) small number   (c) entrance   (d) trickery

4. There are <u>criteria</u> for selection. First, you must be successful in your professional milieu.
    (a) payments   (b) criticisms   (c) standards   (d) problems

5. Up to 300 men apply annually. They must meet only one requirement—that they be <u>well-to-do</u>.
    (a) healthy   (b) wealthy   (c) well-meaning   (d) employed

Video Activities: True Love

Before You Watch.   Work in small groups. Number these causes for couples (dating or married) to end their relationship from 1 (most common) to 5 (least common).

_____ a.   money problems
_____ b.   different priorities
_____ c.   lack of communication
_____ d.   the romance is gone
_____ e.   problems with family or friends

Watch.   Circle the correct answers.

1. What is Dr. Mary Quinn's job?
   a.   a medical doctor   b.   a teacher   c.   a couple's counselor

2. According to the reporter, what does love *not* require?
   a.   bonding   b.   time   c.   loyalty   d.   communication

3. What products can help couples improve their communication skills?
   a.   books   b.   movies   c.   music   d.   games

4. The woman from the dating service says that after people find a partner, they often get _____.
   a.   married   b.   lazy   c.   discouraged

5. Dr. Quinn says that _____ can help keep couples close.
   a.   commitment   b.   marriage   c.   traditions

Watch Again.   Compare answers in small groups.

1. Check Dr. Quinn's four tips for improving communication.
   ____ a.   Ask questions   ____ b.   Choose your words carefully.
   ____ c.   Listen closely.   ____ d.   Pick a good time to talk.
   ____ e.   Put things in terms of yourself.
   ____ f.   Make statements about your needs.

2. The woman with the red hair says that if your partner isn't thoughtful, you should ___.
   a.   be more thoughtful   b.   leave him/her   c.   tell him/her how you feel

3. Match the phrases with their meanings.
   1.   split up   a.   good feeling
   2.   kick back   b.   end a relationship
   3.   a high   c.   get lazy

After You Watch.   Find an article about marriage. First skim the article to get the general idea. Write one sentence about what you think the general idea is. Then scan the article for at least three facts. Circle them. Finally, read the article. How accurate was your guess about the general idea when you skimmed?

Chapter 4

Health and Leisure

IN THIS CHAPTER

In the United States and Canada, people are becoming increasingly interested in their health. They are spending a great deal of their free time in gyms, exercise centers, and health food stores. Americans and Canadians are also traveling more and farther than ever before. The first selection in this chapter discusses the foods we eat and what effects they have on us for good or for ill. The second takes a look at some surprising effects that tourism has on the places being visited.

PART 1   Eat Like a Peasant, Feel Like a King

Before You Read

1   **Using Headings as Guides.** The following article is longer than the ones you have read so far. After the introduction, there are three headings. List them in the following spaces.

1. _____Introduction_____
2. _____
3. _____
4. _____

Picking out the headings in an article is one form of previewing (see page 22). It helps you see the organization and major ideas. Headings are usually of two kinds: they tell the main topic of a section, or they simply give a small detail to catch the reader's interest. The ones that tell the main topic are the most helpful for comprehension.

- Which two of the headings tell the main topic of the section?
- Judging from the headings, what do you think you will read about in sections 2, 3, and 4?

2   **Getting the Meaning of Words from Context.** To help you understand the meaning of words from their context, follow these instructions.

1. The only uncommon word in the title is *peasant*. To infer its meaning, notice how it is in a parallel construction with the word *king*: "Eat Like a ___ , Feel Like a ___." A parallel construction is used either for comparison or for contrast. So *peasant* means either something very similar to *king* or something very different. With this clue in mind, read the sentence on lines 50 to 54, and tell what you think is meant by a *peasant diet*. How does this relate to the title?

   _____

2. Words (often in italics) sometimes follow the title of an article and give a brief summary of its main idea. In this case, the word *elite* is used at the end of the summary. Do you know its meaning? If not, notice the context: "Eat simple foods, not elite treats." The word *not* tells you that *elite treats* are the opposite of *simple foods*. *Elite* is also used in line 2 to describe a group of people. Look at this context too; then, in your own words, explain the meaning of *elite*.

   _____

3. Look at the second word of the second paragraph: *eclectic*. It describes the menu that makes up the entire first paragraph. Read that paragraph and think about what is special and unusual about the grouping of foods described here. Then explain the meaning of the word *eclectic*.

   _____

4.   Scan the first two sections of the essay for the noun *affluence* and its related adjective *affluent*, which are used four times. From the contexts, guess its meaning and write it here. Can you also find in the fifth paragraph a synonym for affluence, beginning with the letter *p*?

   _____

5.   The word *cuisine* is used five times in the essay. Scan for it and, using the contexts, explain what you think it means.

   _____

> "You are what you eat" is a popular American saying, and what you eat can contribute to destroying your health. According to modern research, certain cultures have healthier diets than others. Which cultures are these? What foods should you choose in order to avoid cancer, hypertension, and heart disease? Read the following article from *American Health* magazine to find out.

Read

Eat Like a Peasant, *Feel* Like a King

Research around the globe points to a recipe for well-being: Eat simple foods, not elite treats.

Start with miso soup, a classically simple Japanese recipe. For an appetizer, try a small plate of pasta al pesto. On to the main course: grilled chinook salmon, with steamed Chinese cabbage on the side. End with a Greek salad, sprinkled with olive oil, and a New Zealand kiwi fruit for dessert.

An eclectic menu, to be sure. But it could contain some of the world's healthiest dishes. Miso soup, according to recent Japanese research, may help prevent cancer, as may cabbage. Salmon, olive oil, and the garlic in your pesto can all help fight heart disease. Even the kiwi is rich in fiber, potassium, and vitamin C. In the last few years, nutritionists have been studying such international superfoods—dishes from around the globe that may hold the key to healthy eating. They're building on research that began in the '40s and '50s, when researchers first realized that a country's diet is intimately connected to the health of its people.

Since then, an explosion of medical studies has produced a flood of information on diverse human diets—from the Inuit of the Arctic to the Bushmen of Africa's Kalahari Desert. But the globe-trotting researchers have done more than discover the best features of each country's cuisine. They've also demonstrated broad nutritional principles that apply to people all over the world. And their clearest finding is a sobering one.

In many countries, they've found, the healthiest diet is simple, inexpensive, traditional fare—precisely the diet that people abandon as they move into affluence. Japanese immigrating from the high-carbohydrate Pacific to high-fat America have a greater risk of heart disease the more westernized their diet becomes. The same pattern holds for developing nations that emerge from poverty into prosperity. Poor people who can't get enough to eat are at risk, of course, whatever their diets. But as a country's food becomes richer, the scourges of poverty (infectious disease and malnutrition) are replaced by the "diseases of civilization" (arteriosclerosis, certain cancers, obesity).

The simple, ideal diet—often called the "peasant diet"—is the traditional cuisine of relatively poor, agrarian countries such as Mexico and China. It's usually based on a grain (rice, wheat, corn), fruits and vegetables, small amounts of meat, fish, eggs or dairy products, and a legume.

The advantages are obvious: low fat and high fiber, with most calories coming in the grains and legumes. "A low-fat, high-fiber diet is a preventive diet for heart disease, certain cancers, hypertension, adult-onset diabetes, obesity," says Dr. Wayne Peters, director of the Lipid Consultation Service of Massachusetts General Hospital.

Early Diets: Nuts and Plants

According to Peters, "We evolved eating a low-fat diet, and that's what our genetic composition is really designed to handle." Studies of one of the world's most primitive diets—and one of the healthiest ones—back him up. In southern Africa's Kalahari Desert, some tribes still eat as early humans did, hunting and gathering. Anthropologists say the foods of the Bushmen are probably closest to foods that, over two million years, shaped our intestines, our cutting and grinding teeth, our churning stomachs.

"Hunting and gathering may not have been such a bad way of life," says Richard Lee, an anthropologist at the University of Toronto who has studied the !Kung tribe since the 1960s. "The main element for the !Kung is the mongongo, a superabundant nut eaten in large quantities. They routinely collect

and eat more than 105 edible plant species. Meat is secondary."

Another student of the !Kung—Stewart Truswell, a professor of human nutrition at Australia's University of Sydney—says their eating schedule is really continual "snacking" (the gathering) punctuated by occasional feasts after a successful hunt. They are nutritionally healthy, the only shortfall being fairly low caloric intake. And Bushmen show few signs of coronary heart disease. Those who avoid accidents or other calamities, says Lee, often live to "ripe old age."

Few people, though, would choose a !Kung diet—or even a simple peasant diet from western Europe.... In an affluent society, it takes willpower to keep fat intake down to the recommended maximum: 30% of total calories. (The average American gets more than 40% of his calories from fats.) When a country reaches a certain level of affluence, as the U.S...and Japan...grains and beans give way to beef and butter. And animal protein—in meat and dairy products—usually comes packaged with artery-clogging saturated fats and cholesterol.

In India, for example, many middle-income people are now gaining weight on a rich diet—even though the poor half of the population still can't afford enough to eat. As the middle class has become more affluent, they've been able to indulge, and Indian doctors are reportedly seeing more obesity, hypertension, and heart disease. Many Indian dishes are soaked in ghee (clarified butter) or coconut oil, one of the few vegetable oils that is virtually all saturated fat. Very recently, though, Indians have gone in for the diets and aerobics classes that are popular among the rest of the world's elite.

If it's just too difficult to stay with a really low-fat "peasant" diet, the alternative is to rehabilitate high-calorie dishes. Cut down on overall fat intake and substitute, in the words of one researcher, "nice fats for nasty fats." Americans have already been following this advice. In the past 20 years the consumption of "nasty" saturated fats has declined, while we've taken in more of the polyunsaturated fats, such as corn and safflower oils, that can help lower blood cholesterol. This change may help explain the simultaneous 20% to 30% drop in heart disease in the U.S.

Why Socrates* Loved Olive Oil

An even better strategy for changing our fat intake may come from studying diets in the Mediterranean—Spain, Greece, and southern Italy. With some regional variation, people in these cultures eat small amounts of meat and dairy products (although consumption has increased steadily since World War II) and get almost all of their fat in the form of olive oil, says physiologist Ancel Keys, professor emeritus at the University of Minnesota School of Public Health and leader in international dietary studies.

Keys has noted that farmers sometimes quaff a wineglass of the oil before leaving for the fields in the morning. Elsewhere in the Mediterranean,

---

*Socrates was an ancient Greek philosopher. He is often used to represent a wise man.

bread is dipped in olive oil. Salads are tossed with it. Everything's cooked in it.

130   Though people in some of these countries eat nearly as much total fat as Americans, they are singularly healthy, with very little heart disease. Now laboratory studies of olive oil help explain why. Unlike most other vegetable oils common in the West, olive oil consists mainly of "monounsaturated" fats. Re-
135   cent research indicates that monounsaturates do a better job of preventing heart disease than the more widely touted polyunsaturates.

As Americans become ever more concerned with healthy eating, we're likely to pay more and more attention to world cuisines. The polyglot among nations, we've started to seek out ethnic flavors from everywhere. "Foreign"

140   ingredients, from seaweed and bean curd to tortillas and salsa, are now readily available in large super-
145   markets. And Mexican and Asian restaurants have become more widespread than any other eateries except ice cream parlors,
150   hamburger stands, and pizzerias, according to the National Restaurant Association.

But the trick to finding healthy food, wherever it comes from, is to look
155   carefully at each dish. No single cuisine is all good or all bad. Each has something to teach us.

The moral is simple: Whether you're eating an American beef stew or a French cassoulet, you need to know what's in it. With a little nutritional knowledge, you can sample some of the world's tastiest foods and know you're also
160   eating some of the best.

Healthy Diets from Around the World

China: The Chinese eat a diet that's about 69% carbohydrate, 10% protein, and only 21% fat. That's remarkably close to the mixture that western nutritionists recommend. Rice, noodles, Chinese cabbage, and mushrooms, along
165   with other vegetables and small portions of fish and meat, are staples of Chinese diets. Recent medical research suggests that oriental mushrooms help boost the immune system and also have qualities that may help prevent heart disease. The downside of Chinese cookery, as in Japan, is the excess of salt and the use of monosodium glutamate (MSG). MSG is as bad as salt if you're
170   fighting high blood pressure, and it can also cause allergic reactions. For many people, when dining in Chinese restaurants it is best to ask for the MSG to be cut out.

Mexico: What Mexican dishes are best for health-conscious diners? Though it's high in fat, guacamole is a surprisingly good bet. Most of the fat in avoca-
175   do is monunsaturated, like the fat in olive oil. *Seviche* (fish marinated in lime juice) is low in fat overall; so are some chicken dishes like chicken tostadas,

180

if they're not fried. And in case you're wondering, the hot chili peppers of Mexican cuisine could actually be good for you, if you can take the heat. Chili peppers are an excellent source of vitamins A and C. They may even help you fight a cold, asthma, bronchitis, and sinusitis.

Canada: The tremendous amount of fish that the Inuit eat helps to prevent heart disease. Fish oil is beneficial in that it lowers blood pressure, cholesterol, and the blood's capacity to clot. A recent Dutch study showed that eating as few as two fish meals a week cut the death rate from coronary heart disease by half.

185

Italy: In southern Italy, age-old staples—such as pasta, olive oil, garlic, whole wheat bread—provide a true gift of health: protection from cancer and heart disease. Like oriental mushrooms, garlic is good for the heart and the immune system.

190

Japan: Two products of the lowly soybean—miso and tofu—are healthy staples. Miso soup may fight cancer; tofu gives low-fat protein. Seaweed, the Japanese lettuce, is high in many nutrients. On the other hand, Japan's smoked, salted, and pickled foods lead to a high incidence of stroke and stomach cancer.

Andrew Revkin

After You Read

3 **Recalling Information.** Based on what you read, match each item of food to its effects.

Foods
1. MSG
2. garlic and oriental mushrooms
3. Mexican chili peppers
4. miso soup
5. fish oil
6. smoked, salted, and pickled foods

Probable Effects on Health
a. seems to lower blood pressure, cholesterol, and the blood's capacity to clot
b. rich in vitamins A and C and possibly a help in fighting colds and asthma
c. contributes to high blood pressure and may cause allergic reaction
d. may help fight cancer
e. probably lead to strokes and cancer of the stomach
f. good for the heart and the immune system

4 **Formulating the Key Ideas.** In addition to a main idea, a complex reading selection may have other important, or key, ideas.

1. The main idea of the article is given in simple terms in the title and the italicized sentence that follows it. In your own words, what is the main idea?

_____

_____

2. Another key idea is the relationship between affluence, diet, and health. The article illustrates this by referring to several different societies. In your own words, explain how affluence changes diet and health, and refer to at least two cultures that illustrate it.

_____

_____

_____

_____

_____

_____

5   **Specialized Use of Vocabulary.** Sometimes a particular word is used in a very special way that depends on the meaning of the entire sentence or paragraph. For example, the most common use of the word *sober* is as an antonym of the word *drunk*. A sober person is one who is not under the influence of alcohol or drugs, one who is clear-headed, in full control of his or her senses. Note the specialized use of this word in lines 28 to 34.

Example: "But the globe-trotting researchers have done more than discover the best features of each country's cuisine. They've also demonstrated broad nutritional principles that apply to people all over the world. *And their clearest finding is a sobering one*."

The italicized sentence can be paraphrased (put into clear and direct words) like this:

The main conclusion of the researchers makes us face a serious fact.
_____

First read the vocabulary hints. Then paraphrase the italicized parts of the excerpts.

1. The usual meaning of the word *punctuate* is to put punctuation marks into a piece of writing so as to separate it into meaningful chunks. Think about what it means in the following excerpt from lines 81 to 87 and paraphrase the italicized part.

    "Another student of !Kung…says *their eating schedule is really continual 'snacking' (the gathering) punctuated by occasional feasts after a successful hunt*."

    _____

    _____

2. The word *quaff* is quite unusual, but its meaning can be guessed simply by looking at the two words that follow it and making the obvious inference. Read the following sentence (lines 126 to 127) and tell what common word is usually used in place of *quaff*.

    "Keys has noted that farmers sometimes *quaff* a wineglass of the oil before leaving for the fields in the morning."

    _____

Talk It Over

In small groups, discuss the following questions.

1. What are your favorite cuisines? After reading this article, which cuisine do you think is the most healthful? Why?
2. What kind of restaurant do you like to go to? At what time of day? Why?
3. What do you think of "fast food"? Is it healthful? Why do you think it is so popular?
4. Can you explain what "junk food" is? Give some examples. Do you ever indulge in it?
5. Besides diet, what other factors are important for our health? In your opinion, what is the key to a long and healthy life?

Focus on Testing

Analyzing Compound Words

As we have seen in Chapter 1 (page 6), many English words are made up of two shorter words. These are called compound words, and they are usually adjectives or nouns. Some compound words are written with a hyphen between them, such as *low-fat*; others, such as *wineglass*, are written as one word. Breaking apart compound words can help you understand their meaning. For example, look at the word *well-being* in the introductory quote in the reading selection "Eat Like a Peasant, *Feel* Like a King." What do you think it means? When taking vocabulary tests, try breaking apart the compound words to help understand their meaning.

Circle the word or phrase that best explains the meaning of the underlined word or phrase. Refer back to the selection "Eat Like a Peasant, *Feel* Like a King" if necessary.

1. <u>globe-trotting researchers</u> (line 28)
   a. professors and students of geography
   b. investigators who travel around the world
   c. people who study the movement of the earth
   d. experts in the benefits of exercise

2. <u>shortfall</u> (line 89)
   a. unusual action
   b. change in the way of thinking
   c. shift from bad to good
   d. absence of something needed

3. <u>intake</u> (lines 89, 96)
   a. interference
   b. planning for the future
   c. entering into the body
   d. disease

4. <u>widespread</u> (line 147)
   a. large in size
   b. open to the public
   c. present in many locations
   d. complicated by difficult rules

5. <u>downside</u> (line 168)
   a. negative part
   b. good news
   c. lower section
   d. deep mystery

6. <u>health-conscious</u> (line 173)
   a. smart and strong
   b. bright and informed
   c. interested in not getting sick
   d. always taking medicine

What Do You Think?

Smoking

Medical evidence proves that smoking is a health risk. Smokers have a greater chance of developing cancer, emphysema, and heart problems. Second-hand smoke, which exposes nonsmokers to smoker's fumes, also is said to increase chances of nonsmokers developing serious diseases. Yet, smokers insist on smoking and don't seem to be bothered by health warnings.

■ Do you think people are smoking more or less nowadays?
■ What do you think about restrictions against smoking inside public buildings?
■ Do you smoke? Why or why not?

Look at the chart and answer the question.

What do the countries with high smoking rates have in common? What do the countries with low smoking rates have in common?

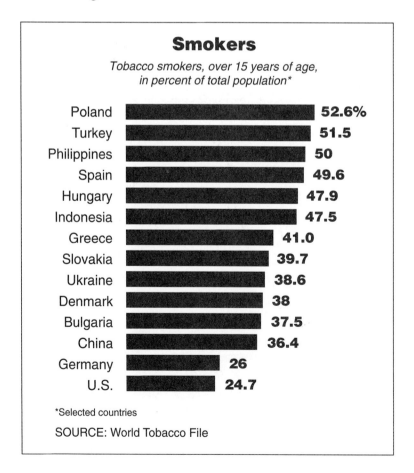

Smokers

Tobacco smokers, over 15 years of age, in percent of total population*

Country	Percent
Poland	52.6%
Turkey	51.5
Philippines	50
Spain	49.6
Hungary	47.9
Indonesia	47.5
Greece	41.0
Slovakia	39.7
Ukraine	38.6
Denmark	38
Bulgaria	37.5
China	36.4
Germany	26
U.S.	24.7

*Selected countries

SOURCE: World Tobacco File

PART 2	# Here Come the Tourists!

Before You Read

1   **Skimming for the Point of View.** A piece of writing presents ideas about a certain sub-ject. It also presents a certain attitude or point of view about the subject. The point of view may be positive, in favor of the person, place, or thing being talked about. On the other hand, it may be negative, against it. The third possibility is a point of view that is somewhere in between and shows both positive and negative aspects of the subject.

It is obvious from the title that the following reading deals with tourism. But what point of view does it express about tourism? Skim the reading to identify its point of view. Then put an X in front of the statement that best expresses the point of view of the article.

_____ 1.   Tourism has a good effect on the places visited.

_____ 2.   Tourism has a bad effect on the places visited.

_____ 3.   Tourism has both good and bad effects on the places visited.

What do you think of this point of view? Is it similar to your own attitude toward tourism? Does the photo on page 66 illustrate the point of view of the selection? Ex-plain.

2   **Getting the Meaning of Words from Context.** Read the analysis following each of these sentences from the reading to learn some new words and methods of figuring out meanings. Then fill in the blank with the letter of the best response.

1.   It was hard to believe that the community began its ecotourism project in 1992 in order to protect natural resources. (line 2)

The word *ecotourism* has only been in use for about the last 20 years. The first part, *eco-*, is taken from the word *ecology*, which means "the relationship between people and their natural surroundings or environment." In recent years, concern for a healthy ecology has become an important theme.

Judging from this, what kind of tourism do you think ecotourism is?

a.   tourism that does not cost much

b.   tourism for the very rich

c.   tourism that does not harm the environment

d.   tourism that uses the environment for adventure

2.   Their repeated "requests" annoyed tourists. (line 5)

Quotation marks are sometimes used to show that a word does not have its usual mean-ing. Usually, a *request* is the action of asking for something politely. Here, an example of a typical "request" made to tourists is given in the first sentence. This gives you a clue about the meaning of *annoyed*.

What does it mean to *annoy* someone?

a.   to make someone happy
b.   to make someone sad
c.   to make someone confused
d.   to make someone angry

3.   Some *locals* were more skilled and playful in their requests, others *up-front* and demanding. (line 5)

Adjectives in English can often be used as nouns if *the* is put in front of them. The word local is used that way here, and then made plural with an *s*. Scan the second paragraph and you will see it used in three other sentences.

What does the word *locals* mean?

a.   people from nearby
b.   people from far away
c.   beggars
d.   workers

The adjective *up-front* is a compound word, so the two short words that make it up can give you some clue to its meaning. Also, it is paired with *demanding* and both words are put in contrast with *skilled* and *playful*. That means they mean something very different from *skilled* and *playful*.

What does *up-front* mean?

a.   tall
b.   direct
c.   smart
d.   funny

4.   Indigenous People in the Andes demand compensation for having their photographs taken. … (line 31)

The word *indigenous* is followed by the word *people* written with a capital letter. This gives you a clue about its meaning. These people live in the Andes mountains, and that gives you another clue.

What does *indigenous* mean?

a.   rude
b.   courteous
c.   foreign
d.   native

5.   These young vacationers like to distinguish themselves as "travelers" not "tourists." (line 52)

In this sentence, two words are put in quotation marks because they are direct quotes of what people say and also because they are used in a special way. The first is said to distinguish people from the second.

What does *distinguish* mean?

a. make similar
b. make different
c. go far away
d. come closer

6. But in "frontiers" like Kathmandu, Goa, and Bangkok, where a backpacking subculture has existed since it became part of the "hippie" routes in the 1960s... (line 54)

Once again we have a word in quotation marks because it is used with a special meaning that is not the usual one. The word *frontier* has two usual meanings: a place near the border of another country, or a new, unexplored area of the world or of knowledge.

What do you think the word *frontiers* means here?

a. very popular places for tourists
b. places where no tourists ever go
c. places where only adventurous tourists go
d. places where tourists may go in the future

The prefix *sub-* means "under" as in the word *submarine* (a vehicle that goes under the water) or "lesser in importance."

What does *subculture* mean in this sentence?

a. a large group of people who are all very different
b. a large group of people with similar customs
c. a small group of people who are all very different
d. a small group of people with similar customs

7. ...such travelers have a reputation for *stinginess* and rude, hard b*argaining*. (line 56)

The suffix *-ness* tells us this is a noun, the quality of being stingy. For clues to the meaning of *stingy* and *stinginess*, look at the examples of how the young vacationers and backpackers act in the sentences before and after this one.

What does *stinginess* mean?

a. practice of insulting people for no reason
b. attitude of kindness and humility
c. custom of not spending or giving money
d. habit of spending and giving money freely

Related to the word *stinginess* is the word *bargaining*. This is the gerund (-ing form) of the verb *to bargain*, which is used in line 62.

What do you think the verb *to bargain* means?

a. to look at something carefully before buying it
b. to try to make the price of something lower
c. to give away one thing in exchange for another
d. to sell something for very little money

This selection is an excerpt taken from a book by Deborah McLaren called *Rethinking Tourism and Ecotravel*. The author is a journalist and director of the Rethinking Tourism Project, a nonprofit group that supports networking and indigenous self-development. She has lived and worked in various parts of Asia and the Americas and has her residence in Washington, D.C. Her book has a subtitle that shows clearly the author's point of view: *The Paving of Paradise and What You Can Do to Stop It*. Read with an open mind to see if you learn something new about travel.

Read

Here Come the Tourists! (excerpt)

"Give me the t-shirt," the woman said to the tourist. The small village in the Amazon was almost filled with beggars. It was hard to believe that the community began its ecotourism project in 1992 in order to protect natural resources. The villagers had lost interest in the land and became enchanted by
5   things the tourists had. Their repeated "requests" annoyed tourists. Some locals were more skilled and playful in their requests, others up-front and demanding. "They have money and many things," said the woman asking for the t-shirt. "It's no problem for tourists."

    It is easy for the locals to perceive tourists as incredibly wealthy. The en-
10   tire tourist experience revolves around money and purchases. The community itself is being purchased. Tourists are superconsumers who bring their foreign languages and communications, strange and inappropriate clothing, and camera into the community. In the context of a brief visit, sometimes an overnight, few real friendships are
15   formed between tourists and locals. Tourists are eager for adventure, or at least the perfect photo opportunity. If the tourist becomes upset in the midst of the excitement, the local
20   usually pays the price. But these strange people sometimes give away token gifts to locals, even money. This results in begging, which becomes increasingly wide-
25   spread as locals begin to see themselves as "poor" and tourists as "rich." The psychological pressure of viewing oneself as poor or backward can manifest itself in crimes not pre-
30   viously common in a community.

    Indigenous Peoples in the Andes demand compensation for having their photographs taken, saying it's intrusive. A woman in Otava-

35 lo, Ecuador, explained to me, "We see ourselves and our children on post-cards and in books. We do not benefit from having our photos taken. A foreigner does. We demand part of the profits." In some Indigenous communities, photography is taboo because it is believed to cause physical and spiritual harm to the person who is photographed. In India young children have had

40 limbs torn from their bodies to make them more pathetic and hence "better" beggars. Adults who commit this violence often have several children who work for them. Other forms of begging sometimes found amusing by tourists offend many locals. An Indigenous leader from Panama told me, "It breaks my heart to see the young boys swimming after the coins the tourists throw in

45 the water. We spent years acquiring our rights to these lands. Now with tourism, the people here do not care about the land anymore. They just want tourist dollars."

While tourists believe they can contribute to destination communities, locals don't always agree. Money spent by budget travelers—especially back-packers—may go into the local economy. They tend to stay in cheaper hotels

50 and eat in cheaper restaurants owned by locals and so get closer to the local culture. These young vacationers like to distinguish themselves as "travelers" not "tourists." They live by budget travel guides and often flock to the same inexpensive areas of villages and cities. But in "frontiers" like Kathmandu,

55 Goa, and Bangkok, where a backpacking subculture has existed since it became part of the "hippie" routes in the 1960s, such travelers have a reputation for stinginess and rude, hard bargaining. In Indonesia I met a British bicyclist who was cycling around the world. He was proud that he had spent virtually no money on his trip. He lived with families that took him in every night

60 from the road and ate what was offered to him by people he met along his way. He had not worked in any of the places he had visited. He was extremely happy that he had just bargained a local merchant down from the equivalent of ten cents to a penny for four pieces of bread. I thought it was rather odd that he was taking advantage of everyone he met and wouldn't even pay a

65 fair price to a poor baker.

After You Read

3 **Separating Fact from Opinion.** The distinction between fact and opinion often is not clear. Events taken to be common knowledge, statements supported by scientific evidence, or statements about something that can be verified (checked out) are generally taken to be facts. Beliefs expressed by only one person are usually considered opinions, unless the person is judged to be an authority on the matter.

Which of the following statements from the reading do you think are facts and which ones are opinions? Why? Write F in front of the facts and O in front of the opinions. Compare your answers with those of your classmates. Line numbers are given so you can examine the contexts.

_____ 1. The community began its ecotourism project in 1992. (line 2)

_____ 2. The villagers lost interest in the land. (line 4)

_____ 3. The entire tourist experience revolves around money and purchases. (line 9)

_____ 4. Few real friendships are formed between tourists and locals. (line 14)

_____ 5. If the tourist becomes upset, the local usually pays the price. (line 18)

_____ 6. Indigenous People in the Andes demand compensation for having their photographs taken. (line 31)

_____ 7. In some communities photography is taboo because it is believed to cause harm. (line 37)

_____ 8. Tourists believe they can contribute to destination communities. (line 48)

_____ 9. Budget travelers tend to stay in cheaper hotels and eat in cheaper restaurants. (line 50)

_____ 10. In Kathmandu, Goa, and Bangkok, a backpacking subculture has existed since the 1960s. (line 54)

4   **Scanning for Vocabulary.** Find the following words in the article, using your scanning skills and the clues given here. Words are asked for in order of their appearance in the selection. (If necessary, review instructions for scanning, page 20.)

1. A two-word phrase meaning "things that a country has and can use to its benefit, such as coal and petroleum":
   n _____ r _____

2. An adjective that starts with *e* and means "delighted, pleased as if by magic":
   _____

3. An adjective starting with the prefix *in-* and meaning "not correct for the occasion": _____

4. A synonym for the verb *show* that starts with the letter *m*: _____

5. An adjective that came into English from the islands of Tonga and means "considered not acceptable and so forbidden": t_____

6. A synonym for getting or obtaining that begins with the letter *a*:
   _____

7. A verb starting with the letter *f* that means to move together in a group (like birds):
   _____

8. An adjective starting with the prefix *in-* and meaning "not costing very much":
   _____

9. A word in quotation marks that refers to the group of young people in the late 1960s who wore flowers and strange clothes, reacted against traditional values and took mind-altering drugs: _____

10. An adverb beginning with a *v* that means "almost completely, for the most part":
    _____

Talk It Over

In small groups, discuss the following questions.

1. The village in the Amazon brought in tourists in order to protect its natural resources. What natural resources do you think the villagers wanted to protect? What went wrong?

2. What kinds of jobs does tourism bring to a small village? Do these jobs sometimes benefit the local people or not? Explain.

3. Is begging a problem only in developing countries? What are some ways to deal with it?

4. Why does the woman in Otavalo, Ecuador, want compensation for having photos taken? Why is photography taboo in some communities?

5. Do you ask permission before taking photos of strangers? Why or why not?

6. What is a "budget traveler" and why do such travelers sometimes bring money into the local economy?

7. What types of travelers do not bring much money into the local economy? Why?

8. Does the British tourist who was cycling around the world have a good attitude? Why or why not?

---

5 **Brainstorming.** Brainstorming means trying to pull out a lot of ideas from your brain and that of someone else (or of several others) on a difficult problem. Do not keep quiet about ideas that seem wild or doubtful. If they have any possibility at all, put them down. Later you can cut down your list. Do not write carefully with correct grammar and punctuation. Just write fast. You want a lot of suggestions in any form. Keep the ideas flowing.

Certainly there are places in the world where tourism "works" by benefiting both locals and tourists. Brainstorm in pairs or small groups on what is necessary for good tourism. Imagine that you are leaders in a small community near a pristine (clean and untouched) beach in a place of great natural beauty. Write a list of rules or ideas for economic development. (For example: What activities would you permit? Which would you forbid? What kinds of tourists would you try to attract?) Think fast. The developers are coming!

6 **Supporting a Position.** The reading presents one point of view about tourism and its impact on tourist destinations. Of course, there are other valid (correct) points of view. What is your point of view on this topic? Choose either *good* or *bad* in the following topic sentence and complete the paragraph with details or examples to support your opinion. (You may wish to say "...has both a good and bad impact" and in that case you should mention details to show both.)

In my opinion, tourism usually has a (good/bad) impact on the places visited.

_____

_____

_____

_____

_____

_____

_____

_____

_____

_____

_____

7   **Scanning Charts.** Do people from the United States go as tourists to the home countries of the tourists who visit the United States? (Or do they go to completely different countries?) In other words, is it a two-way street?

Work in a group to find information on the two charts to help you to answer this question. Follow these steps:

- First of all, does everyone in the group understand the question? Try to explain it in different words.

- Look carefully at the two charts about tourism. What kind of information does each one give? Does either chart exclude some groups of tourists? If so, is that relevant to answering the question?

- Try to find a way of using the charts to get information relating to the question. How can you do this? Copy down relevant information.

- Working together, write down an answer to the question. It may not be a complete answer, but it is often true that we can only find partial answers to complex questions.

- Compare your group's answer to those of other groups. Which group has the best answer? Why is it the best?

Top 20 Nationalities of Overseas Travelers to the U.S.

Rank	Country of residence	1997 total	1998 total	1997/1998 % change	Rank	Country of residence	1997 total	1998 total	1997/1998 % change
1.	Japan	5,367,578	4,885,369	−9.0%	11.	Switzerland	410,209	410,900	0.2%
2.	United Kingdom	3,720,979	3,974,976	6.8	12.	Taiwan	442,780	386,413	−12.7
3.	Germany	1,994,296	1,901,938	−4.6	13.	Colombia	317,736	367,968	15.8
4.	France	978,327	1,013,222	3.5	14.	South Korea	746,550	364,061	−51.2
5.	Brazil	940,698	909,477	−3.3	15.	Spain	328,024	326,339	−0.5
6.	Italy	580,261	610,796	5.3	16.	Sweden	292,424	300,925	2.9
7.	Venezuela	487,981	540,685	10.8	17.	Israel	260,052	269,752	3.7
8.	Argentina	503,393	523,909	4.1	18.	Bahamas	319,240	251,929	−21.1
9.	Netherlands	473,420	490,198	3.5	19.	Ireland	217,278	232,391	7.0
10.	Australia	500,615	460,705	−8.0	20.	Belgium	241,366	230,190	−4.6

NOTE: Excludes arrivals from Mexico and Canada. *Source*: U.S. Dept. of Commerce, International Trade Administration.

Top 20 International Destinations of American Tourists

Rank	Country	1996 travelers (000)	1997 travelers (000)	Percent change 1996/1997	Rank	Country	1996 travelers (000)	1997 travelers (000)	Percent change 1996/1997
1.	Mexico	19,616	17,700	−10%	12.	Hong Kong	752	671	−11%
2.	Canada	12,909	13,401	4	12.	Switzerland	693	671	−3
3.	United Kingdom	2,869	3,570	24	14.	South Korea	554	649	17
4.	France	1,860	2,098	13	15.	Republic of China (Taiwan)	495	562	14
5.	Germany	1,642	1,796	9					
6.	Italy	1,385	1,471	6	16.	Turkey	475	519	9
7.	Jamaica	1,029	1,341	30	17.	Brazil	376	498	32
8.	Japan	871	1,082	24	18.	People's Republic of China	396	476	20
9.	Bahamas	1,504	1,017	−32					
10.	Netherlands	772	822	7	18.	Philippines	475	476	0
11.	Spain	613	714	16	20.	Australia	534	454	−15

Source: U.S. Dept. of Commerce, International Trade Administration; Statistics Canada; Mexican Ministry of Tourism

Video Activities: Bottled Water

Before You Watch.   Answer and discuss these questions in small groups.

1. Where do you get your drinking water?
    a. buy it from a store   b. from the city water supply   c. from a well

2. Which kind of water is better in these ways? Write T for tap water or B for bottled water.

    _____ a. price   _____ c. taste
    _____ b. safety   _____ d. convenience

Watch.   Circle the correct answers.

1. The NRDC is probably a _____.
    a. water bottling company
    b. consumer group
    c. doctors' organization

2. The NRDC study found that _____.
    a. tap water is often the same as bottled water
    b. tap water contains harmful chemicals
    c. bottled water is safer than tap water

3. Sonia Scribner (the owner of The Water Lady) believes that consumers should _____.
    a. go right to the source   b. buy bottled water   c. drink tap water

4. The NDRC thinks that it's time for _____.
    a. the public to drink bottled water
    b. the government to make tap water safer
    c. people to realize that bottled water is not always better

Watch Again.   Compare answers in small groups.

1. What did the NRDC find in water?
    a. lead   b. mercury   c. bacteria   d. arsenic

2. Complete the statements with the numbers.

    4   ⅓   1,000   103   25

    a. The public spent _____ billlion dollars on bottled water in 1997.
    b. The NRDC tested _____ kinds of bottled water.
    c. Some bottled water is _____ times as expensive as tap water.
    d. The NRDC found that _____ % of bottled water is tap water.
    e. _____ of the water tested was the same quality as tap water.

After You Watch.   Look for an article on health and/or nutrition. Find several words that you do not understand. Make a list of the words. Try to guess the meanings of the words from the context in which they are set. Were you able to guess their meanings?

Chapter 5

High Tech, Low Tech

IN THIS CHAPTER

Technology keeps transforming our world. The first article talks about this transformation and its far-reaching consequences that may be threatening to cut our world in two. The second article discusses a somewhat old-fashioned technology that has gone through its own kind of high-tech transformation and is making a comeback on a worldwide scale.

| PART 1 | # Wired World Leaves Millions Out of the Loop |

Before You Read

1   **Skimming for the General Idea.** Before reading about something complex, skim the whole selection for the general idea. This will give you a context to help with understanding new vocabulary. Skim the following article by quickly reading (without looking up any words) the title and subtitle, the first paragraph, the first sentence of some of the middle paragraphs, and the last paragraph. Then circle the letter of the most appropriate ending to the following statement.

In general, the article is about

   a.   the many ways that developing countries are using modern telecommunications and the Internet to improve life and business.

   b.   whether it is a good or bad idea for developing countries to become wired to technology in the same ways that developed countries are.

   c.   the large difference in technology between the developing and developed countries and what can be done to make this smaller.

2   **Making Inferences about Vocabulary.** An inference can also be called an "educated guess." You guess what something means based on what you know about the general idea or context behind it. Now that you know the general idea of the article, try to infer (make an inference about) the meaning of the phrases or expressions in these questions.

   1.   The title includes the common everyday expression *out of the loop*. What does it mean for a person to be "left out of the loop"?

   It means a person is not included in some things that other people are doing.

   Maybe the person does not get some information or some product or cannot

   participate in some activities that others are doing.

   2.   A *gap* is an empty space between two things. The subtitle refers to the "technological gap." What does that mean?

   _____

   _____

   3.   The first sentence talks about electronic communications in the developed world. It says that people "take them for granted." What does it mean if we take something for granted?

   _____

   _____

   4.   In line 50 there is a reference to "virtual universities." You can tell this is a somewhat new term because the author puts it in quotation marks. You are given clues to its meaning in the second part of the sentence. What is a "virtual university"?

   _____

   _____

3   Figuring Out the Meaning of Compound Words. Figure out the meaning of the compound words in the following sentences by breaking them up into parts or by looking at the context. Circle the letter of the one word or phrase that best expresses the meaning of each underlined compound word. (See page 6 for an explanation of compound words.)

1. Electronic communications have become <u>commonplace</u> in the developed world.
    a. useless and out of date
    b. <u>present in large numbers</u>
    c. hard to find
    d. placed in unusual areas

2. In <u>less-developed</u> countries, telecommunications are of a different order of availability.
    a. poorer countries
    b. richer countries
    c. countries that are far away
    d. countries that are close by

3. Still, vast stretches of the world remain woefully <u>underserved</u>.
    a. with no telecommunications
    b. with some telecommunications but not enough
    c. with more than enough telecommunications
    d. with no understanding of the need for telecommunications

4. Despite tremendous efforts by private suppliers, governments, international development groups and <u>non-governmental</u> organizations,…
    a. organizations that are part of the government
    b. organizations that are not part of the government
    c. organizations that work against the government
    d. organizations that cooperate with the government

5. If you look at the developing nations, they really don't have the <u>infrastructure</u>.
    a. people who are interested in working in technical careers
    b. buildings designed especially to hold machines
    c. roads constructed to transport the parts needed for replacement
    d. underlying foundation or basic framework necessary for operating

6. When markets are far away and advertising prohibitively expensive, the Internet opens doors to small and <u>medium-sized</u> enterprises.
    a. big
    b. small
    c. big and small
    d. neither big nor small

7. Where medical specialists are rare, <u>tele-medicine</u> projects have saved lives.
    a.   medical cures performed by electricity and electronic machines
    b.   computerized robots programmed to give medical treatments
    c.   doctors and nurses giving medical advice by telephone and television
    d.   doctors and nurses being transported to far-away places on a regular basis

8. Catching up with the computer, Internet, and telecommunications revolutions requires a culture of <u>know-how</u>.
    a.   engineering
    b.   intelligence
    c.   training and education
    d.   money and investment

Read

What difference does it make if you have telephones, computers, fax machines, or access to the Internet, or if you don't have them? People in the developed world hsometimes feel these machines take too much time away from them, and choose not to use them. But there is a large part of the world where people do not have that choice. The absence of technology in a whole society can make an enormous difference, not only in business but also in other ways involving health, education, and quality of life. Read the following article to find out more about the "technological gap" and how it is dividing the world in two.

Wired World Leaves Millions Out of the Loop
The Technological Gap Is Getting Larger

Brian Knowlton

WASHINGTON—Electronic communications of every form have become so commonplace in the developed world that we take them for granted. In any busy hour, we may be paged, place a mobile phone call, use an electronic cash machine, send a fax, receive an e-mail and perform an Internet search—
5   using technologies that have emerged largely in the last 20 years.

In less-developed countries, telecommunications are of a different order of availability, but
10 with the same ability to transform lives. In the mountains of Burma, yak drivers can call ahead on their mobile
15 phones to find the best road for their caravans to take to market in the rainy season. Shop owners in rural Africa

20 can phone orders to sup-
    pliers rather than traveling
    to the capital city.

        Still, vast stretches of
    the world remain woefully
25 underserved. Despite
    tremendous efforts by
    private suppliers, govern-
    ments, international de-
    velopment groups and
30 non-governmental organ-
    izations, the risk looms
    that as some countries
    vault forward on the back
    of new technologies,
35 other will fall painfully far-
    ther behind.

        "If you look at the developing nations," said Nanette Levinson, an Amer-
    ican University professor specializing in telecommunications and develop-
    ment, "they really don't have the infrastructure. The gap is getting larger."

40   In Cambodia, only seven inhabitants in 10,000 had main phone lines as
    of l996, the latest year for which statistics could be obtained. In highly wired
    Singapore, the government has set a goal of providing high-speed Internet
    access to every home, business, and school. Thailand's yearly growth rates
    in Internet use have reached 1,000 percent. China is predicted to pass the
45 U.S. level of Internet use by 2005 and leads the world pager market.

        In the United States, roughly one person in three uses the Internet. In
    South Asia, only one in every 10,000 does....

        Yet, no one doubts the enormous potential benefits of modern telecom-
    munications for the poorer countries. When there are too few teachers and
50 schools are too far apart, "virtual universities" using video, television and In-
    ternet can fill a huge gap: when markets are far away and advertising pro-
    hibitively expensive, the Internet opens doors to small and medium-sized
    enterprises; where medical specialists are rare, tele-medicine projects have
    saved lives; where the press faces repression, the Internet has provided new
55 freedoms.

        From rural Mexico and Chile to Zambia and Zimbabwe, the Food and
    Agriculture Organization has helped farmers' associations use Internet links
    to plan planting, follow the weather and find buyers.

        A World Bank report predicts that modern information infrastructure can
60 create the "end of geography" and bring economic progress to isolated coun-
    tries and regions. But progress for those most in need has come slowly....

        The World Bank predicts that international aid can provide barely one-
    thirtieth of the estimated $60 billion that developing countries would need to
    develop telecommunications networks over five years.

65   Much thought, considerable creativity and some money have been
    brought to the problem by international organizations, from the World Bank to
    the UN Food and Agriculture Organization to UN-associated International
    Telecommunication Union, or ITU. Japan has its own telecoms aid program,
    focusing on Asia.

70 　　The ITU recently announced a $2.7 million fund to set up electronic commerce centers in developing countries.

　　But the funding of programs like the ITU's is dwarfed by the problem. And bridging the digital divide is not just costly. Catching up with the computer, Internet and telecommunications revolutions requires layers of infrastructure,

75 financing institutions and equipment, and a culture of know-how.

　　Several trends offer hope. Prices of personal computers have tumbled. Internet-based communications are a small fraction cheaper than those via traditional telephone or faxes. In many cases, a remarkable array of locally initiated Internet services has emerged in developing countries without out-

80 side help. Some governments are easing regulatory restrictions.

　　Across the developing world, thousands of public access points for phone, fax and computer or Internet use are springing up. Schools often use their computers for teaching by day, then open them to the community by night for Internet access.

The Wall Street Journal

After You Read

4　**Identifying Support for Ideas.** Most pieces of factual writing contain a number of general ideas that are supported by details and examples. Tell which details on the right give support to each of the general ideas listed on the left. (You might find some details that you feel do not really support any of the ideas or that may support more than one general idea.)

General Ideas

_____ 1.　Electronic communications are commonplace in the developed world.

_____ 2.　There are large areas of the world that are very underserved in telecommunications.

_____ 3.　There are great benefits that can be obtained from telecommunications for poorer countries.

_____ 4.　There are some hopeful trends related to closing the technological gap.

Supporting Details

a.　"Virtual universities" can be used when there are not enough schools or teachers.

b.　Prices of personal computers have tumbled.

c.　In any busy hour people in some places may use a pager, computer, mobile phone, fax and cash machine.

d.　In South Asia, only 1 person in every 10,000 uses the Internet.

e.　People in some developing countries have set up a lot of Internet services all by themselves.

f.　In the United States, roughly one person in three uses the Internet.

g.　Tele-medicine projects save lives when there are few medical specialists available.

h.　In Cambodia, only 7 inhabitants in 10,000 had main phone lines as of 1996.

i.　Farmers' associations use Internet links to plan planting, follow the weather and find buyers.

j.　Shop owners in rural Africa can phone orders to suppliers instead of traveling to the capital.

k.　Schools in the developing world often open up at night to give Internet access to the community.

5   **Colorful Verbs.** Good writers use interesting verbs to add "color" to their writing. Often they suggest a picture, sound, or feeling. Scan the article for the colorful verbs used by the author and write them in the blanks to replace the ordinary verbs in italics. (The sentences are in the order of their appearance in the article.)

1.   Despite tremendous efforts…, the risk *exists as a possibility*… <u>looms</u>.

2.   …as some countries *move quickly* _____ forward on the back of new technologies, others will fall painfully farther behind.

3.   The ITU recently *made known* _____ a $2.7 million fund to set up electronic commerce centers in developing countries.

4.   But the funding of programs like the ITU's, *is made small* _____ by the problem.

5.   And *getting across* _____ the digital divide is not just costly.

6.   Prices of personal computers have *gone down* _____.

7.   Across the developing world, thousands of public access points for phone, fax and computer or Internet use are *appearing* _____.

6   **Making Inferences About the Audience.** Some ideas are not directly stated, but they can be inferred or concluded from what is stated. These are called inferences.

Every article is written for a specific audience, or group of readers. The article does not tell us who these people are, but you can make inferences about them. Write Yes in front of inferences that can be made from the article. Write No in front of inferences that cannot be made from the article. (If you are not certain, skim the whole article again.)

____Yes____ 1.   The people reading this article are from the developed world.

_____ 2.   The people reading this article do not want the developing world to catch up to the developed world in telecommunications.

_____ 3.   The people reading this article know what the World Bank and the United Nations are and understand something about how they work.

Talk It Over

As a class or in small groups, discuss the following questions.

1.   How often do you use e-mail? Do you prefer talking with friends on e-mail or on the telephone? Why?

2.   In your opinion, does e-mail make life easier or harder for people nowadays? Explain.

3.   When do you use the Internet? What do you use it for?

4.   Under what circumstances would you consider using the Internet for romance? Do you think this is dangerous or foolish? Or is it an efficient way to make new friends?

7 **Paragraphs With Supporting Examples.** One common, "classic" style of paragraph contains a general idea with supporting examples. The general idea is in the first sentence (the topic sentence). Two or more examples supporting the general idea follow.

The following three paragraphs from the article are written in this style. Fill in the blanks.

1. Paragraph 1 (lines 1–12)

> In less-developed countries, telecommunications are of a different order of availability, but with the same ability to transform lives. In the mountains of Burma, yak drivers can call ahead on their mobile phones to find the best road for their caravans to take to market in the rainy season. Shop owners in rural Africa can phone orders to suppliers rather than traveling to the capital city.

a. In simple words, state the general idea: <u>In less-developed countries, telecommunications can transform lives.</u>

b. How many examples are given to support this idea? <u>two</u>

2. Paragraph 2 (lines 13–23)

> Yet, no one doubts the enormous potential benefits of modern telecommunications for the poorer countries. When there are too few teachers and schools are too far apart, "virtual universities" using video, television and Internet can fill a huge gap: when markets are far away and advertising prohibitively expensive, the Internet opens doors to small and medium-sized enterprises; where medical specialists are rare, tele-medicine projects have saved lives; where the press faces repression, the Internet has provided new freedoms.

a. In simple words, state the general idea: _____

b. How many examples are given to support this idea? _____

3. Paragraph 3 (lines 24–33)

> Several trends offer hope. Prices of personal computers have tumbled. Internet-based communications are a small fraction cheaper than those via traditional telephone or faxes. In many cases, a remarkable array of locally initiated Internet services has emerged in developing countries without outside help. Some governments are easing regulatory restrictions.

a. In simple words, state the general idea: _____

b. How many examples are given to support this idea? _____

8 **Writing a Paragraph with Supporting Examples.** Choose one of the following three topic sentences and support it by writing two or more examples.

- Some days I feel that technology is my best friend.
- Some days I feel that technology is my worst enemy.
- I think I am one of the luckiest people in the world.

What Do You Think

Using Cellular Phones

An estimated one-tenth of the world's population owns a cellular phone. This means that any time day or night, these people can call or be called if the phone is on. Their phones can ring at the theater, in the coffee shop, in the classroom, in the car, in the bedroom.

- Do you think it's a good idea that a person can be reached at anytime? Why or why not?
- Where and when do you think that sending or receiving calls should not be allowed? In restaurants? At the movies? At a concert? In the classroom? Explain your point of view.
- What kind of restrictions should be put on phone calls while a person is driving?

PART 2   Tracks to the Future

Before You Read

1   **Identifying the Pattern of Organization.** Look at the title, illustrations, and the synopsis (brief summary) before the beginning of the article. What problem is being discussed? What solution is being offered?

Now that you know the topic, try to identify the way the article is organized. This can help you to read it more easily. Look at the following three patterns. Then take a couple of minutes to skim the article and tell which pattern it uses.

Pattern 1: From General to Specific
- General statement of a problem
- Specific examples of the problem
- History of why the problem exists
- Discussion of the possible solution(s)

Pattern 2: From Specific to General
- Description of specific examples of a larger problem
- History of why the problem exists
- General Statement of the problem
- Discussion of the possible solution(s)

Pattern 3: From Personal to General to Specific
- Personal story of author's connection to the problem
- General statement of the problem
- History of why the problem exists
- Discussion of the possible solution(s)

2   **Scanning to Complete Common Phrases.** Learn some common phrases that will expand your vocabulary and help you to read the article. Scan for the words to complete the following phrases and fill in the blanks. (The phrases are given in the same order as they appear in the article.

1. getting on (a train, plane, or boat): climbing on <u>board</u>
2. starting out as one of the first to act: leading the _____
3. crowding together of many vehicles so that they move very slowly: traffic _____
4. spreading out of neighborhoods to places only reached by cars: suburban _____
5. a group of streetcars used together in one city: a _____ of streetcars
6. the arrangement of workers and operations in a factory to put together machines or appliances: the _____ line
7. the decorative style of the 1920 and 30s, using bold lines: the Art _____ look
8. moving in a steady decrease of number that can not be reversed: in an _____ decline
9. an international fashion or tendency: a worldwide _____
10. the areas that are situated away from the center of the city: the _____ of the city

Read

Nowadays, some people are choosing low tech over high tech because they think it improves their quality of life. They prefer to walk, ride a bicycle, or take the bus to work, rather than driving a car and having a parking problem. They like chatting with someone on the telephone, rather than writing an e-mail message. One example of a low-tech solution to current problems is the streetcar. This was a popular form of transportation about 80 or 90 years ago. Later, it disappeared, but now urban planners say we should bring it back.

■   If the streetcar is so great, why did it disappear?

■   What problems would be solved by using streetcars for public transportation?

Read to find out the answers to these questions and to learn more about the problems of our cities.

Tracks to the Future
All Over The World, Commuters Are Climbing On Board.
The Modern Streetcar Is Leading the Charge Against Traffic Congestion, Pollution and Suburban Sprawl.

Peter Boisseau

At Rio Vista Junction near San Francisco, the old railway station has been transformed into the Western Railway Museum—a sort of retirement home for all things rail, including a fleet of streetcars. I have travelled from Toronto to see one streetcar in particular. Once known as KC551, the TTC4752 and finally, MUNI 1190, it sits in a field of gnarled yellow grass, still wearing the

5

faded cream and burgundy colours of the Toronto fleet of the 1950s. "They're like time machines," museum curator John Plytnick says quietly.

From the day it was introduced as a novelty ride by inventor John Wright at the Canadian Industrial Exhibition in Toronto in 1883, the electric streetcar spread to cities across the continent. By the early 1920s, it dominated urban travel in North America, Europe and parts of Asia, carrying billions of passengers a year.

My streetcar rolled off the assembly line in 1946—one of the last batches of the Presidents Conference Committee (PCC) class cars. Their comfortable ride and distinctive Art Deco look had been a welcome boost to the industry in the late 1930s. But by the time my streetcar took to the tracks in Kansas City as KC551, that city's once-mighty fleet was in irreversible decline, reflecting a worldwide trend.

The reasons are still hotly debated. Ridership had never recovered to pre-Depression levels. Meanwhile, maintenance bills on aging fleets rose, profits suffered and, in North America, the car was becoming the preferred mode of transport. There's little doubt that an alliance of oil, tire and auto companies led by General Motors played a large part in the disappearance of the streetcar, especially in the United States. Between 1936 and 1950, through a company called National City Lines, the alliance snapped up 100 privately owned streetcar lines in 45 cities and replaced them with routes plied by buses—made mostly by GM.

The U.S. government had also started an aggressive freeway construction scheme to help move people and their automobiles from the cities to the rapidly swelling suburbs. Ironically, some say the streetcar lines were used to spur development on the outskirts of cities. A case in point is Kansas City's Country Club line: KC551 was one of the last streetcars to run this route, which ended at the site of America's first suburban shopping mall.

It wasn't until the late 1960s that urban planners began to realize that their highway-building schemes were actually adding to congestion by encouraging more people to drive. In the developed world, there is now one car for every two people. Each year thousands of deaths are attributed to air pollution largely caused by smog from engine exhaust. And it only stands to get worse. If China and India reach half the level of car ownership of the developed countries, the world's population of automobiles will double, says Hirotaka Koike, an

40   urban-planning professor from Utsunomiya University in Japan, a country that is also seeking to bring back its abandoned streetcar systems.

     A growing body of evidence also suggests streetcars play a dynamic role in restoring the quality of urban life—much more so than a bus. In the U.K., Manchester reduced traffic by 2.6 million car journeys a year thanks to its new

45   tramway and now plans an expansion to revitalize the city's docklands area. In Edinburgh, a proposed tramway along the waterfront would share existing bus lanes.

     Car traffic fell 17 percent in downtown Strasbourg, France, after city planners gave light rail priority. "The coming of the tram has been both an urban

50   and ecological success," says Bertrand Wipf-Scheibel of Compagnie des Transports Strasbourgeois. Elsewhere in France, engineers are experimenting with a less expensive system for smaller towns—a rubber-tired streetcar guided by a single grooved rail.

     In the United States, the resurgent streetcar industry has greatly bene-

55   fited from billions of dollars in federal money earmarked for new transit, leading some critics to suggest the revival is fuelled by politics. The government, however, may simply be searching for a more effective way to ease traffic congestion.

En Route, Air Canada Magazine

After You Read

3   **Adding Suffixes to Form Nouns and Adjectives.** Many nouns and adjectives are formed by adding a suffix to the root of a related verb or noun. Fill in the blanks with nouns or adjectives from the article that are related to the words in italics. (See pages 5 and 6 for examples of suffixes.) The words are given in the order of their appearance in the article.

1. Just like people, old machines need to *retire* and the Western Railway Museum is a sort of ____retirement____ home for old streetcars.
2. *Comfort* is necessary in public transportation. People want a _____ ride.
3. The streetcar was *invented* for the Canadian Industrial Exhibition in Toronto in 1883. John Wright was the _____.
4. It is not easy to *maintain* an aging fleet. The cost of _____ is high.
5. Auto, oil, and tire companies were *allies* in the fight for more highways in the 1930s and 40s. They formed an _____ to kill the streetcar.
6. Tracks began to *disappear* in the cities and more roads were built. General Motors played a large part in the _____ of the streetcar.
7. The U.S. government started to *construct* more highways. It had an aggressive _____ scheme.
8. Developers began to *develop* more land for housing. Much of this _____ was on the outskirts of the city.
9. These new places were called *suburbs*. This was the start of the _____ trend.

10. In developing countries many people want to be *owners* of cars. If they greatly increase their level of car _____ , there could be problems for the world's ecology.

11. Some cities want to *expand* their public transportation system. This kind of _____ helps to bring life to the city centers.

12. Governments are trying to *revive* the streetcar industry. This _____ may be an effective way to ease traffic congestion.

4   **Paraphrasing Key Ideas.** One of the best ways to test our comprehension is to paraphrase (explain in our own words) the key ideas from a reading. Use the questions as a guide and write a short paragraph to explain each of the following ideas.

- *Changes by vested interests.* Often changes are made in society by vested interests (groups who make money from these changes). The public does not know what these groups are doing until many years later. The article describes a change like this during the 1930 and 40s in cities in the United States (lines 18–26). Who were these vested interests? What did they do, and why?

_____

_____

_____

_____

- *Unforeseen consequences.* Even with the best of intentions, governments sometimes make programs that bring bad results or consequences. Often these are consequences that no one expected or foresaw (saw in advance). The article tells about a government program like this (lines 27–41). What did the government do? Why? What bad consequences occurred?

_____

_____

_____

_____

Talk It Over

1. Is there a problem with traffic congestion in the place where you live? If so, when and where does it happen?

2. Have you ever experienced gridlock (being in a car when there is so much traffic that all movement stops)? How do people feel when that happens? In what ways can this be a dangerous situation?

3. Have you ever taken a streetcar? Which do you prefer: a streetcar, a bus, or a subway? Why? In your opinion, would it help cities to bring back streetcar systems?

4. Do you sometimes choose low tech in your life rather than high tech? Can you give some examples of this? Do you think that low tech can improve our quality of life?

5 **Doing a Street Interview.** Pretend that your classroom is a street and you are a news reporter. Ask three or more people what their opinions are on one of the following questions. (Other people may ask you questions too and you will have to take time to answer—politely, of course!) Copy down the answers and report on your findings.

- ■ Life in the Suburbs. Would you like to live in the suburbs? Why or why not? Describe the kind of house that would be your dream house. Would you have trees, a dog, a big garage, a swimming pool? Explain. What disadvantages are there in the suburbs?

- ■ Living downtown in the heart of the city. Would you like to live in a nice apartment in the heart of the city? Why or why not? What would your apartment be like? Where would it be located? Where would you go and what would you do in the evenings? What disadvantages would there be to urban life?

- ■ Road rage. Have you heard about road rage (intense anger and violence that people feel while driving a car)? What do you think causes this? What makes you angry when you are driving or riding in a car? Do you love cars or hate them? What would your ideal car be like, the car of your dreams?

Focus on Testing

Computerized Testing

The latest innovation in testing is the computerized test. Test questions and answer choices are presented on the screen and students can answer with a tap of the keyboard or a click of the mouse. Before the actual test begins, there usually is a tutorial showing how to use the computer to respond to the questions. Scores are displayed on the screen at the end of the test so that a student has immediate feedback rather than having to return several days later for results.

Some computerized tests are "adaptive." This means that a test question is selected from a large pool of items based on how the test taker has responded to the prior question. The first question presented is of medium difficulty. If the test taker answers correctly, the next item will be more difficult. If he or she answers incorrectly, the next question will be easier. The computer sorts questions by level of difficulty and many other factors, such as gender, ethnic and age references, area or discipline it is drawn from, and format of the question, before presenting it on the screen. In this way, the questions are "adapted" to find the true skill level of the test taker.

Among all the conveniences of computerized testing, there are some drawbacks. No longer can you get a quick overview of the test, answer the easy questions first, and come back later to finish the difficult ones. Test items are presented one at a time, and you *must* choose an answer in order to move on to the next question. On adaptive tests, once you have confirmed your answer, you cannot go back to change it if, later on, you realize that your answer was wrong.

Here are some helpful tips to remember when taking computerized tests.

1. Always read everything that appears on the screen. Understanding the directions for answering the question can be as important as knowing the correct answer.
2. Take as much time as you need to familiarize yourself with how to take the test by paying attention to the tutorial. Many computerized tests are untimed and those that are timed do not start the timer until the tutorial is finished.
3. Be as certain as you can about your answer choice because you cannot go back to change it once it is confirmed.
4. Use only the keys that you have been told to use in the tutorial or test instructions. Pressing other combinations of keys may interfere with the test.
5. It won't bite! If you are using a computer for the first time, do not hesitate to ask the examiner or test proctor for help in getting started. Most of all, do not be afraid of the mouse; it won't bite!

Angelia Jovanovic, Assessment Counselor
Sacramento City College

Scan the article for the correct terms to replace the words or phrases in italics, and write them in the blanks.

1. Test questions appear on the screen and students answer with a tap of the keyboard or a click of the *pointing device* mouse.
2. Before the test begins there is usually a *program teaching you how to take the test* _____.
3. Some computerized tests are *progressively adjusted to the ability of the test taker as he or she gives right or wrong answers* _____.
4. In this kind of test, the computer sorts questions by level of difficulty but also by factors such as *whether the prior question was about a male or female* _____.
5. Some other factors the computer uses for sorting questions are ethnic and age references, discipline that the question is drawn from, and the *manner of presentation, that is, true/false, multiple choice, and so on* _____ of the question.
6. One of the drawbacks of computerized testing is that you can no longer make a quick *skimming of all items* _____ so that you can answer the easy questions first.
7. On some tests, once you have *indicated for a second time* _____ your answer, you cannot go back and change it.
8. The most important tip of all, according to the author, who has worked for 20 years in the field of testing, is to always read everything that appears on the *surface for viewing* _____.
9. You should take as much time as you need to go through the instructional program at the beginning because computerized tests do not start the *device that measures how long you take* _____ until the tutorial is finished.

Video Activities: Internet Publishing

Before You Watch.

1. Match the words with their meanings.
    1. online   a.   part of a story usually published in chronological order
    2. download   b.   on the Internet
    3. installment   c.   to move information from the Internet to your computer
2. Do you use the Internet? What do you use it for?

Watch.   Circle the correct answers.

1. What kinds of things does William Bass download onto his computer?
    a. music   b. research   c. sports articles   d. pictures
2. What is true about Stephen King's book, *The Plant*?
    a. It was published online.   b. It was free.
    c. It was published in parts.   d. It was a bestseller.
3. According to William Bass, the best thing about books online is that they're
    _____.
    a. cheap   b. convenient   c. easy to read
4. What did Stephen King threaten to do if not enough people paid for his
    book?
    a. charge more for the rest of the book
    b. not write another book online
    c. not finish rest of the book
5. Gillian McCombs says that electronic books will _____.
    a. help sell regular books
    b. let authors make more money
    c. never replace paper and ink books

Watch Again.   Compare answers in small groups.

1. How much did Stephen King charge for *The Plant*?_____
2. What was the minimum percentage of paid downloads would Stephen King
    accept?
    a. 25%   b. 75%   c. 95%
3. The male publishing expert says that Stephen King's book will _____.
    a. be the death of paper and ink books
    b. not change the publishing industry
    c. not be a success

After You Watch.   Find an article in which the writer gives his/her opinion about
technology. Answer these questions:

1. Who was the intended audience? How do you know?
2. What is the writer's opinion?
3. What support does he/she give for this opinion?

Chapter 6

Money Matters

IN THIS CHAPTER

The first selection describes the success story of a business that is making money and creating jobs across many national borders. The second selection, written by one of the great short story writers of the English language, focuses on a more personal aspect of the financial question: the embarrassment and difficulties that a lack of money can cause in a social situation.

PART 1

Executive Takes Chance on Pizza, Transforms Spain

Before You Read

1   **Skimming for the General Idea.** Try to get a general idea of what an article is about before beginning it. This will help you comprehend it better. Look at the title and photo. Then take one minute to skim the whole article and answer the following question. Compare your answer with those of your classmates.

What are three factors that helped this man succeed?

2   **Scanning for Members of Word Families.** A good way to expand vocabulary is through word families—groups of words related in form and meaning, such as *combine, combined,* and *combination.* Scan the reading selection for words related to the given words and write them underneath. The words are in the order of their appearance in the article.

1.   pizza

  ___pizzeria___   A noun meaning "a place that produces or sells pizza"

2.   convenient

  _____   A noun meaning "quality of being convenient, easy, or suitable"

3.   modern

  _____   A verb meaning "becoming modern"

4.   manage

  _____   A noun meaning "the act or manner of managing"

5.   prosperous

  _____   A verb meaning "did well or became prosperous (wealthy)"

6.   special

  _____   A noun meaning a "types of food, or other products, that are special"

7.   afford

  _____   An adjective meaning "can be afforded by a person's financial means, not too expensive"

8.   mental

  _____   A noun meaning "mental outlook, way of thinking"

9.   mature

  _____   A verb meaning "growing older and wiser, becoming more mature"

Read

Unlike the trend of the last century, when most people stayed in one job or profession for a lifetime, the people in business today change jobs frequently as they try to climb the ladder to success. Sometimes they do succeed; sometimes they fail. Leopoldo Fernandez Pujols changed from being a salesman for a medical supply company to opening his own business. Read the following article to see how he managed to become successful.

Executive Takes Chance on Pizza, Transforms Spain

MADRID, Spain—Leopoldo Fernandez was earning $150,000 a year as an executive in Spain with Johnson & Johnson when he decided to open a pizzeria on the side.

"Keep in mind, I knew nothing about pizza. My job was about selling
5   heart valves, heart monitors, surgical instruments," said the 47-year-old Cuban-American, a former marketing director for the U.S. medical supply company.

Six years later, Fernandez is the president of TelePizza, a multinational with projected sales of $120 million this year. By year's end, the Madrid-based
10   pizza businessman's name will adorn more than 200 outlets in 10 countries. The company, one of the first to answer a need for convenience goods in modernizing Spain, may even be the world's fastest growing pizza chain, according to a recent issue of the trade magazine *Pizza Today* and research by TelePizza.

15   "I thought I'd just open five little stores and keep my job at Johnson & Johnson," recalled Fernandez in an interview as he puffed a $5 Cuban cigar. Two small Cuban flags are placed on his desk top.

Success came "so quickly my biggest problem has been keeping on top of the growth-money management, people management, training. Most new
20   businesses grow at 10–20 percent yearly. We've grown at 10 percent a month since we opened," Fernandez said.

After his first shop prospered in Madrid, Fernandez left his job, sold his house and stocks, and cobbled together $300,000 to put into the business. From then on, new pizzerias opened rapidly, first in Spain and then abroad.

25   At the time TelePizza began in the late 1980s, pizzas were available in Spain only in Italian restaurants, and home delivery of any food was rare. But with more women in the workplace and Spain still modernizing, there was a growing need for convenience foods. TelePizza's success is widely credited with setting off a boom in home-delivered fast food in Spain.

30   Hundreds of motorbikes now ply Madrid's streets delivering everything from pizza to traditional specialities like Spanish tortillas (egg and potato omelettes) and paella.

Like the Domino's chain of U.S. fame, TelePizza's pies come fast—the company guarantees that pizzas will arrive in under 30 minutes, depending
35   on where customers live. They are fairly affordable, with a pie for up to four people costing $13, compared with $6 for a McDonald's quarter-pounder, fries and Coke, undelivered.

Some say Spain's growing appetite for fast food is undermining the country's healthy Mediterranean diet. "There's a saying, when we were poor we
40 made better eating choices than we do now," said Consuelo Lopez Nomdedeu, a nutritionist with the government-run National College of Health. But Fernandez dismissed such complaints. "The key is variety in the diet," he said. "I wouldn't eat pizza daily or hamburgers (nor would I eat) Spanish dishes like lentils or garbanzos."

45 Along with crediting the untapped Spanish market for his success, Fernandez noted that growing up as an immigrant in the United States probably also helped. Like many other refugees fleeing the Castro revolution, Fernandez moved to Florida from Cuba in 1960 with his parents.

"An immigrant has to find ways to succeed because he's on the bottom,"
50 said Fernandez, who also has worked for Procter & Gamble Co., the leading U.S. consumer products company.

"Here, my advantage is that I understand Spanish mentality better than Americans do and I understand Americans better than Spaniards do," Fernandez said.

55 So far, his recipe for success is working. Fernandez said TelePizza outsells its three biggest rivals in Spain—Domino's, Pizza Hut and Pizza World—combined. The company has a fleet of more than 2,000 motorbikes in Spain and sells 25,000 pizzas daily in the Spanish market.

About two-thirds of TelePizza outlets in Spain are franchises while 90 per-
60 cent of the 40 stores abroad are company-owned. In addition to Spain, there are TelePizza outlets located in Mexico, Colombia, Chile, Portugal, Belgium, Greece and Poland—with stores in France and Brazil set to open before year's end.

"We plan to go into the U.S. in due time," Fernandez said. "For now we
65 are maturing and learning from growth markets."

Stephen Wade

CLOSE TO HOME   JOHN McPHERSON

PIZZA SHACK

"Didn't that pizza delivery kid used to be our paperboy?"

After You Read

3 **Using the Context to Explain Business Terms.** Use the context and the clues to explain the following business terms.

1. executive (line 2) The verb *to execute* means "to carry out or put into effect"
   administrator or manager in a company

2. multinational (line 8) Break the word apart to find its meaning.
   _____

3. projected sales (line 9) Think about what a project is and the time frame it refers
   to. _____

4. outlets (line 10) Break the word apart and remember we are talking about a product that is being marketed. _____

5. chain (line 12) Imagine a picture of a chain, made up of separate parts called links.
   _____

6. boom (line 39) The meaning can be inferred partly from the sound of this word.
   _____

7. untapped market (line 45) *To tap* something means "to open or start" it, as in tapping an oil well Do you know the meaning of the prefix *un-*?

    _____

8. franchises (line 59) Notice these stores are contrasted with others that are company-owned. _____

9. growth markets (line 65) Take a guess from the words themselves.

    _____

4   Answer these questions in small groups.

1. What problems did Mr. Fernandez have at first?
2. Why do you think that TelePizza is doing so well?
3. What does the Spanish nutritionist think of the recent changes in Spanish eating habits? Do you agree with her opinion or with that of Mr. Fernandez?
4. What kinds of "fast food" are popular where you live? What do you think of them?
5. How does Mr. Femandez's nationality as a Cuban-American help him?

Talk It Over

Since Leopoldo Fernandez opened his first Telepizza outlet, the company owns or franchises more than 760 pizza outlets. Telepizza restaurants are mainly in Spain, but now also in seven other countries: Germany, Sweden, Chile, Mexico, Morocco, Poland and Portugal. Fernandez recently bought a failed Domino's franchise in France and hopes to crack the U.S. market in the near future. A short time ago he branched out into U.S. style food courts that serve other types of food such as grilled chicken and ribs, and Chinese dishes. His fleet of mopeds has grown to over 15,000.

In a small group, discuss this approach to business with the following questions. Compare your answers with those of other groups.

1. Do you think that it is wise to expand as much and as fast as Telepizza has been doing recently?
2. How do you know when you are taking too much of a risk? When is it good not to take a risk?
3. What factors, besides luck, could cause problems for a business like this one?
4. Would you like to have your own business some day, or do you prefer to work for someone else? Explain your choice.

Around the Globe

Successful entrepreneurs (people who start new businesses) from around the world offer advice about how to succeed in business in the following quotes. Write a paragraph about one of the quotes telling in your own words what you think it means and why you like it or dislike it. Be sure to write the quote and its author at the beginning.

- "Lead, follow, or get out of the way."
  " Never get discouraged and quit. Because if you never quit, you're never broken."
  —Ted Turner, founder of CNN and TNT

- "Develop a product where there is no market, then create one."
  —Akio Morita, Sony Electronic

- "Success is the one percent of your work that results from the 99 percent that is called failure."
  —Soichiro Honda, Honda cars and motorcycles

- "Build 'em strong and sell 'em cheap."
  "Concentrate on one product used by everyone, every day."
  —Baron Marcel Bich, Bic pens, razors

- "A computer on every desk and in every home."
  —Bill Gates, Microsoft Corporation

Focus on Testing

Reading Between the Lines

In many reading comprehension tests, you are asked to read a passage and choose the best answer to some questions about it. Often these questions ask you to make an inference about the reading. Remember that an inference is a true idea that is not stated directly but can be inferred (concluded or deduced) from what is stated. In English, this is often called "reading between the lines."

Look at the first question of the following exercise. In order to choose the correct inference, you must decide why three of the ideas are not correct inferences. The test is trying to fool you, so be careful! First, one of the choices is false. Another is true, but we don't have enough information to decide. Another of the choices may be true but is already directly stated in the passage in different words. So it is not an inference. Now, through the process of elimination, we have cut out three choices and are left with the one correct answer. So, circle the letter for that answer.

Following are three passages from the article "Executive Takes Chance on Pizza, Transforms Spain." Each passage is followed by a question about it. Circle the one best answer.

Question 1

Leopoldo Fernandez was earning $150,000 a year as an executive in Spain with Johnson & Johnson when he decided to open a pizzeria on the side. "Keep in mind, I knew nothing about pizza. My job was about selling heart valves, heart monitors, surgical instruments," said the 47-year-old Cuban-American, a former marketing director for the U.S. medical supply company.

1. What can be inferred from the passage about Leopoldo Fernandez?
    a. He is middle-aged.
    b. He was born in Cuba.
    c. He is a risk taker.
    d. He was poor before starting a business.

Question 2

At the time TelePizza began in the late 1980s, pizzas were available in Spain only in Italian restaurants, and home delivery of any food was rare. But with more women in the workplace and Spain still modernizing, there was a growing need for convenience foods. TelePizza's success is widely credited with setting off a boom in home-delivered fast food in Spain.

2. What can be inferred from the passage about TelePizza's customers?
    a. They like to buy on credit.
    b. They do not like Italian restaurants.
    c. Many are very traditional.
    d. Many are working women.

Question 3

Along with crediting the untapped Spanish market for his success, Fernandez noted that growing up as an immigrant in the United States probably also helped. Like many other refugees fleeing the Castro revolution, Fernandez moved to Florida from Cuba in 1960 with his parents.

"An immigrant has to find ways to succeed because he's on the bottom," said Fernandez, who also has worked for Procter & Gamble Co., the leading U.S. consumer products company.

3. What can be inferred from the passage about Fernandez's opinion of immigrants?
    a. Immigrants usually don't work as hard as others.
    b. Immigrants usually work harder than others.
    c. Immigrants are employed by big companies.
    d. Immigrants receive support from their families.

The Luncheon

Before You Read

1 **Identifying the Setting, Characters, and Conflict.** Reading a story is easier if you first identify the key narrative elements that every story must have.

- setting, the time and place
- characters, the main people who act in the story
- plot, the action that starts with a conflict, develops into a complication, and ends with a resolution

1. Find the setting by looking at the illustration and skimming the first few paragraphs. When does the story take place (more or less)? _____ Where? _____

2. Who are the main characters? There is of course the narrator (the one speaking) since the story is written in the first person (using "I" and "me"). The other character is a woman whose name we are never told. What do we know about this woman?

    _____

    _____

3. We cannot identify in advance the whole plot, but we can find out where it starts. The action always starts with a conflict (a problem or difficulty) because if everything were fine, there would be no story. Read quickly up to line 23 and find the conflict. Explain it here.

    _____

    _____

You will have to read the story to see how this conflict gets complicated, rises to a climax (the most difficult and intense moment of the action), and then ends in the resolution.

2 **Getting the Meaning of Words from Context.** The author uses exact adjectives and adverbs to describe the feelings of the characters and the appearance of their surroundings. Look for clues in the context and underline the word or phrase closest to the meaning of the word in italics.

1. But I was *flattered* and I was too young to have learned to say no to a woman. (line 18)
    a. worried about the future
    b. <u>pleased by the praise</u>
    c. confused about what to do
    Notice the clue in line 13 where the woman praises the young man.

2. She was not so young as I expected and in appearance *imposing* rather than attractive. (line 25)
    a. notable
    b. good looking
    c. unattractive

3. I was *startled* when the bill of fare was brought, for the prices were a great deal higher than I had anticipated. (line 32)
    a. depressed by sad memories
    b. scared by a sudden surprise
    c. filled with hope

4. "What would you like?" I asked, hospitable still, but not exactly *effusive*. (line 55)
    a. enthusiastic
    b. silent
    c. timid

5. She gave me a bright and *amicable* flash of her white teeth. (line 56)
    a. angry
    b. false
    c. friendly

6. It would be *mortifying* to find myself ten francs short and be obliged to borrow from my guest. (line 92)
    a. embarrassing
    b. boring
    c. tiring

7. The asparagus appeared. They were enormous, *succulent*, and appetizing. (line 99)
    a. too ripe
    b. dry
    c. juicy

8. I knew too—a little later, for my guest, going on with her conversation, *absent-mindedly* took one. (line 121)
    a. with a cruel intention
    b. without thinking
    c. in a careful way

9. The bill came and when I paid it I found that I had only enough for a quite *inadequate* tip. (line 126)
    a. generous
    b. small
    c. exact

10. But I have had my revenge at last. I do not believe that I am a *vindictive* man, but... (line 134)
    a. forgiving and peaceful
    b. filled with contentment
    c. set on getting revenge

The following selection is a narrative (story) by one of the master short story writers of the English language, William Somerset Maugham (1874–1965). Born in Paris and educated in England, he worked as a secret agent for the British government in World War I and then spent the rest of his life writing and traveling throughout many parts of the world.

Read

3 **Predicting Events in a Narrative.** It is helpful while reading a narrative to think a bit ahead of the action. As you read, try to predict what is going to happen next. The story will be interrupted at a few points and you will be asked some questions to guide you. Do not worry about understanding every word. Just try to follow the main thread of the action. The narrator starts out by describing how he went to the theater and met a woman he had not seen in 20 years. This brings to his mind the memory of that time long ago and so he tells the story of that earlier meeting.

The Luncheon

I caught sight of her at the play and in answer to her beckoning I went over during the interval and sat down beside her. It was long since I had last seen her and if someone had not mentioned her name I hardly think I would have recognized her. She addressed me brightly.

5   "Well, it's many years since we first met. How time does fly! We're none of us getting any younger. Do you remember the first time I saw you? You asked me to luncheon."

Did I remember?

It was twenty years ago and I was living in Paris. I had a tiny apartment in
the Latin Quarter overlooking a cemetery and I was earning barely enough
money to keep body and soul together. She had read a book of mine and had
written to me about it. I answered, thanking her, and presently I received from
her another letter saying that she was passing through Paris and would like
to have a chat with me; but her time was limited and the only free moment she
had was on the following Thursday: she was spending the morning at the Lux-
embourg and would I give her a little luncheon at Foyot's afterwards? Foyot's
is a restaurant at which the French senators eat and it was so far beyond my
means that I had never even thought of going there. But I was flattered and I
was too young to have learned to say no to a woman. (Few men, I may add,
learn this until they are too old to make it of any consequence to a woman
what they say.) I had eighty francs (gold francs) to last me the rest of the
month and a modest luncheon should not cost more than fifteen. If I cut out
coffee for the next two weeks I could manage well enough.

*What do you think of the request that the woman has made of the main char-
acter? Why do you think that he accepted it? Do you think he is going to get
into trouble? Why or why not?*

I answered that I would meet my friend-by-correspondence at Foyot's on
Thursday at half past twelve. She was not so young as I expected and in appearance imposing rather than attractive. She was in fact a woman of forty (a
charming age, but not one that excites a sudden and devastating passion at
first sight), and she gave me the impression of having more teeth, white and
large and even, than were necessary for any practical purpose. She was talk-
ative, but since she seemed inclined to talk about me I was prepared to be
an attentive listener.

I was startled when the bill of fare was brought, for the prices were a great
deal higher than I had anticipated. But she reassured me.

"I never eat anything for luncheon," she said.

"Oh, don't say that!" I answered generously.

"I never eat more than one thing. I think people eat far too much nowadays. A little fish, perhaps. I wonder if they have any salmon."

Well, it was early in the year for salmon and it was not on the bill of fare,
but I asked the waiter if there was any. Yes, a beautiful salmon had just come
in—it was the first they had had. I ordered it for my guest. The waiter asked
her if she would have something while it was being cooked.

*What did the man notice about the woman's appearance? Does it perhaps give
a clue to her character? From what she has said so far, do you expect her to
order any more food? Why?*

"No," she answered. "I never eat more than one thing. Unless you had a
little caviar. I never mind caviar."

My heart sank a little. I knew I could not afford caviar, but I could not very
well tell her that. I told the waiter by all means to bring caviar. For myself I
chose the cheapest dish on the menu and that was a mutton chop.

"I think you're unwise to eat meat," she said. "I don't know how you can expect to work after eating heavy things like chops. I don't believe in overloading my stomach."

50   Then came the question of drink.

What do you think the woman is going to say about the question of drink? What do you think she is going to do? And the man? Why?

"I never drink anything for luncheon," she said.

"Neither do I," I answered promptly.

"Except white wine," she proceeded as though I had not spoken. "These French white wines are so light. They're wonderful for the digestion."

55   "What would you like?" I asked, hospitable still, but not exactly effusive.

She gave me a bright and amicable flash of her white teeth.

"My doctor won't let me drink anything but champagne."

I fancy I turned a trifle pale. I ordered half a bottle. I mentioned casually that my doctor had absolutely forbidden me to drink champagne.

60   "What are you going to drink, then?"

"Water."

She ate the caviar and she ate the salmon. She talked gaily of art and literature and music. But I wondered what the bill would come to. When my mutton chop arrived she took me quite seriously to task.

65   "I see that you're in the habit of eating a heavy luncheon. I'm sure it's a mistake. Why don't you follow my example and eat just one thing? I'm sure you'd feel ever so much better for it."

"I *am* only going to eat one thing," I said, as the waiter came again with the bill of fare.

The waiter has come once again. What will happen next?

70   She waved him aside with an airy gesture.

"No, no, I never eat anything for luncheon. Just a bite, I never want more than that, and I eat that more as an excuse for conversation than anything else. I couldn't possibly eat anything more—unless they had some of those giant asparagus. I should be sorry to leave Paris without having some

75   of them."

"Madame wants to know if you have any of those giant asparagus," I asked the waiter.

I tried with all my might to will him to say no. A happy smile spread over his broad, priestlike face, and he assured me that they had some so large, so

80   splendid, so tender, that it was a marvel.

"I'm not in the least hungry," my guest sighed, "but if you insist, I don't mind having some asparagus."

I ordered them.

"Aren't you going to have any?"

85   "No, I never eat asparagus."

"I know there are people who don't like them. The fact is, you ruin your palate by all the meat you eat."

Something is ironic when it is the opposite of what is true or expected. What is ironic about what the woman keeps saying? How do you think the man feels about this? Do you think the man or the woman will order more food?

We waited for the asparagus to be

90   cooked. Panic seized me. It was not a question now of how much money I should have left over for the rest of the month, but whether I had enough to pay the bill. It would be mortifying to find myself ten francs short and be obliged to borrow from my guest. I could not bring myself to do that. I knew exactly how much I had and if the bill came to more I had made up my mind

95   that I would put my hand in my pocket and with a dramatic cry start up and say it had been picked. Of course it would be awkward if she had not money enough either to pay the bill. Then the only thing would be to leave my watch and say I would come back and pay later.

The asparagus appeared. They were enormous, succulent, and appe-

100   tizing. The smell of the melted butter tickled my nostrils as the nostrils of Jehovah were tickled by the burned offerings of the virtuous Semites. I watched the abandoned woman thrust them down her throat in large voluptuous mouthfuls and in my polite way I discoursed on the condition of the drama in the Balkans. At last, she finished.

105   "Coffee?" I asked.

"Yes, just an ice cream and coffee," she answered.

I was past caring now, so I ordered coffee for myself and an ice cream and coffee for her.

"You know, there's one thing I thoroughly believe in," she said, as she ate

110   the ice cream. "One should always get up from a meal feeling one could eat a little more."

"Are you still hungry?" I asked faintly.

"Oh, no. I'm not hungry; you see, I don't eat luncheon. I have a cup of coffee in the morning and then dinner, but I never eat more than one thing for

115   luncheon. I was speaking for you."

"Oh, I see!"

Then a terrible thing happened. While we were waiting for the coffee, the head waiter, with an ingratiating smile on his false face, came up to us bearing a large basket full of peaches. They had the blush of an innocent girl; they

120   had the rich tone of an Italian landscape. But surely peaches were not in season then? Lord knew what they cost. I knew too—a little later, for my guest, going on with her conversation, absentmindedly took one.

125   "You see, you've filled your stomach with a lot of meat"—my one miserable little chop—"and you can't eat any more. But I've just had a snack and I shall enjoy a peach."

The bill came and when I paid it I found that I had only enough for a quite inadequate tip. Her eyes rested for an instant on the three francs I left for the waiter and I knew that she thought me mean. But when I walked out of the restaurant I had the whole month before me and not a penny in my pocket.

So far the luncheon has gone badly for the man. Since you know that Somerset Maugham likes irony and surprise endings, can you think of some way he might turn the situation around? Will the man somehow get his revenge?

130   "Follow my example," she said as we shook hands, "and never eat more than one thing for luncheon."

"I'll do better than that," I retorted. "I'll eat nothing for dinner tonight."

"Humorist!" she cried gaily, jumping into a cab. "You're quite a humorist!"

But I have had my revenge at last. I do not believe that I am a vindictive
135   man, but when the immortal gods take a hand in the matter it is pardonable to observe the result with complacency. Today she weighs twenty-one stone.*

---

*The stone is a British unit of measurement. One stone equals fourteen pounds.

After You Read

4   **Recalling Idioms and Expressions.** Fill in the following summary of the story with idioms or expressions used in the selection. To help you, either the meaning is given in parentheses or the first or last word is given in italics.

He (saw) _____ her at a play. She said to him, "How *time* _____ and he remembered twenty years earlier when he was so poor that he could hardly keep _____ *together*. She had asked him to take her to a restaurant that was far (too expensive for him) _____ . He agreed, but *his heart* _____ when she ordered a very expensive meal. Ironically, she (scolded him) _____ for ordering one small chop. Afterward, he ordered coffee because he was *past* _____. Twenty years later, he saw that the immortal gods had (participated) _____ in his revenge: She was enormous!

Talk It Over

With a partner, discuss the following questions.

1. Why do you think the woman behaved as she did? Did she want to take advantage of the young man, or was she simply ignorant of his money problems? Or didn't she care if he had problems?

2. What should the young man have done to get out of this difficult situation? Do you think that he was trapped by the rules of courtesy and good manners? What would you have done in similar circumstances?

3. How has the author used irony in this story to create humor?

4. Have you ever been in an embarrassing situation because of money? If so, how did you get out of it?

5. Why do you think some people continually have money problems? Is it the fault of credit cards? Of lack of experience or training?

6. What is the best rule for managing your money?

What Do You Think?

Buying on the Internet

People love to shop, and more and more of them are shopping on the Internet. Some are pleased with the variety of goods offered, and the ease of shopping in the comfort of their own homes.

■ Have you ever shopped on the Internet? If so, what products have you bought?

■ Do you prefer to shop on the Net, use a catalog, or go to a store in person? Why?

■ Some consumers think it's not safe to buy on the Internet. Do you agree or not? What precautions would you take before completing a transaction on the Internet?

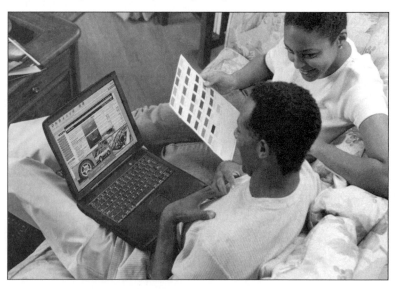

Video Activities: Welfare Payments

Before You Watch.   Discuss these questions in small groups.

1. What kinds of problems do you think that the Department of Social Services (DSS) takes care of?

    a. health   b. poverty   c. traffic   d. tax

2. A grand jury listens to evidence and decides _____.

    a. if a person is guilty or innocent
    b. on appropriate punishment for a criminal
    c. whether a crime has been committed

3. What kind of crime is graft?

Watch.   Circle the correct answers.

1. What was the grand jury's decision about DSS?

    a. They weren't giving poor families enough help.
    b. They often gave money to people that shouldn't get it.
    c. They needed a new director.

2. The grand jury felt that DSS's slogan <u>should</u> be, "When in doubt, _____ it out."

    a. check   b. give   c. put

3. What does the DSS's slogan in Question #2 mean?

    a. If you aren't sure about whether to give people money or not, get more information.
    b. If you don't know who should get help, ask your supervisor.
    c. If you have facts about a case, tell the people in charge.

4. What is Jake Jacobson's job?

    a. a lawyer for DSS   b. a client of DSS   c. director of DSS

5. The grand jury _____ Jacobson.

    a. praised   b. criticized   c. fired

Watch Again.   Complete the statements using the numbers.

20–30   7   20   60

1. DSS gives out $_____ million in overpayments a year.
2. The county board of supervisors will have _____ days to study the report.
3. The grand jury said that nothing had changed at DSS for the past ____ years.
4. The report said that _____ % of the DSS payments were fraudulent.

After You Watch.   Find an article about money or finance.

1. First skim it for the general idea and write one sentence about this idea.
2. Read it and compare the general idea with your sentence.
3. Find at least six words for which you know other forms (finance/financial, money/monetary, etc.).

Chapter 7

Remarkable Individuals

IN THIS CHAPTER

People can be remarkable in many ways. The first reading in this chapter is about a man who has had a lasting influence through the greatness of his intellect, the second about a woman well known for the power of her personality. The last selection deals with five heroes of extraordinary courage who have fought ardently on four different continents for the rights and dignity of the oppressed.

PART 1   # Confucius, 551 B.C.E.–479 B.C.E.

Before You Read

1   **Skimming for the General Idea.** Who was Confucius? Skim the following article for the answer to this question. (To refresh your memory about how to skim for the general idea of a reading, see page 40.) After you skim, circle the letter of the statement that best expresses the overall idea of the reading. Why is it better than the other two?

a. Confucius is a historical figure famous for his brilliant invention of a new philosophy that transformed the society of his times and has remained popular in China continuously until the present day.

b. Confucius was a powerful leader of ancient China whose ideas about mathematics, science, and human behavior formed the basis for traditional values and later inspired the communist government.

c. Confucius was the learned teacher responsible for a book of ethical and moral principles that has influenced Chinese society for many centuries, surviving attacks by different groups opposed to them.

2   **Figuring Out Words from Structure Clues.** Separate the following words into smaller words or affixes (prefixes or suffixes). Then, use the clues to make up a working definition, a definition that is helpful but not perfectly written.

1. childhood

    The affix -*hood* can extend something through space or time. So *neighborhood* is a space where neighbors are, and *childhood* is ___a time when you are a child___.

2. background

    The *ground* is the place where things are done, and *back* can refer to going back in space or time, so a person's *background* refers to _____.

3. principality

    A *kingdom* is a country ruled by a king, and a *principality* is a _____.

4. cornerstones

    The stones in the corners give the main support for a building. So the *cornerstones* of a philosophy are _____.

5. benevolent

    The root *bene-* means "good" (as in *benefit*, a good thing), and the root *vol* means "wishing" or "willing" (as in *volunteer*, one willing to do something), so *benevolent* means _____.

6. outlook

    Breaking the word into two smaller words, your *outlook* is the way you _____.

7. defender

The suffix *-er* means "one who ...," so a *defender* is _____.

8. innovator

The suffix *-or* is sometimes used in place of *-er* and means the same thing, so an *innovator* is _____.

9. commoners

Commoners are people who _____.

Read

Confucius, 551 B.C.E.–479 B.C.E.
Michael H. Hart

No other philosopher in the world has had more enduring influence than Confucius. For over two thousand years his concept of government, and his ideas about personal conduct and morality,
5   permeated Chinese life and culture. Even today, his thoughts remain influential.

There was little in his childhood background to predict the remarkable prestige that Confucius eventually achieved. He was born in a small prin-
10   cipality in northeastern China, was reared in poverty, and had no formal education. Through diligent study, however, he educated himself and became a learned man. For a while he held a minor government post; but he soon resigned
15   that position and spent most of his life as a teacher. Eventually, his most important teachings were gathered together into a book, the *Analects*, which was compiled by his disciples.

The two cornerstones of his system of personal conduct were *jen* and *li*. *Jen*
20   might be defined as "benevolent concern for one's fellow men." *Li* is a term less easily translated: it combines the notions of etiquette, good manners, and due concern for rituals and customs. Confucius believed that a man should strive after truth and virtue rather than wealth (and in his personal life he seems to have acted on that principle). In addition, he was the first major philosopher to state the Gold-
25   en Rule, which he phrased as "Do not do unto others that which you would not have them do unto you."

Confucius believed that respect and obedience are owed by children to their parents, by wives to their husbands, and by subjects to their rulers. But he was never a defender of tyranny. On the contrary, the starting point of his political out-
30   look is that the state exists for the benefit of the people, not the rulers. Another of his key political ideas is that a leader should govern primarily by moral example, rather than by force.

Confucius did not claim to be an innovator, but always said that he was mere-ly urging a return to the moral standards of former times. In fact, however, the

35   reforms which he urged represented a change from—and a great improvement over—the governmental practices of earlier days.

At the time of his death, Confucius was a respected, but not yet greatly influential, teacher and philosopher. Gradually, though, his ideas became widely accepted throughout China. Then, in the third century B.C. Shih Huang Ti united all

40   of China under his rule, and decided to reform the country entirely and make a complete break with the past. Shih Huang Ti therefore decided to suppress Confucian teachings, and he ordered the burning of all copies of Confucius' works. (He also ordered the destruction of most other philosophical works.)

Most Confucian books were indeed destroyed; but some copies survived the

45   holocaust, and a few years later, after the dynasty founded by the "First Emperor" had fallen, Confucianism re-emerged. Under the next dynasty, the Han, Confucianism became the official state philosophy, a position it maintained throughout most of the next two millennia.

Indeed, for much of that period, the civil service examinations in China were

50   based primarily on knowledge of Confucian classics. Since those examinations were the main route by which commoners could enter the administration and achieve political power, the governing class of the largest nation on Earth was largely composed of men who had carefully studied the works of Confucius and absorbed his principles.

55   This enormous influence persisted until the nineteenth century, when the impact of the West created revolutionary changes in China. Then, in the twentieth century, the Communist party seized power in China. It was their belief that, in order both to modernize China and to eliminate economic injustice, it was necessary to make radical changes in society. As the ideas of Confucius were highly

60   conservative, the communists made a major effort to eradicate his influence, the first such effort since Shih Huang Ti, twenty-two centuries earlier.

After You Read

3   **Identifying Key Terms.** From the column on the right, choose the best explanation for each of the following terms taken from the reading. Some explanations will be left over.

_c_	1. Analects	a.	A leader must sometimes use tyranny to achieve benefits for the state.
____	2. Confucian politics		
		b.	benevolent concern for other people
____	3. Golden Rule	c.	collection of the teachings of Confucius, made by his disciples
____	4. *jen*		
____	5. *li*	d.	Don't do to others what you don't want them to do to you.
____	6. Shi Huang Ti	e.	emperor of China in the third century who suppressed Confucianism
		f.	etiquette, good manners, and concern for rituals and customs
		g.	system of civil service examinations in China based mainly on Confucian ideas
		h.	The state exists for the people, and leaders should govern by example, not force.

4 **Forming Related Words.** Write the word from the reading related to each word in italics, according to the description.

1. the adjective related to *endure* _____ *enduring*
2. the adjective related to *influence* _____
3. the adverb related to *easy* _____
4. the adjective related to *politics* _____
5. the adverb related to *primary* _____
6. the adjective related to *government* _____
7. the adjective related to *Confucius* _____
8. the adjective related to *philosophy* _____
9. the verb related to *modern* _____

5 **Inferring Meaning.** The words on the left are listed in the order of their appearance in the reading. Match each word with the correct synonym or definition. For a word you are not sure about, scan the reading for it, and use the context to infer its meaning.

__j__	1.	enduring	a.	terrible destruction of one group of people
_____	2.	permeated	b.	fame, good reputation
_____	3.	reared	c.	try hard, make an effort, attempt
_____	4.	diligent	d.	get rid of completely, erase, do away
_____	5.	prestige	e.	filled, were present in all parts of
_____	6.	resigned	f.	abuse of power, cruel treatment of people under you
_____	7.	notions	g.	rule, government
_____	8.	etiquette	h.	hardworking, industrious, persistent, reliable
_____	9.	strive	i.	took control of, grabbed
_____	10.	tyranny	j.	lasting, continuing
_____	11.	suppress	k.	ideas, concepts
_____	12.	holocaust	l.	gave up, quit
_____	13.	dynasty	m.	push down, stop something from having an influence
_____	14.	seized	n.	raised, brought up
_____	15.	eradicate	o.	good manners, correct way of acting

6 **Supporting General Statements.** Working with a partner or in a small group, find specific facts to support the following statements about Confucius taken from the reading.

1. There was little in his childhood background to predict the remarkable prestige that Confucius eventually achieved.
2. But he was never a defender of tyranny.
3. Shih Huang Ti therefore decided to suppress Confucian teachings.
4. This enormous influence persisted until the nineteenth century, when the impact of the West created revolutionary changes in China.

Talk It Over

In small groups or with the class, discuss the following questions.

1. In your opinion, why has Confucianism had such an enduring influence?
2. Even in the world of today, *jen* and *li* are still the two most important principles for human social behavior. True or false? Explain.
3. Do you think that governments should exert control over their citizens? Should some ideas be prohibited? Can ideas be prohibited? Explain.

Around the Globe

Look at the photos and read the brief descriptions of two men who have been called leaders for the new millennium. Then, with a partner or in a small group, answer the questions.

Leaders Governing Change

Mexican President Vicente Fox took office in December, 2000, after defeating the candidate of the party that had ruled Mexico for 71 years.

Fox promised to concentrate development efforts in the poorer areas of Mexico's south and to treat Mexico's Indian population with more respect. He has introduced an Indian Bill of Rights to the Mexican legislature.

President Fox, a former Coca-Cola executive, has outlined a national micro-lending program and wants to channel profits from Mexico's growing economy into improving education and health services.

The 6-foot-5-inch president has big plans for the Mexican people. Of his economic program he said, " It is going to be an economic project to improve the life of each person."

Kim Dae-jung won the year 2000 Nobel Peace Prize for his work in expanding democracy and human rights in South Korea and East Asia in general. The Nobel Committee especially noted his work towards peace and reconciliation with North Korea.

Kim Dae-jung, along with his North Korean counterpart, Kim Jong-il, discussed security issues and signed an agreement to work toward eventual reunification of the Korean Peninsula. Initial steps were taken towards the reunification of families that have been separated for 50 years, since the end of the Korean War. South Korean financial investment in the North was also discussed.

"To us, a new day is beginning," said President Kim Dae-jung. "We are at a juncture of opening a new chapter in our history, putting an end to 55 years of division and hostility."

1. What great achievement of Vicente Fox has won the attention of the world?
2. What great achievement of Kim Dae-jung has won the attention of the world?
3. Do you think that these men will continue to make key changes in their countries? Why or why not? In your opinion, which man has the harder task?
4. What other leader do you think may bring about important changes in the near future? Explain.

Making Connections

Work by yourself or with a partner on one of the following tasks. Try to find some interesting facts on the Web, at the library, or in a local bookstore, and report back to the class.

* How do modern Chinese people view the teachings of Confucius? Are his books still selling? Does he influence movies or popular culture? What other Chinese philosophers can you find information on?
* How well is Vicente Fox doing as president of Mexico? Is he still popular? Does he travel a lot? Has he been able to make any important changes? What books has he written? Does his party have a Website?
* Who is Kim Dae-jung, really? What kind of life does he lead since winning the Nobel Peace Prize? Does he spend a lot of time with his family? Has he written a book? Does he continue to work toward reconciliation with North Korea?

Beating the Odds

Before You Read

1 **Using a Title and Illustrations to Predict.** Look at the title of the next selection. It's a phrase often used in reference to gambling (horseracing, poker, blackjack). People say, "What are the odds of winning? Is it one in two or one in a million?" Beating the odds means that you win, even when there is a very small chance of doing so.

Skim the article and look at the photos of Oprah Winfrey.

- What do you think the title tells us about her life?
- What do you learn about her by looking at the photographs?

2 **Using Context and Structure to Get Meaning.** Use your intuition, knowledge of word structure, and inference to select the meanings closest to the words in italics in the phrases taken from the reading. Underline the one correct choice for each item.

1. There is little question Oprah Winfrey has become one of the most *revered* celebrities of our time.
   a. unknown
   b. disliked
   c. <u>admired</u>
   d. remembered

2. …it is probably her *grueling* path to fame and fortune that has *endeared* her to millions of fans.
   grueling
   a. easy
   b. difficult
   c. enjoyable
   d. famous

3. *endeared* (Notice the small word inside this word.)
   a. made her unpopular
   b. made her dear
   c. made her known
   d. made her wealthy

4. … she also had a wild and *uncontrollable side* that forced her to move from relative to relative
   a. side that can not be controlled
   b. side that tries to control everyone
   c. side that is too much controlled
   d. side that sometimes controls

5. …until she ended up in the custody of her father, a strict *disciplinarian*.
   a. person without discipline
   b. person who hates discipline
   c. person who doesn't need discipline
   d. person who gives discipline

6. Despite all the *hardships* of her childhood, Oprah fused education, ambition, and talent into a vehicle for success as she rose from a position of poverty and a *disadvantaged* youth to become one of the most successful women in America.
   hardships
   a. happiness
   b. schools
   c. difficulties
   d. violence

7. *disadvantaged* (The prefix *dis-* means "not.")
   a. with many advantages
   b. with few if any advantages
   c. with the normal number of advantages

8. Her story is a *poignant* modern example of living the American Dream. (There aren't many clues here, so this is a good word to look up in the dictionary.)
   a. totally unbelievable
   b. sharply painful to the feelings
   c. hard to understand
   d. impossible to imitate

9. Still, she continued to *excel* academically, which, just as in Mississippi, earned her the *contempt* of her classmates.
   excel (Think of the related word *excellent*.)
   a. perform better than others
   b. perform worse than others
   c. perform the same as others
   d. not be able to perform at all

10. *contempt* (Here is another word worth looking up in the dictionary.)
    a. affection and friendship
    b. good will, help, cooperation
    c. indifference and lack of interest
    d. disdain, mockery, disrespect

Read

Oprah Winfrey is the wealthiest female entertainer in the world. She owns her own television and film production studio and her own magazine. Her TV talk show is watched by 22 million domestic viewers each week. Oprah's influence extends beyond the world of television into social awareness, publishing, film, philanthropy, and education. Her book club has revived interest in reading, and her Angel Network raised over $3.5 million in its first year to fund 150 scholarships for students in need. Her photo was featured on the cover of *Newsweek* magazine in January, 2001, as the leading woman of the new century.

To understand just how surprising Oprah's success is, you have to know something of the recent history of the United States. When she was growing up, African-Americans (then referrred to as Negroes) were subjected to a great deal of discrimination and prejudice (negative attitudes toward people of certain races and groups). In the South, they were forced to use separate, inferior washrooms and elevators from those of white people. When using public transportation, they had to sit in the back of the bus. Even in Northern cities, such as New York or Chicago, there were many restaurants, theaters, swimming pools, and other places where they were not allowed. All over the country, young people of color were segregated (placed in separate schools) and given inferior education and few job opportunities. All of this changed because of the Civil Rights movement in the 1960s and 70s. New laws were brought in to *desegregate* the schools and open up opportunities for *minorities* (groups that were not part of the white majority). There is still discrimination in some sectors, but in general, it has been greatly reduced.

Read the following article to find out more about Winfrey's early years and the influences that helped her to triumph over prejudice and achieve success.

Beating the Odds
Ben Muzabaugh

There is little question Oprah Winfrey has become one of the most revered celebrities of our time. But while her skills as an actress, host and producer have been widely acknowledged by critics, it is

5   probably her grueling path to fame and fortune that has endeared her to millions of fans.

Born in the poverty and oppressive racial climate of the Deep South in 1954, Oprah was the great-great granddaughter of Constantine and Vi-

10   olet Winfrey, a Mississippi slave couple who was freed after the Civil War. Although Oprah exhibited an exceptional aptitude, she also had a wild and uncontrollable side that forced her to move from relative to relative until she ended up in the

15   custody of her father, a strict disciplinarian.

Despite all the hardships of her childhood, Oprah fused education, ambition and talent into a

vehicle for success as she rose from a position of poverty and a disadvantaged youth to become one of the most successful women in America. Her story is a poignant modern example of living The American Dream, and it has served as an extraordinary source of motivation for women and men throughout the world.

Hard Times

Oprah was the child of Vernita Lee, a struggling single mother living deep in the heart of Mississippi at the beginning of the tumultuous Civil Rights Era. Vernita, wary of the poverty and prejudice of the South, decided to make a change. She moved north in hopes of earning better wages while facing fewer social obstacles than she would at home in Mississippi.

While she hoped the North would be more hospitable, Vernita was worried that bringing along her baby would prove exceedingly difficult. Vernita left Mississippi for Milwaukee in 1954, where she became a housekeeper for affluent white suburban families. But Oprah remained in the South under the care of her grandmother, Hattie Mae Lee.

From the very beginning, Hattie Mae stressed the importance of education to young Oprah, teaching her arithmetic, reading and writing by the age of three. It also did not take long for Oprah to show a penchant for narrating and performing. Even at her young age, she earned the admiration of church parishioners by performing in plays and reciting biblical passages with remarkable poise and confidence. Likewise, Oprah quickly excelled in school and was advanced directly to first grade after just a few days of kindergarten.

Northward Bound

In 1960, at age six, things changed dramatically for Oprah. Finally established in Milwaukee, Vernita Lee decided it was time for her daughter to join her. The world that Oprah discovered in the North was dramatically different than the one she had become accustomed to in the South. While Vernita was doing better financially in Milwaukee than she had in Mississippi, doing so required that she spend most of the day traveling to and from the distant suburban home where she cleaned house. This meant little direct supervision of Oprah, who now was forced to share a small one-room apartment with her mother, her mother's boyfriend and a younger child that came out of that relationship.

Oprah was no longer getting the attention she had received at Hattie Mae's farm. Still, she continued to excel academically, which, just as in Mississippi, earned her the contempt of her classmates. Just two years after bringing Oprah to Milwaukee, Vernita Lee found herself unable to give her daughter the care she deserved. Vernita's live-in boyfriend had reneged on promises to marry, and, desperate for a solution, Vernita called Vernon Winfrey to see if he could help.

Although his identity has never been confirmed, Vernon Winfrey is the man that Vernita believed to be Oprah's father. Vernon himself had only learned that he may have fathered the child when he received a news clipping of Oprah's birth, along with an ambiguous note from Vernita that read. "Send clothes."

Nonetheless, Vernon and his wife Zelma accepted Oprah into their Nashville home with open arms. Vernon and Zelma were strict guardians, determined to see Oprah live up to her potential. Vernon charged his daughter—now in the third grade—with the task of reading one book per week, with a written book report to follow.

When the next summer came, Oprah boarded a bus back to Milwaukee to visit her mother. Vernita was determined to keep custody of her daughter and refused to let Oprah return to Nashville.

70   Vernita's crowded apartment served as a boarding house for various relatives who used it when they had no place else to go. Unfortunately for Oprah, now entering her teen years, this scenario opened the door for one of the most difficult chapters of her life. Oprah has since maintained that several male family members sexually abused her during this time.

About this time, desegregation had begun at schools across the nation. Oprah was accepted into the Upward Bound program, which aimed to bring minorities to white private schools. With a full scholarship, Oprah began attending an upper
75   middle-class school in suburban Milwaukee. While the school was superior to the rough public school she had attended in the city, the transition was a difficult one. Oprah became acutely aware of the differences between her and her affluent white classmates.

The turmoil at home, coupled with her alienation in the classroom, led Oprah
80   to become increasingly rebellious. She became more difficult for Vernita to handle and finally ran away from home—remaining on the lam for a week before returning home after she ran out of money.

Vernita came to the conclusion that she could not handle Oprah. Vernon Winfrey agreed to take Oprah back into his home, where his strict discipline quickly
85   set his daughter back on a path that helped her become the media superstar she is today.

After You Read

3   **Identifying Positive and Negative Points.** The article describes both positive and negative influences in the early life of Oprah Winfrey. It does not separate these into two categories, but mixes them together in the form of a narrative. Work with a partner to make two lists: 1) the people, places, and events that had a positive influence and 2) the people, places, and events that were obstacles and negative influences. Compare your list with the lists of others.

4   **Recalling Vocabulary.** Follow the clues and fill in the blanks with the words missing from the phrases taken from the reading. The first letter of each word is given, and they are given in order of their appearance.

1.   Word meaning "famous people": one of the most revered c _elebrities_____ of our time

2.   Word meaning "the condition of being poor": born in the p_____ and oppressive racial climate of the Deep South

3.   Adjective describing something which is not peaceful or calm: the t_____ civil rights era

4.   The adjective related to the word *hospitality*: she hoped the North would prove more h_____.

5.   Another way of saying "very" or "to a great degree": e_____ difficult

6.   A synonym for *rich* or *wealthy*: a_____ white suburban families

7.   A word meaning "composure" or "ease and dignity of manner": with remarkable p_____ and confidence

8. A word meaning "vague, unclear, suggesting different meanings": along with an a_____ note

9. A noun meaning "a feeling of being alone and different from others": her a_____ in the classroom

10. The adjective related to the verb *rebel*: r_____

11. A word meaning "a condition of extreme disturbance and confusion": the t_____ at home

12. A three-word phrase meaning "in the act of running away": remaining o_____ t_____ l_____ for a week before returning home

Talk It Over

In a small group or with the class, discuss the following questions.

1. How much do you know about Oprah Winfrey? What skills and talents does she have? Why is she famous? In what ways did she "beat the odds"?

2. What do you think is meant by the reference to "the American Dream"? How does Oprah Winfrey symbolize this?

3. Do you think it builds character to have a difficult childhood? Can children be ruined by having it too easy or getting too much love? Explain.

3. What causes prejudice and discrimination against certain groups of people? What's the best way to fight prejudice and discrimination?

4. In Canada and the United States, people of color and gays have gained more rights in recent years. But they have gained even more rights in some European countries. What countries do you know about where people of color and gays enjoy more rights than in Canada and the United States?

5   **Making a Comparison and Contrast.** Confucius and Oprah Winfrey are separated by millennia of time and thousands of kilometers of distance. Still, it is possible to compare them since both are outstanding figures who have had a great impact on world culture. Work with a partner or in a small group to make a list of the most important similarities and differences between these two remarkable human beings. If time permits, use this list as a basis to write a brief essay of comparison and contrast between them, following this general outline.

Paragraph 1: Introduction describing each person and his or her importance and influence.

Paragraph 2: Similarities between the two.

Paragraph 3: Differences between the two.

Paragraph 4: Your own personal reaction and a general conclusion.

After you have finished, be sure to think of a good title and write it at the center top of your essay.

PART 3   Courage Begins with One Voice

Before You Read

1 **Previewing for Organization.** As you can see from the title and illustrations, the following article is about people who show great courage in working for the human rights of oppressed people. An article like this usually includes a general description of the subject and specific examples, but these can be organized in various ways. Look at the following three patterns of organization. Then skim the article and decide which pattern is used. Circle the number of the correct one.

1. Two or more specific examples / General description
2. General description / Two or more specific examples
3. One lively specific example / General description / Other specific examples

2 **Using Expressive Synonyms.** Good writers have large vocabularies. They don't have to repeat the same word over and over. They use words that are more exact and expressive than the common ones. Find synonyms from the reading to replace the common words and phrases in italics.

1. There is a common *complaint* _lament_ that there are no more heroes...
2. ...these women and men spoke to me with compelling *speaking ability* _____...
3. Their determination, *bravery* _____ and commitment...
4. ...in the face of *great* _____ danger...
5. ...to *work* _____ for a more decent society. (Look for a three-word expression.)
6. The crisis of authority is one of the causes for all the *cruel acts* _____...
7. ...and a writer of *strong* _____ essays on repression and dissent.
8. ...they are still ready to *give up* _____ their lives...
9. Today, she *keeps track of* _____ rights violations...
10. ...the two greatest *barriers* _____ to human progress...
11. The decisions we make about how to *lead* _____ our lives...
12. ...to *pay* _____ for the alleged crimes of their relatives.

Read

Now read the essay to learn more about courage and five heroes who possess this quality.

Courage Begins with One Voice
Kerry Kennedy Cuomo

There is a common lament that there are no more heroes.... That perception is wrong. I have spent the last two years interviewing 51 people from 40 countries about the nature of courage. Imprisoned, tortured, threatened with death, these women and men spoke to me with compelling eloquence on the subjects to which they have devoted their lives and for which they are willing to sacrifice them— from free expression to women's rights, from environmental defense to eradicating slavery.

Among them are the internationally celebrated, including Nobel Prize laureates. But most of them are unknown and (as yet) unsung beyond their national boundaries…. Their determination, valor and commitment in the face of overwhelming danger challenge each of us to take up the torch for a more decent society.

Kailash Satyarthi, India

"Small children of 6, 7 years and older are forced to work 14 hours a day without a break or a day for rest," says Kailash Satyarthi of the more than 6 million children in India who work in bonded labor— a form of slavery where a desperate family is forced to hand over a child as guaranty for a debt. "If they cry for their parents, they are beaten and tortured. They are often kept half-fed and are not permitted to talk or laugh out loud." Since 1990, Satyarthi has helped to free more than 40,000 people, including 28,000 children, from overcrowded, filthy and isolated factories, particularly in the massive carpet industry. "I have faced threats, and two of my colleagues have been killed," says Satyarthi, who heads the South Asian Coalition on Child Servitude. "But I think of it all as a test. If you decide to stand up against such social evils, you have to be fully prepared— physically, mentally and spiritually."

Vaclav Havel, Czech Republic

"The crisis of authority is one of the causes for all the atrocities we are seeing in the world today," says Vaclav Havel, 63, Czechoslovakia's leading playwright and a writer of compelling essays on repression and dissent. "The post-Communist world presented a chance for new moral leaders. But gradually people were repressed, and much of that opportunity was lost." In 1989, he was elected president of the newly formed Czech Republic, the first non-Communist leader in more than 40 years. Havel remains one of democracy's most principled voices. "There

are certain leaders one can respect, like the Dalai Lama," he says. "Although often they have no hope, they are still ready to sacrifice their lives and their freedom. They are ready to assume responsibility for the world—or the part of the world they live in. Courage means going against majority opinion in the name of the truth."

Kek Galabru, Cambodia

"There are around 600 to 900 people tortured by the police in custody every year to whom we give medical assistance," say Kek Galabru, 58. "Without us they would die." A medical doctor, Galabru played a key role in opening negotiations that led to the 1991 peace accords ending the Cambodian civil war, which left more than a million people dead.

Today, she monitors rights violations through the Cambodian League for the Promotion and Defense of Human Rights, which she founded. "Many times with our work, we are so depressed," she says. "It could be so easy for us to take out suitcases, take an airplane and not look back. But then we say, 'Impossible, they trust us.' When a victim comes to see us and says, 'I know I would have died if you were not here,' that gives us more energy. If we only save one person, it's a victory."

Oscar Arias Sanchez, Costa Rica

"War, and the preparation for war, are the two greatest obstacles to human progress, fostering a vicious cycle of arms buildups, violence and poverty," says Oscar Arias Sanchez, 60, the former president of Costa Rica. Arias was awarded the Nobel Peace Prize in 1987 for his role in ending conflict in Central America. He continues to campaign for democracy and demilitarization worldwide. "Three billion people live in tragic poverty," he says, "and 40,000 children die each day from diseases that could be prevented. War is a missed opportunity for humanitarian investment. It is a crime against every child who calls out for food rather than for guns. The decisions we make about how to conduct our lives, about the kind of people we want to be have important consequences. It is clear that one must stand on the side of life."

Juliana Dogbadzi, Ghana

"When I was 7, my parents sent me to a shrine where I was a slave to a fetish priest for 17 years," says Juliana Dogbadzi, 26, referring to the religious and cultural practice known as *Trokosi*, in which young girls, mostly virgins, are sent into servitude to atone for the alleged crimes of their relatives. "Each day, we woke up at 5 a.m., cleaned the compound, prepared a meal for the priest, worked until 6 and returned to sleep without food," she says. Sexual services also were required, resulting in unwanted pregnancies.

"Unlike most of the others, " says Dogbadzi, "I got over the fear instilled by the *Trokosi* system. This was my weapon." Today, after a daring escape, she travels the country speaking out against *Trokosi* and trying to win freedom for other slaves. "What I do is dangerous," she says, "but I am prepared to die for a good cause."

After You Read

3 **Identifying the Voices in a Reading.** An author sometimes presents different voices in an article by quoting (repeating) the exact words of other people. In this case, all five of the human rights heroes are quoted. Read the quotations from the reading and match the letter of the correct speaker to each quotation.

a. Kailash Satyarthi, India

b. Vaclav Havel, Czech Republic

c. Kek Galabru, Cambodia

d. Oscar Arias Sanchez, Costa Rica

e. Juliana Dogbadzi, Ghana

_____ 1. "War, and the preparation for war, are the two greatest obstacles to human progress, …"

_____ 2. "I have faced threats, and two of my colleagues have been killed … But I think of it all as a test."

_____ 3. "The post-Communist world presented a chance for new moral leaders. But gradually people were repressed, and much of that opportunity was lost."

_____ 4. "Each day, we woke up at 5 a.m., cleaned the compound, prepared a meal for the priest, worked until 6 and returned to sleep without food,…"

_____ 5. "Many times with our work, we are so depressed, It could be so easy for us to take out suitcases, take an airplane and not look back."

Focus on Testing

Previewing the Questions

Use the following True / False Comprehension Exercise to practice reading under the stress of test conditions. Imagine that you are taking an exam and must finish the exercise as fast as possible. What is the first thing you should do before beginning? Preview. Quickly look over all the questions to see what kind of information is asked for.

■ Is it small details or large ideas?

■ Where is the information you need for these questions?

■ Is it in one section, or will you have to reread two or more sections to answer some questions?

After previewing, start in right away and scan the reading for the answers you don't remember. Don't spend too much time on any item that seems hard or tricky. Just take a guess. (In True / False, you have a 50–50 chance of being right.) Keep your eye on the clock! How long did it take you too finish? Compare yourself with your classmates in terms of speed and accuracy. How well do you work under stress?

Write T for true or F for false in front of each statement about the reading. Correct the false statements to make them true.

_____ 1. The author spent two years interviewing 40 people from 51 countries about the nature of courage.

_____ 2. Most of these people are not well known, but a few of them are international celebrities.

_____ 3. Bonded labor is a system by which a poor child is taken care of by a host family and taught a trade in exchange for moderate work.

_____ 4. Kailash Satyarthi of India stopped working to free child workers after two of her colleagues were killed.

_____ 5. Vaclav Havel is a playwright and writer who became president of the Czech Republic in 1989.

_____ 6. Havel believes that a true leader like the Dalai Lama stands up for the opinions of the majority.

_____ 7. Kek Galabru helped to negotiate an end to the Cambodian Civil War in 1998, a war in which more than a million people died.

_____ 8. Today she gives medical assistance to victims of torture, and works for the Cambodian League for the Promotion and Defense of Human Rights.

_____ 9. Oscar Arias Sanchez, a former president of Costa Rica, was awarded the Nobel Peace Prize in 1997.

_____ 10. Arias Sanchez believes that the way to end conflict in Central America is to create a strong and just multinational military force.

_____ 11. _Trokosi_ is a cultural and religious practice in which young girls in Ghana are given away as slaves when they are very young.

_____ 12. Juliana Dogbadzi escaped from the _Trokosi_ system and left Ghana and now travels the world speaking against this practice.

4   **Using Noun Suffixes.** Various suffixes (-*ance, -ence, -itude, -ity, -ment, -tion*) are commonly added to verbs or adjectives to turn them into nouns. Sometimes small spelling changes are also necessary. Follow the model and write the correct nouns from the reading in the blanks.

1.   That (way to perceive) _perception_ is wrong.
2.   From free (actions to express) _____ to women's rights,…
3.   Their determination, valor and (choice to commit) _____ in the face of overwhelming danger…
4.   …and a writer of compelling essays on (acts to repress) _____ and dissent.
5.   They are ready to assume (the attitude of being responsible) _____ for the world…
6.   …we give medical (actions to assist) _____ ,…
7.   A medical doctor, Galabru played a key role in opening (actions to negotiate) _____…
8.   War, and the (action to prepare) _____ for war, …
9.   He continues to campaign for democracy and (the acts to demilitarize) _____ worldwide.
10.   War is a missed opportunity for humanitarian (actions to invest) _____ .
11.   The (choices to decide) _____ we make…
12.   …young girls, mostly virgins, are sent into (obligation to serve) _____ …

What Do You Think?

Remarkable leaders, history makers, can be either good or bad. Brainstorm some examples of those leaders who most people would consider good and those who most people would consider bad. Then discuss these questions.

■   What makes the difference between a good leader and a bad leader?
■   Do both types have some of the same characteristics? What are they?
■   Can a leader be both good and bad? Give some examples.

Video Activities: Overcoming Serious Illness

Before You Watch.   Discuss these questions in small groups.

1. When you are paralyzed, _____.
   a. you cannot move some muscles
   b. you are in a lot of pain
   c. your bones are broken
2. A stroke affects your _____.
   a. heart   b. brain   c. lungs

Watch.   Circle the correct answers.

1. Brian Davis became paralyzed when he had _____.
   a. an accident   b. a stroke   c. a heart attack
2. What part of Brian Davis's body was paralyzed?
   a. his arms   b. his left leg   c. his right side
3. What did Brian Davis have to relearn?
   a. walking   b. thinking   c. talking   d. swallowing
4. What part of Brian Davis's body is still paralyzed?
   a. one arm   b. one leg   c. one hand
5. Who promised to ride with Brian?
   a. his brother   b. his friend   c. his doctor
6. Circle the adjectives that describe Brian.
   determined   depressed   courageous   weak   hardworking   content

Watch Again.   Compare answers in small groups.

1. How long ago was Brian's accident?
   a. 1 year   b. 6 months   c. 5 years
2. What is Brian's advice to people in his situation?
3. What is Brian's next challenge?
   a. to climb a mountain
   b. to become a doctor
   c. to ride without training wheels

After You Watch.   Read about Helen Keller, or someone else who has faced great physical problems, on the Internet or in an encyclopedia. Write a summary that answers these questions.

1. What were her physical problems?
2. How did she overcome them?
3. What did she accomplish despite her problems?

Chapter 8

Creativity

IN THIS CHAPTER

Exactly what makes a person creative? A precise answer to that question will always remain a mystery, but this chapter presents readings about three creative people who have worked in very different fields: architecture, writing, and film making. By learning about them, we can observe different kinds of creativity in action. Then, at the end of the chapter, the What Do You Think? section offers a brief opinion written by one of the world's best-known anthropologists on a controversial topic: are men more creative than women?

PART 1

Guggenheim Museum U.S.A.

Before You Read

1   **Vocabulary of Shapes and Forms.** When you read the following article, you will notice references to geometric forms (like the circle, polygon, and so on) and how they change in two or three dimensions. To understand the ideas of the architect of the Guggenheim Museum, it helps to have some vocabulary relating to these forms. So here is a brief review of the names of some basic shapes. Study the illustrations; then complete sentences 1 to 6 appropriately.

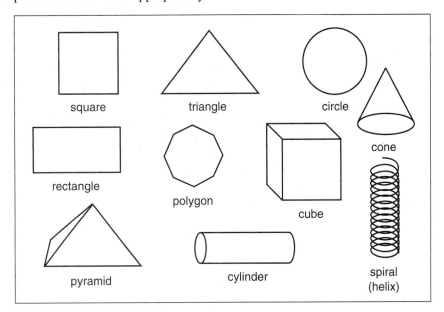

1. A square extended into three dimensions is a _____ .
2. A _____ extended into three dimensions is a pyramid.
3. Any two-dimensional figure with four sides and four right angles is a _____.
4. A closed, two-dimensional figure that usually has more than four sides is a _____.
5. The combination of a cylinder and a pyramid is a _____ . (Ice cream is often served in these.)
6. Some seashells (and bed springs and screws) are in the form of a _____ , which may also be called a _____ .

2   Discuss these questions in small groups.

1. What beautiful or outstanding buildings do you have in your city?
2. What ones have you seen in other cities, in books or on the Internet?
3. What makes these buildings remarkable?
4. Do you know anything about the architects who designed them?

Read

A common characteristic of many creative works is innovation, the creation of something new. This quality is apparent in the famous Solomon R. Guggenheim Museum, as you can see by looking at the photos illustrating the following article. Although it opened in 1959, the museum still strikes the eye as new and unusual. What kind of person do you think would design a building like this and why? The following article tells us about this famous and controversial man.

Guggenheim Museum U.S.A.

In 1932, New York's Museum of Modern Art assembled what was clearly meant to be a definitive exhibition of modern architecture. It presented the work of Frank Lloyd Wright along with that of Le Corbusier,* Ludwig Mies van der Rohe, and Walter Gropius, two leaders of Germany's revolutionary design
5 school, the Bauhaus.† On that occasion, Wright commented, "I warn you that having made an excellent start, I fully intend not only to be the greatest architect that has ever been but also the greatest of all future architects."

Wright's pride in his own work was understandable. When his three co-exhibitors were still in grade school, he was already designing remarkably in-
10 novative houses, any one of which could have established him as first among

*Le Corbusier (1887–1965) was a Swiss architect and city planner who lived in France. His buildings are characterized by daring and original design.

†A school of design founded in Germany in 1919 and continued in Chicago after 1937. The Bauhaus taught the importance of technical mastery and craftsmanship.

contemporary architects. With the help of devoted assistants, Wright had created dozens of these houses, year after year. By 1932, Wright's work had become highly individualistic—often with hints of expressionism* that would surface in his design for the Guggenheim Museum.

15   Frank Lloyd Wright's childhood had been shaped by a New England heritage of liberal Protestantism and an acceptance of the "natural philosophy" that was expressed in the writings of Walt Whitman and Henry David Thoreau. These two American writers believed that much of modern human anguish was due to urban environments and loss of contact with nature. The human

20   foot had been made to touch earth, not concrete, and human dwellings were meant to be in harmony with their natural surroundings. In the spirited and energetic atmosphere of the times, it is perhaps not surprising that Wright also developed that insistence upon absolute freedom of mind that marks the true pioneer as well as the renowned artist. This is why he so often seemed more

25   concerned with finding the proper form for an idea than with pleasing his clients. To Wright, the artistic integrity of his work was far more important than its practical function. Once, when the owner of one of his houses called to say that rain was dripping on him from a crack in the ceiling, Wright is said to have suggested that the man move his chair.

30   Both Wright's genius and obstinacy came to play their roles in his design for the Guggenheim Museum in New York City. In the early 1940s, Solomon R. Guggenheim, who was committed to the development of modern painting, found himself in need of more space to house a growing collection of pictures. He decided that a museum of modern art ought to be the work of a leading

35   modern architect. Ironically, he turned to Wright, a man known to have little liking for twentieth-century painting, and commissioned him to design the new museum. Wright's creation is one of the most original buildings in the world, a museum with its own place in the history of art. Yet as a picture gallery, it is a failure. Ultimately, the only thing it displays well is itself.

---

*A style of painting developed in the twentieth century, in which the expression of emotion is considered more important than the representation of reality. Colors and forms are often distorted or exaggerated.

40   Perhaps at the time that the plans for the Guggenheim were being drawn up, the administrators of the museum were unaware of Wright's growing rejection of conventional square and rectangular forms of city buildings and blocks. Wright was continually searching for natural forms appropriate to human needs, forms that he described as "organic architecture, opening onto
45   the world rather than insulating people from it." So he had begun to explore the possibilities of the triangle, the polygon (recalling the form of mineral crystals), and even the circle. For some time, he had been ready to take the logical step from the circle to the spiral, the form of conch shells, "plastic and continuous." This form is more properly called a helix, and is really a circle
50   carried to the third dimension. Wright boldly designed the new building in the shape of an inverted conical spiral, and convinced Solomon Guggenheim that this form would make a magnificent museum.

The museum is essentially a long ramp that starts at ground level and spirals upward in five concentric turns, continually growing wider so that it
55   opens out toward the top. Within the spiral is a vast central space, illuminated primarily by a huge skylight. At the first-floor level, the main spiral is joined with a smaller, round building, used for readings, lectures, and offices. A broad horizontal rectilinear base connects both elements and also relates the museum as a whole to its rectilinear environment of city blocks and conven-
60   tional buildings.

In defense of his stunningly original design, Wright declared that he was not merely playing a game with forms: He believed that the helix was really the best shape for a picture gallery. He claimed that the conventional manner of displaying paintings in one dreary room after another distracts the atten-
65   tion of visitors by making them concerned with the condition of their feet rather than the masterpieces on the walls. According to Wright, this museum fatigue was the result of bad architecture. At the Guggenheim, visitors would enter on the ground floor and be carried by elevator up to the top, where they would begin to slowly wind down along the spiral. Any weariness would be coun-
70   teracted by the natural form of the shell, which would gently "spiral" visitors

75

down to the first floor. As they descended, they would be able to study the paintings hung along the outward-leaning walls. In this way, each work of art would be viewed at an angle—as Wright believed the artist himself had seen it on the easel. But in reality, the museum is a challenge. Visitors must make their way down a ramp at an angle, studying paintings hung on a wall that both curves and slopes.

80

As a building, however, the Guggenheim Museum defines a magnificent space and has become a compulsory stop on even the most basic tour of New York. The startling effect of the Guggenheim lies in its unusual form and stark simplicity. While it was under construction—and remaining upright in apparent defiance of gravity—Wright would smirk happily and say of his colleagues, "They'll spend years trying to work it out."

Flavio Conti

After You Read

3   **Making Inferences and Drawing Conclusions.** With a partner or in a small group, read the following statements taken from the article. What inferences can you make or conclusions can you draw about Wright and his relationships with people from them?

1.   Wright commented, "I warn you that having made an excellent start, I fully intend not only to be the greatest architect that has ever been but also the greatest of all future architects." (lines 5 to 7)
     Wright has a lot of confidence in himself. He also has a lot of ambition. He wants
     to get ahead of others. He is very competitive.

2.   With the help of devoted assistants, Wright had created dozens of these [innovative] houses, year after year. (lines 11 to 12)
     _____
     _____

3.   Once, when the owner of one of his houses called to say that rain was dripping on him from a crack in the ceiling, Wright is said to have suggested that the man move his chair. (lines 27 to 29)
     _____
     _____

4   Find the following words in the article, using the clues given here and the number of blanks as aids.

1.   An adjective beginning with c that means "present-day" (Paragraph 2)
     contemporary

2.   A noun beginning with p that means "a person who goes before, preparing the way for others in a new region or field of work." This word is often used to refer to the early settlers of the American West. (Paragraph 3)
     _____

3. A synonym for *stubbornness* that begins with o (Paragraph 4)

   _____

4. The opposite of *original* or *unusual*, beginning with c (Paragraph 5)

   _____

5. Two synonyms for *tiredness*, one beginning with f and the other with w (Paragraph 7)

   _____

6. A smile is not always nice: a noun that begins the same way as the word *smile* but means a smile that is offensive, insulting, or irritating (Paragraph 8)

   _____

Talk It Over

In small groups, discuss the following questions.

1. Exactly what is innovative about Wright's design for the Guggenheim? Why did he choose to build it this way?
2. Referring to the Guggenheim Museum, the article states: "Yet as a picture gallery, it is a failure. Ultimately, the only thing it displays well is itself." Is this a fact or an opinion? Explain. (For a brief explanation of the difference between fact and opinion, see page 67.)
3. When you travel to new cities, do you pay attention to their architecture? Does it have an influence on you? In which city or region has the architecture impressed you the most? Why?
4. If you have seen the Guggenheim Museum, describe your reaction to it. If you have not seen it, tell what you think of it based on the article and photos.
5. What museum(s) have you been in? What did you like about it (them)?
6. For you, what is most important about a building?

Focus on Testing

Thinking Twice About Tricky Questions

The multiple-choice exercise is a common test format for reading comprehension. Usually it requires that you look back and scan for information.

The items generally follow the order of appearance, so when you do the following exercise, look for the answer to question 1 at the very beginning of the selection "Guggenheim Museum U.S.A." in the first two paragraphs.

You will see that question 1 is "tricky" because the answer is not given directly. You must make inferences. Look at each of the possibilities. Two of them relate to age, but the other is different. Check that one first. Is there evidence that Wright was "unknown" at that time? If not, how can you infer his age, compared to the other participants in the exhibit?

Look at the rest of the items in the exercise. Which ones are straight memory questions with answers given directly in the reading? Which ones are "tricky" and require inferences?

Circle the letter of the best response, according to the reading selection "Guggen-heim Museum U.S.A."

1. When the exhibition of modern architecture was presented in New York in 1932, Frank Lloyd Wright was _____ .
   a. the oldest of the participants
   b. the youngest of the participants
   c. unknown

2. In his architectural work Wright was most concerned with _____ .
   a. expressing his heritage of liberal Protestantism
   b. finding the correct form for an idea
   c. making his clients happy

3. It is ironic that Solomon Guggenheim chose Wright to design his museum of modern art because _____ .
   a. it is one of the most original buildings in the world
   b. he found himself in need of more space for his collection
   c. Wright did not like modern art very much

4. Wright was searching for an "organic architecture" that would use forms found in nature, such as the _____ .
   a. square
   b. cube
   c. polygon

5. One of the strikingly original aspects of the Guggenheim Museum is that it follows the form of an upside-down cone in a _____ .
   a. spiral
   b. pyramid
   c. rectangle

6. Another unusual characteristic of the Guggenheim is that _____ .
   a. it is illuminated only by five huge skylights
   b. visitors view paintings while they walk down a ramp
   c. paintings are displayed in one dreary room after another

PART 2

If You Invent the Story, You're the First to See How It Ends

Before You Read

1   **Getting the Meaning of Words in Context.** Use the form or context to guess the meaning of the words in italics. (To use the context, find the word in the reading and look at the sentences before and after it.) Underline the word or phrase closest to the meaning of each word.

1. You can't go very fast on a dirt road so we were *poking along*. (lines 3–4)
    a. going very fast
    b. <u>going very slow</u>
    c. not moving
    d. getting ready to move

2. The driver was a *middle-aged* man wearing glasses … (lines 5–6) (Combine the meanings of the two small words that make up this compound word.)
    a. young
    b. old
    c. not very young and not very old
    d. dressed to look very old

3. I thought she might be arrogant and imperious, coldhearted, the way a beautiful woman, *spoiled* by her beauty, can be. (lines 17–18) (Notice the meaning of the compound word *coldhearted*.)
    a. made into a good person
    b. made into a bad person
    c. frightened
    d. excited

4. I thought that the man might be her husband, or her lover, and that he was *pleading with* her. (lines 18–20) (Notice also the same words in another context, lines 27–29.)
    a. giving directions to
    b. saying insulting words to
    c. trying to anger
    d. trying to influence

5. Maybe she was sitting sullenly still, not *heartlessly*. (line 29) (Think about what the heart represents in most Western cultures and the meaning of the suffix *-less*.)
    a. in a cruel manner
    b. in a kind manner
    c. tirelessly
    d. mindlessly

6. Perhaps he was trying to comfort her for a young man's cruelty or some other terrible teenage *disappointment*. (lines 31–33)
    a. bad occurence that takes you by surprise
    b. happy event that is not expected
    c. medical appointment
    d. business deal

7. I watched them closely, trying to *decipher* the story. (line 34)
    a. forget
    b. deliver
    c. understand
    d. invent

8. How odd an occupation it is, how *unpredictable* and how humbling. (line 42)
    a. able to be predicted
    b. unable to be predicted
    c. pardonable
    d. unpardonable

9. I carry these things around inside my head until I'm *compelled* to write them down *to get rid* of them. (lines 54–55)
    compelled
    a. afraid
    b. unable
    c. forced
    d. told

10. *to get rid of*
    a. to bring into my imagination
    b. to combine with other ideas
    c. to push away from me
    d. to say in the right way

2 **Finding the Basis for Inferences.** Scan the sections of the reading indicated in parentheses to find the basis (reasons that give support) for the following inferences. Write the words that suggest each inference and an explanation.

1. Inference: The narrator (the person telling the story) lives in the country, not in the city.
    Basis for the inference: *"driving along the narrow dirt road on which I live"* You do not have dirt roads in the city.

2. Inference: The man in the car in front was very interested in his partner in the front seat.
    Basis for the inference: _____

    _____

3. Inference: His partner in the front seat did not seem interested in him.
    Basis for the inference: _____

    _____

4.   Inference: The narrator has an active imagination.
     Basis for the inference: _____

     _____

5.   Inference: The narrator does not have a calm temperament.
     Basis for the inference: _____

     _____

3   Discuss the following questions in small groups.

1.   Who are your favorite authors and what have they written?
2.   Have you ever tried to imagine how they get the ideas for their stories or articles?

Read

In this article from *The New York Times*, a writer writes about writing. Roxana Robinson tells us about the way the writing process begins in her own case and the reasons she has for writing. Read to find out more about the creative process of writing.

If You Invent the Story, You're the First to See How It Ends

You begin for yourself. The reader comes later.

One afternoon I was driving along the narrow dirt road on which I live. Ahead of me was a small red car with two people in the front seat. You can't go very fast on a dirt road so we were poking along. As we did, I began to
5   watch the car in front of me. The driver was a middle-aged man wearing glasses, and beside him sat a woman with long, wavy blond hair.

I could see the man's face because he kept turning and talking to the woman, but I couldn't see her face because she never turned to look at him or answer.

10   As we drove along, the man turned again and again, talking to the woman. He had thinning hair and a kindly face. Everything about him, his gestures, the way he spoke, seemed friendly and affectionate: he leaned toward her, he smiled. But she sat without movement or response, staring straight ahead. She never once looked in his direction, and I wondered why.

15   I supposed of course that they were fighting. The long blond hair suggested someone who was beautiful, or anyway someone who invited admiration and was used to it. I thought she might be arrogant and imperious, coldhearted, the way a beautiful woman, spoiled by her beauty, can be. I thought that the man might be her husband, or her lover, and that he was
20   pleading with her. I thought she was turning cold to him: perhaps she was ending things completely, and he was trying to win her back. I felt sorry for the man, who was trying so hard to reach her, to save things.

We both slowed down to cross a little stone bridge, and once past it, on the straight, he turned again to her. I wondered then if I'd gotten it wrong. The

25 | man was definitely middle-aged, and the woman's long, thick blond hair suggested youth. Perhaps the man was not her husband but her father.

Perhaps he was pleading with her about something else: maybe about her behavior toward her mother, for example, or her grades or her attitude in school. Maybe she was sitting sullenly still, not heartlessly. Or maybe it was
30 | something else: maybe she was not stony-faced and implacable or sullen, but miserable. Maybe she was weeping and unable to look at her father. Perhaps he was trying to comfort her for a young man's cruelty or some other terrible teenage disappointment.

I watched them closely, trying to decipher the story. The man turned to
35 | her, smiling, tilting his head coaxingly. She still did not look at him. I felt sympathy for the man, making such a tender and dedicated effort; and sympathy for the woman, locked in such a paralyzed and miserable state.

We reached the stop sign at the end of Mount Holly Road, and the man turned once more to the blond woman. This time, at last, she turned toward
40 | him. She leaned over and licked his nose. She was a golden retriever.

The reason for this story is to give you some idea of what it's like to be a writer. How odd an occupation it is, how unpredictable and how humbling.

I am often asked when I started writing. But the important question is not when do writers start, but why.

45 | My own reasons for writing, for setting down the story, are to a large extent selfish. With each story—and by story I mean anything I write—I am trying simply to work something out for myself. You, the reader, play no part here: this is a private matter.

I write about the things that trouble me. I write about the things that disturb
50 | me, the things that won't let me alone, the things that are eating slowly at my brain at 3 in the morning, the things that unbalance my world. Sometimes these are things I've said or done: sometimes they're things I've heard about or seen. Sometimes they're only sentences, sometimes scenes, sometimes complete narratives. I carry these things around inside my head until I'm com-
55 | pelled to write them down to get rid of them. I sit down and begin.... I really write to free myself....

After You Read

4 **Building Suspense.** The author starts out by offering us a mystery. This awakens our curiosity, our desire to find out what is going on. The author then builds suspense (a feeling of anticipation and excitement) about what will happen next. She does this by presenting some different possibilities to explain the mystery. Finally she surprises us with a trick ending and ends the suspense. Fill in the blanks to show these steps.

1. The mystery that the author offers us is this: _the one-sided interactions between two people driving in a car_.

2. The first possible explanation the author gives is the following: the man is with his _____ and he is _____.

3. The second possible explanation is the following: the man is with his _____ and he is _____.

4. The real truth is shown in the surprise ending: the man is really with
   _____.

5. The reason the author does all this is to tell us something about writing stories.
   What doe she want to show us about the process of writing? _____
   _____

5 **Identifying Synonyms from Parallel Constructions.** Often synonyms (words meaning the same thing or almost the same thing) appear in parallel constructions. These are
usually, but not always, linked by the word *and*. Look at the following sentences from
the reading. Identify the word(s) in parallel construction with the word in italics. Explain what you think is the meaning of that word.

1. Everything about him, his gestures, the way he spoke, seemed friendly and
   affectionate…
   friendly   Affectionate means friendly, filled with good feelings or affection for
   someone or something.

2. I thought she might be arrogant and *imperious*. (The word in parallel construction
   may not be known to you. In that case, think of the word *empire*, which is related
   to the word in italics and look at the context.)
   _____
   _____

3. Or maybe it was something else: maybe she was not stony-faced and *implacable*…
   _____
   _____

4. I felt sympathy for the man, making such a tender and *dedicated* effort…
   _____
   _____

5. … and sympathy for the woman, locked in such a paralyzed and *miserable* state.
   (Here the word in parallel construction is not an exact synonym, but it gives you
   an idea of part of the meaning of the word in italics.)
   _____
   _____

6. I write about the things that trouble me. I write about the things that *disturb* me,
   the things that won't let me alone, the things that are eating slowly at my brain at
   3 in the morning, the things that unbalance my world. (This time the word in italics
   is a verb, not an adjective. One verb in parallel construction is a synonym, but
   there are also some other verb phrases that give you more information on the
   meaning.)
   _____
   _____

6   **Writing Your Own Group Mystery.** Working in a small group, invent your own mystery in the form of a chain story. Each person writes one part. Then you combine all the parts and put a good title at the beginning, one that will make people want to read it. Choose one of the following topics or make up your own. In the first part you describe the situation and tell why it is mysterious, in the second part (or parts) you build suspense with some possible explanations, then, in the third part, surprise your readers with an unusual ending!

1. Three odd-looking people sitting at a table across from me in a restaurant who are not talking at all or even looking at each other
2. An old woman dressed in expensive clothes who is holding hands at the theater with a handsome young man in his twenties
3. My neighbors who live next door and never go outside during the day, but come and go all night long, carrying suitcases and boxes
4. My friend Sam who always has lots of money but rarely goes to work and says that he is employed by a "technical company," but won't tell its name

Talk It Over

In small groups, discuss the following questions.

1. Roxana Robinson uses a mystery and suspense to make a point about writing. These are the usual elements of horror films. They scare the viewers with a mystery, build suspense and then finish with a surprise ending. What horror films do you know about? Why are they scary? How do they build suspense?
2. What are some of the different reasons that people have for writing? Why does the author of this selection write?
3. Do you think that being a writer is an easy life or a difficult one? What would be some advantages to this profession? What would be some disadvantages?
4. Are there some books you think should definitely *not* be written? Explain.
5. Would you like to be a writer? If you were going to write a book, what would you write about?

PART 3

We Can't Just Sit Back and Hope

Before You Read

1   **Previewing for Point of View.** An interview gives the reader a double point of view: that of the interviewer and that of the person being interviewed. (For an explanation of point of view, see page 63.) We can make judgments about the person from that person's own words (enclosed in quotation marks) and also from the interviewer's comments. Of course, the interviewer cannot tell us everything, so she or he selects topics and quotes to project a particular image of the person interviewed. Look at the title and skim the interview. Then decide which of the following descriptions fits the image of Steven Spielberg that the author, Dotson Rader, intends to show.

1. A hard-working, ambitious man who wants fame and money above all else
2. A sensitive, emotional man influenced by family and traditional values
3. A temperamental genius with strong mood changes and a deep desire to create beauty

Read

Steven Spielberg is one of today's most successful Hollywood movie directors. A mark of his creativity is the great diversity of his films. With your class, make a list of all the Steven Spielberg films you have heard of. How many different types of movies are on it? The following interview with Spielberg presents a personal view of the man and his motivation for making films.

We Can't Just Sit Back and Hope

Very early on, when he was eight, Steven Spielberg was drawn to filmmaking, although he had seen few movies, mostly Disney features. He recalls being fascinated by visual images—comic books, art and TV, even though his parents let him watch very little, instead keeping a blanket over the set. He was a slow reader. He didn't read as a boy, he says, he gazed. Out of his obsession with the visual came a gift for storytelling. I asked what compelled him to tell stories.

"I was always drawn to stories because my need was I wanted to be the center of attention," he replied, smiling. "It's as simple as that. I'd be in a new school, and needed to stand out. What I discovered was I love telling stories. I come from a family of three younger sisters, and we were all fighting for our position in the family, and we were all trying hard to be recognized by our parents. My sisters did things that were unique, but I did something that was more unique than all of them put together. I had a movie camera, and I could make movies."

His first movie camera was an 8-mm Kodak borrowed from his father.

"I could use my sisters as actors in my films, I could trash them in any way I felt like," he explained with boyish delight. "Kill them over and over and it was all in the interest of telling a good story. And then I could show my little 8 mm films to my parents and get them to react. It was how I originally found my position in the family. I discovered something I could do, and people would be interested in it and me. I knew after my third or fourth little 8 mm epic that this was going to be a career, not just a hobby. I had learned that film was power."

When Spielberg was a teenager, his parents divorced, and the hurtful impact of that event would become a recurring theme in his movies—children uprooted by divorce, young lives suddenly rendered incomplete. He has said

35

that his film *E. T.—The Extraterrestrial* was born of his longing for an older brother and a father who slipped away.

In his late teens, Spielberg moved with his family from Arizona to northern California, where he attended high school and continued making his movies. He neglected his academic studies, and his grades reflected it. After gradu-

40

ation, he wasn't accepted by any major film school, so he attended Cal State at Long Beach. During this period, he made a 22-minute short, *Amblin'*, a road picture about a girl and boy hitching from the Mojave Desert to the ocean. This small movie changed his life.

Amblin' won awards at the Venice and Atlanta film festivals, and it caught the eye of Sidney Sheinberg, then head of TV production at Universal. Shein-

45

berg signed Spielberg to a seven-year contract.

What makes so many of his films so successful? What makes them different?

"I don't know what makes them different," he replied. "Ninety percent of my movies are old-fashioned in the way a Frank Capra or a Preston Sturges

50

movie is. A lot of the films I've made probably could have worked just as well 50 years ago, and that's just because I have a lot of old-fashioned values.

"I'm a fuddy-duddy. I'm a real stick-in-the-mud fuddy-duddy. I'm very 'retro,' as my son calls me. I don't let my kids watch a lot of television, as my parents didn't let me. But I do think it's a mistake to censor from my children

55

the news. I don't want them coming of age and suddenly realizing that there's a whole world out there that they missed and they're ill-prepared to accept."

Spielberg is a doting and …protective father. Given that, I said, how can he defend the sex and violence in American entertainment?

"I don't," he answered, "but neither do I want government censorship.

60

We [in show business] have to be responsible for the content of what we put

on the airwaves, in theaters, or sell in video and record stores. But there's a
fine line between censorship and good taste and moral responsibility."

Given the suffering of this century and given the violence in our own
American towns, I asked if he saw much hope.

65   "I've always been very hopeful," Spielberg replied. "But we can't sit back
and be inactive. We all have to be more active in our groups, communities,
religions, in affecting world opinion. We can't just sit by and hope the guns
and drugs will go away. We have a responsibility. We have a duty to voice our
opinion and to work to fix the world."

After You Read

2 **Finding Synonyms.** Find the words in the article that are close in meaning to the italicized words or phrases. The line numbers of the words you are looking for are given.

1. As a boy, Spielberg didn't read very much; he *watched intently*. (line 9)
    _____gazed_____

2. Out of his *great preoccupation* with the visual came his gift for storytelling.
    (line 9)
    _____

3. He wanted to do something more *special and different* than the things his sisters
    did. (line 20)
    _____

4. Many of his movies have certain *repetitive* themes. (line 32)
    _____

5. Spielberg didn't do very well at *scholarly* studies. (line 38)
    _____

6. He has a lot of *traditional* values that are reflected in his films. (line 49)
    _____

7. As a father, he is concerned about violence but does not want to *remove the op-
    portunity of viewing* the news from his children. (line 54)
    _____

3 **Paraphrasing Main Ideas.** In a small group, discuss the following ideas presented in
the interview. Then write down an explanation for each in simple words.

1. The relationship between Spielberg's position in the family and his career
2. The divorce of his parents and the influence it had on him
3. Spielberg's views on censorship
4. His feelings about hope and responsibility
5. In summary, what kind of a man is Spielberg?

Making Connections

Alone or with others, do one of the following projects.

■ From the library or the Internet find out what different kinds of movies Spielberg makes and what themes he presents in them. Give the titles and a brief description of movies from each type. What themes are common in his work?

■ Choose your favorite (or at least one that you like) Steven Spielberg movie. With facts from the Web or the library explain why you like it or show a short scene from the movie on video and tell why you like that scene.

■ Choose a film by Steven Spielberg that you do not like and follow the same procedure as in the previous instruction, except this time explain or show why you do not like it.

Talk It Over

In small groups, discuss the following questions.

1. In your opinion is the position of a child in the family (as oldest, youngest, and so on) important for the child's character? Explain.
2. Did luck play a role in Spielberg's becoming a director?
3. What are "old-fashioned values"? Are they necessary for good films?
4. Do you think there should be more censorship of films to eliminate a lot of the sex and violence? Why or why not?
5. What movie do you consider a creative work of art? Why?

What Do You Think?

Creativity in Men and Women

Margaret Mead, one of the most famous and widely read writers in the field of anthropology, expressed her ideas on creativity in men and women. In the two following paragraphs, she gives her opinion on why men have achieved more than women in almost every field throughout history. Read the selection by Mead and answer the questions that follow it.

Are Men More Creative Than Women?

Throughout history it has been men, for the most part, who have engaged in public life. Men have sought public achievement and recognition, while women have obtained their main satisfactions by bearing and rearing children. In women's eyes, public achievement makes a man more attractive as a marriage partner. But for men the situation is reversed. The more a woman achieves publicly, the less desirable she seems as a wife.

There are three possible positions one can take about male and female creativity. The first is that males are inherently more creative in all fields. The second is that if it were not for the greater appeal of creating and cherishing young human beings, females would be as creative as males. If this were the case, then if men were permitted the enjoyment women have always had in rearing young children, male creativity might be reduced also. (There is some indication in the United States today that this is so.) The third possible position is that certain forms of creativity are more congenial to one sex than to the other and that the great creative acts will therefore come from only one sex in a given field.

Margaret Mead, *Some Personal Views*, 1979

Questions

1. Do you agree with Margaret Mead when she says that "the more a woman achieves publicly, the less desirable she seems as a wife"? Why or why not?
2. What does Mead say about men who achieve publicly and their desirability as husbands?
3. What are the three possible positions given about male and female creativity?
4. Which of these positions do you think is correct? Can you think of any other position on this question?

Video Activities: A Life of Painting

Before You Watch.   Discuss these questions in small groups.

1.   At what age do people usually retire?
2.   Do you know any elderly people who are still working? If so, how do they feel about their work?

Watch.   Answer the following questions.

1.   What was Harry Sternberg's occupation? _____
2.   What is his occupation now? _____
3.   Why did he move from New York City to Escondido, California?
     a.   for health reasons   b.   for financial reasons
     c.   to be near his children   d.   to be near his wife's family
4.   The narrator uses a nickname for New York City. What is it?
     _____
5.   How did Harry feel when he first moved to Escondido?
     "It was a _____!"
6.   What did Harry discover when he drew pictures of people on the New York City subway? Most people hated _____.
7.   How do we know that Harry loves his work?
     a.   He sleeps in his studio.
     b.   He sometimes forgets to eat.
     c.   When he goes away, he can't wait to get back.
     d.   He paints every day.
     e.   He gets excited before he starts every new painting.

Watch Again.   Compare answers in small groups.

1.   What are the names of the first two paintings? _____ and
     _____
2.   Complete the name of the exhibition in the beginning of the video.
     "No _____ Without _____"
3.   Listen for the numbers.
     1.   the number of years Harry Sternberg has been painting _____
     2.   the number of years he lived in New York City _____
     3.   the year he moved to Escondido _____
     4.   the number of self-portraits he has painted _____
     5.   his age _____
4.   Complete the quotation.
     "I'm as _____ now when I _____ as I was _____."

After You Watch.   Find an article about art or creativity in general.

1.   Find five words that you know synonyms for.
2.   Find three words that you know antonyms for.
3.   Find five words that you can relate to other words. (for example, create/creativity).

Chapter 9

Human Behavior

IN THIS CHAPTER

The way people behave can be viewed in many ways. Human behavior is studied in a disciplined and sometimes scientific way by anthropologists, psychologists, and sociologists. It has also been observed and recorded for centuries in literature. Here we start with a selection from an anthropology textbook that examines the way people evaluate their own culture and other cultures. Next come a short story and a poem that focus on people's attitudes toward their environment.

| PART 1 |

Ethnocentrism

Before You Read

1   **Skimming for the Main Idea.** *Ethnocentrism* is a term commonly used by anthropologists, but the average English-speaking reader may not be familiar with it. In fact, the purpose of the whole selection is to give you an idea of what this term means and why it is important. Skim the first two paragraphs to find the author's explanation of *ethnocentrism* and write it here.

_____

_____

2   **Scanning for the Development of the Main Idea.** Scan the article to answer the following questions.

1. Like most readings taken from textbooks, this one is written in rather long paragraphs. How many of the seven paragraphs begin with a sentence containing the word *ethnocentrism*?

2. The main idea is the meaning and importance of ethnocentrism. It is developed through examples. Put a check in front of the aspects of human culture that are discussed in the reading as examples of ethnocentrism.

____   choice of clothing
____   food preferences
____   language
____   marriage ceremonies
____   myths and folktales

3   Discuss these questions in small groups.

- What do you imagine when you think of anthropologists?
- Have you ever taken a course in anthropology or read an article about it?
- Why do you think people study this subject?

Read

> The following reading is taken from an anthropology textbook. Anthropology is defined in the dictionary as "the science that deals with the origins, physical and cultural development, racial characteristics, and social customs and beliefs of humankind."

Ethnocentrism

Culture shock can be an excellent lesson in relative values and in understanding human differences. The reason culture shock occurs is that we are not prepared for these differences. Because of the way we are taught our culture, we are all *ethnocentric*. This term comes from the Greek root *ethnos*, meaning a people or group. Thus, it refers to the fact that our outlook or world view is centered on our own way of life. Ethnocentrism is the belief that one's own patterns of behavior are the best: the most natural, beautiful, right, or important. Therefore, other people, to the extent that they live differently, live by standards that are inhuman, irrational, unnatural, or wrong.

Ethnocentrism is the view that one's own culture is better than all others; it is the way all people feel about themselves as compared to outsiders. There is no one in our society who is not ethnocentric to some degree, no matter how liberal and open-minded he or she might claim to be. People will always find some aspect of another culture distasteful, be it sexual practices, a way of treating friends or relatives, or simply a food that they cannot manage to get down with a smile. This is not something we should be ashamed of, because it is a natural outcome of growing up in any society. However, as anthropologists who study other cultures, it is something we should constantly be aware of, so that when we are tempted to make value judgments about another way of life, we can look at the situation objectively and take our bias into account.

Ethnocentrism can be seen in many aspects of culture—myths, folktales, proverbs, and even language. For example, in many languages, especially those of non-Western societies, the word used to refer to one's own tribe or ethnic group literally means "mankind" or "human." This implies that members of other groups are less than human. For example, the term *eskimo*, used to refer to groups that inhabit the arctic and subarctic regions, is an Indian word used by neighbors of the Inuit people who observed their strange way of life but did not share it. The term means "eaters of raw flesh," and as such is an ethnocentric observation about cultural practices that were normal to one group and repulsive to another. On the other hand, if we look at one subgroup among the Alaskan natives, we find them calling themselves *Inuit*, which means "real people" (they obviously did not think eating raw flesh was anything out of the ordinary). Here, then, is a contrast between one's own group, which is real, and the rest of the world, which is not so "real." Both terms, *eskimo and inuit, are* equally ethnocentric—one as an observation about differences, the other as a self-evaluation. However, *Inuit* is now seen as a more appropriate term because of its origin.

Another example of ethnocentrism in language can be found in the origin of the English term *barbarian*. Originally a Greek word, the term was used to refer to tribes that lived around the edge of ancient Greek society. The Greeks referred to these people as barbars because they could not understand their speech. *Bar-bar* was the Greek word for the sound a dog makes, like our word *bow-wow*. The Greeks, in a classic example of ethnocentrism, considered those whose speech they could not understand to be on the same level as dogs, which also could not be understood. They did not grant such people the status of human being, much as the word *eskimo* gives those people subhuman status.

Shifting from language to myths and folktales, we find a good example of ethnocentrism in the creation myth of the Cherokee Indians. According to this story, the Creator made three clay images of a man and baked them in an oven. In his haste to admire his handiwork, he took the first image out of the oven before it was fully baked and found that it was too pale. He waited

55 a while and then removed the second image; it was just right, a full reddish-brown hue. He was so pleased with his work that he sat there and admired it, completely forgetting about the third image. Finally he smelled it burning, but by the time he could rescue if from the oven it had already been burnt, and it came out completely black!

Food preferences are perhaps the most familiar aspect of ethnocentrism.
60 Every culture has developed preferences for certain kinds of food and drink, and equally strong negative attitudes toward others. It is interesting to note that much of this ethnocentrism is in our heads and not in our tongues, for something can taste delicious until we are told what it is. We have all heard stories about people being fed a meal of snake or horse meat or something
65 equally repugnant in American culture and commenting on how tasty it was—until they were told what they had just eaten, upon which they turned green and hurriedly asked to be excused from the table.

Certain food preferences seem natural to us. We usually do not recognize that they are natural only because we have grown up with them; they are
70 quite likely to be unnatural to someone from a different culture. In southeast Asia, for example, the majority of adults do not drink milk. To many Americans it is inconceivable that people in other parts of the world do not drink milk, since to us it is a "natural" food. In China, dog meat is a delicacy; but the thought of eating a dog is enough to make most Americans feel sick. Yet we
75 can see how this is a part of a cultural pattern. Americans keep dogs as pets and tend to think of dogs as almost human. Therefore, we would not dream of eating dog meat. Horses, too, sometimes become pets, and horse meat is also rejected by most Americans, although not because of its taste. You may have eaten it without knowing it, and you probably would not recognize it if
80 someone didn't tell you what you were eating. On the other hand, we generally do not feel affection for cows or pigs, and we eat their meat without any feel-

85 │ ing of regret. In India a cow receives the kind of care that a horse or even a dog receives in our country, and the attitude of Indians toward eating beef is similar to our feeling about eating dog meat. On the other hand, in China dogs are not treated as kindly as they are in the United States. Since they are not pets, the attitude of Chinese people toward dogs is similar to our attitude toward cows.

John Friedl

After You Read

4 Working alone or with a partner, scan the reading selection for the words that correspond to the following clues.

1. Two synonyms that mean "the way one looks at the world" (Paragraph 1)
   outlook, world view

2. Two antonyms for "narrow-minded," one beginning with *l* and one with *o* (Paragraph 2)

3. A short word beginning with *b* that means "subjective viewpoint or slanted opinion."

4. A hyphenated term that means "an estimate about the worth or goodness of oneself" (Paragraph 3)

5. Two adjectives beginning with *r* and meaning the opposite of "pleasing" (Paragraphs 3 and 6)

6. A noun that means "a crude, ignorant person" and has its origin in the sound made by a dog (Paragraph 4)

7. Another word for "shade" in reference to colors (Paragraph 5)

8. An adjective meaning "impossible to believe" (Paragraph 7)

5 **Finding Support for Main Ideas.** Either orally or in writing, according to your teacher's instructions, give examples from the selection to support the following main ideas.

1. Ethnocentrism is present in language.
2. Ethnocentrism is present in myths.
3. Ethnocentrism is present in food preferences.

Talk It Over

In small groups, discuss the following questions.

1. What is the meaning of the term *culture shock*, which is used in the first paragraph of the selection? When does culture shock occur? Is it a good or a bad experience for the person to go through? Or can it be both? Explain.
2. Can you think of any examples of ethnocentrism, besides the ones given in the article?
3. What do you think is the main purpose of the article?
4. If you were visiting a foreign country and were asked to eat dog or snake meat, what would you do?
5. What has been your most difficult experience involving unusual food or other customs?

Focus on Testing

Finding Statements and Implied Ideas in Passages

Reading-comprehension tests often ask you to choose answers to questions about a selection, or passage, on the basis of what is stated or implied. The correct answer is stated directly in the passage (sometimes in different words), or it is suggested (implied) as a logical result of what is stated. In the second case—when the answer is implied—it is more difficult to choose.

For questions 1–4, choose the letter of the correct answer on the basis of what is stated in the passage "Ethnocentrism." Then look back at the paragraphs referred to. In what lines did you find the answers?

1. (Paragraph 1) The Greek root of the word *ethnocentric* means _____ .
   a. lesson
   b. difference
   c. group
   d. outlook
   Answer found _____
2. (Paragraph 1) An ethnocentric person believes that his or her culture is
   a. as good as other cultures
   b. better than some cultures
   c. worse than many cultures
   d. the best of all cultures
   Answer found _____

3. (Paragraph 2) Who is ethnocentric?
   a. evil people with no education
   b. liberal anthropologists
   c. members of societies far away
   d. everyone to some degree
   Answer found _____

4. (Paragraph 3) What does *inuit* mean
   a. eaters of raw flesh
   b. real people
   c. subarctic
   d. strangers
   Answer found _____

For questions 5 and 6, choose the letter of the correct answer on the basis of what is implied in the passage "Ethnocentrism." Then look back at the paragraphs referred to. Where and how is each answer implied?

5. (Paragraph 5) What makes the Cherokee Creator myth ethnocentric?
   a. It shows the Creator as a Cherokee.
   b It shows reddish skin as the ideal.
   c. It presents god as a person who makes mistakes.
   d. It presents the white, the red, and the black.
   Answer implied _____

6. (Paragraphs 6 and 7) What is the cause of the differing food preferences among different cultures?
   a. Some foods are naturally pleasing and others distasteful to the human tongue.
   b. Each group has a different body type and mental makeup that needs certain foods.
   c. People tend to like what is familiar to them and to dislike what is unfamiliar.
   d. Human beings have delicate constitutions and reject meat unless forced to eat it.
   Answer implied _____

PART 2   A Clean, Well-Lighted Place

Before You Read

1   **Previewing for Characters and Plot.** The following story takes place in a café in Paris. It was written by the American writer Ernest Hemingway (1899–1961), who lived in Paris for many years. Hemingway is not the sort of writer who describes his characters in great detail. Therefore, the reader must infer a lot about the characters from what they say and do. Skim the story to answer these questions.

1. How many characters are there in the story?
2. Which predominates (has a bigger place): dialog (speaking) or action?
3. Do you feel the general tone of the story is happy or sad? Why?

2   **Getting the Meaning of Words from Context.** Read the following excerpts from the story and decide from context which meaning corresponds best to each italicized word. Even though some of the words are Spanish, the meaning should still be clear from the context. Underline the correct answer.

1. "Last week he tried to commit suicide," one waiter said.
   "Why?"
   "He was in *despair*."
   "What about?"
   "Nothing."
   "How do you know that it was nothing?"
   "He has plenty of money."
   a. poor health
   b. <u>a sad state of mind</u>
   c. financial trouble

(In this case you are told the man has money, so c is not correct. Also, if the man were in poor health, the waiter would not have said he was in despair about "nothing," so a is not correct. That leaves letter b, the right answer.)

2. The waiter took the bottle back inside the café. He sat down at the table with his *colleague* again.
   a. client
   b. boss
   c. co-worker

3. "Finished," he said, speaking with that *omission of syntax* stupid people employ when talking to drunken people or foreigners. "No more tonight. Close now."
    a. shortening of phrases
    b. strange accent
    c. blurred speech

4. "Are you trying to insult me?" (younger waiter speaking)

    "No, *hombre*, only to make a joke." …

    "Each night I am reluctant to close up because there may be someone who needs the cafê." (older waiter speaking)

    "*Hombre*, there are bodegas open all night long."
    a. a funny insult
    b. a word you say to a friend
    c. the name of one of the waiters

5. "A little cup," said the waiter.

    The barman poured it for him….

    "You want another *copita*?" the barman asked.
    a. a small alcoholic drink
    b. a tiny saucer
    c. a spicy Spanish food

6. Now, without thinking further, he would go home to his room. He would lie in the bed and finally, with daylight, he would go to sleep. After all, he said to himself, it is probably only *insomnia*. Many must have it.
    a. a serious illness
    b. severe nervous depression
    c. the inability to sleep

Read

Ernest Hemingway (1899–1961) is one of the most widely read of all modern American authors. His books have been translated into many languages.

A Clean, Well-Lighted Place

It was late and everyone had left the café except an old man who sat in the shadow the leaves of the tree made against the electric light. In the daytime the street was dusty, but at night the dew settled the dust and the old man liked to sit late because he was deaf and now at night it was quiet and he felt
5   the difference. The two waiters inside the café knew that the old man was a little drunk, and while he was a good client they knew that if he became too drunk he would leave without paying, so they kept watch on him.

"Last week he tried to commit suicide," one waiter said.

"Why?"
10 "He was in despair."

"What about?"

"Nothing."

"How do you know it was nothing?"

"He has plenty of money."
15 They sat together at a table that was close against the wall near the door of the café and looked at the terrace where the tables were all empty except where the old man sat in the shadow of the leaves of the tree that moved

slightly in the wind. A girl and a soldier went by in the street. The street light shone on the brass number on his collar. The girl wore no head covering and hurried beside him.

"The guard will pick him up," one waiter said.

"What does it matter if he gets what he's after?"

"He had better get off the street now. The guard will get him. They went by five minutes ago."

The old man sitting in the shadow rapped on his saucer with his glass. The younger waiter went over to him.

"What do you want?"

The old man looked at him. "Another brandy," he said.

"You'll be drunk," the waiter said. The old man looked at him. The waiter went away.

"He'll stay all night," he said to his colleague. "I'm sleepy now. I never get into bed before three o'clock. He should have killed himself last week."

The waiter took the brandy bottle and another saucer from the counter inside the café and marched out to the old man's table. He put down the saucer and poured the glass full of brandy.

"You should have killed yourself last week," he said to the deaf man. The old man motioned with his finger. "A little more," he said. The waiter poured on into the glass so that the brandy slopped over and ran down the stem into the top saucer of the pile. "Thank you," the old man said. The waiter took the bottle back inside the café. He sat down at the table with his colleague again.

"He's drunk now," he said.

"He's drunk every night."

"What did he want to kill himself for?"

"How should I know."

"How did he do it?'

"He hung himself with a rope.'

"Who cut him down?"

"His niece."

"Why did they do it?"

"Fear for his soul."

"How much money has he got?"

"He's got plenty."

"He must be eighty years old."

"Anyway I should say he was eighty.'

"I wish he would go home. I never get to bed before three o'clock. What kind of hour is that to go to bed?"

"He stays up because he likes it."

"He's lonely. I'm not lonely. I have a wife waiting in bed for me."

"He had a wife once too."

"A wife would be no good to him now."

"You can't tell. He might be better with a wife."

"His niece looks after him."

"I know. You said she cut him down."

"I wouldn't want to be that old. An old man is a nasty thing."

"Not always. This old man is clean. He drinks without spilling. Even now, drunk. Look at him."

"I don't want to look at him. I wish he would go home. He has no regard for those who must work."

The old man looked from his glass across the square, then over at the waiters.

"Another brandy," he said, pointing to his glass. The waiter who was in a hurry came over.

"Finished," he said, speaking with that omission of syntax stupid people employ when talking to drunken people or foreigners. "No more tonight. Close now."

"Another," said the old man.

"No. Finished." The waiter wiped the edge of the table with a towel and shook his head.

The old man stood up, slowly counted the saucers, took a leather coin purse from his pocket and paid for the drinks, leaving half a peseta tip.

The waiter watched him go down the street, a very old man walking un-steadily but with dignity.

"Why didn't you let him stay and drink?" the unhurried waiter asked. They were putting up the shutters. "It's not half-past two."

"I want to go home to bed."

"What is an hour?'

"More to me than to him."

"An hour is the same."

"You talk like an old man yourself. He can buy a bottle and drink at home."

"It's not the same."

"No, it's not," agreed the waiter with a wife. He did not wish to be unjust. He was only in a hurry.

"And you? You have no fear of going home before your usual hour?"

"Are you trying to insult me?"

"No, *hombre*, only to make a joke."

"No," the waiter who was in a hurry said, rising from pulling down the metal shutters. "I have confidence. I am all confidence."

"You have health, confidence, and a job," the old waiter said. "You have everything."

"And what do you lack?"

"Everything but work."

"You have everything I have."

"No. I have never had confidence and I am not young."

"Come on. Stop talking nonsense and lock up."

"I am of those who like to stay late at the café," the older waiter said. "With all those who do not want to go to bed. With all those who need a light for the night."

"I want to go home and into bed."

"We are of two different kinds," the older waiter said. He was now dressed to go home. "It is not only a question of youth and confidence although those things are very beautiful. Each night I am reluctant to close up because there may be someone who needs the café."

"*Hombre*, there are *bodegas* open all night long."

"You do not understand. This is a clean and pleasant café. It is well light-ed. The light is very good and also, now, there are shadows of the leaves."

"Good night," said the younger waiter.

"Good night," the other said. Turning off the electric light he continued the conversation with himself. It is the light of course but it is necessary that the place be clean and pleasant. You do not want music. Certainly you do not want music. Nor can you stand before a bar with dignity although that is all that is provided for these hours. What did he fear? It was not fear or dread. It was nothing that he knew too well. It was all a nothing and a man was nothing too. It was only that and light was all it needed and a certain cleanness and order. Some lived in it and never felt it but he knew it all was *nada y pues nada y nada y pues nada.** Our *nada* who are in *nada, nada* be thy name thy kingdom *nada* thy will be nada in *nada* as it is in *nada*. Give us this *nada* our daily *nada* and *nada* us our *nada* as we *nada* our *nada* and *nada* us not into *nada* but deliver us from n*ada*; *pues nada*. Hail nothing full of nothing, nothing is with thee. He smiled and stood before a bar with a shining steam pressure coffee machine.

"What's yours?" asked the barman.

"*Nada*."

"*Otro loco mâs†*," said the barman and turned away.

"A little cup," said the waiter.

The barman poured it for him.

"The light is very bright and pleasant but the bar is unpolished," the waiter said.

The barman looked at him but did not answer. It was too late at night for conversation.

"You want another *copita*?" the barman asked.

"No, thank you," said the waiter and went out. He disliked bars and *bodegas*. A clean, well-lighted cafê was a very different thing. Now, without thinking further, he would go home to his room. He would lie in the bed and finally, with daylight, he would go to sleep. After all, he said to himself, it is probably only insomnia. Many must have it.

Nada is the Spanish word for "nothing." *Y pues nada* means "and then nothing." The older waiter then recites the most famous of all Christian prayers, the "Lord's Prayer," which begins "Our Father which art in Heaven, hallowed be Thy name...." However, instead of saying the correct words, he replaces many of them with the word *nada*. Afterward, he does the same with a small part of another prayer.

†Another crazy one

After You Read

3   **Making Inferences About Characters.** Working alone or with others, make inferences about the characters in the story from the following words and actions. To express your inferences about the characters, you can use words like *maybe, perhaps, probably, must.*

1.   We are told that the old man who is drinking tried to commit suicide the week before. (line 8)

     The old man:

     The old man must be very sad about something. He has problems. He is probably trying to forget his problems by drinking a lot and getting drunk. Then maybe he can go to sleep. Maybe he is afraid to go home if he is not very sleepy. Perhaps he is afraid he will try to commit suicide again.

2.   When asked what the old man was in despair about, this conversation follows:
     "Nothing."
     "How do you know it was nothing?"
     "He has plenty of money." (lines 12 to 14)

     The waiter who spoke last:

     _____
     _____
     _____
     _____

3.   The younger waiter says, "He'll stay all night.... I'm sleepy now. I never get into bed before three o'clock. He should have killed himself last week." (lines 31 to 32)

     The younger waiter:

     _____
     _____
     _____
     _____

4.   After the younger waiter has told the old man that the café is closed, the older waiter says, "Why didn't you let him stay and drink?... It's not half-past two." (lines 83 to 84)

     The older waiter:

     _____
     _____
     _____
     _____

5.   After the man and the younger waiter leave, the older waiter stays for a while and thinks. He recites a prayer in his mind but substitutes the word *nada* for many of the important words. (lines 125 to 129)

The older waiter:

_____

_____

_____

_____

4   **Expressing the Theme.** A story presents specific characters with their problems, feelings, and interactions. From these specifics, you can make a generalization about human behavior or human nature; this is the theme or main idea of the story. Here are three possible expressions of the theme of "A Clean, Well-Lighted Place." With a partner or a small group, decide which of the three you think is the best theme statement for the story, and why. If you do not like any of them, write your own theme statement.

• Those who are sad and alone depend on the kindness of others to keep going.

• Some people have understanding and compassion for others and some don't.

• Very small details can sometimes make the difference between life and death.

Talk It Over

In small groups, discuss the following questions.

1.   At one point, the older waiter says to the younger one, "We are of two different kinds." What does he mean by this? Do you believe there are two different kinds of people?

2.   Why do you think that Hemingway used some Spanish words in the story?

3.   What element do you think is the most important in this story: the characters, the plot, or the setting? Why?

PART 3

The Spell of the Yukon

Before You Read

1   **Previewing for Rhyme and Rhythm.** Like most poems, "The Spell of the Yukon" should be recited aloud and not just read silently. Only then will you get its full flavor. That way you can hear its rhyme and rhythm. *Rhyme* means that some lines end with the same sounds. *Rhythm* means that the lines have a steady number of beats. Read the poem aloud several times or listen to your teacher or a friend read it. Also, listen to the reading on the tape that accompanies this book. Try to hear the patterns of the rhyme and rhythm. Then answer these questions.

1. Which lines rhyme? Is there a regular pattern?
2. Can you hear the strong beats in each line? Although the rhythm in this poem is somewhat irregular, most lines have the same number of strong beats. How many do you hear in each line?

2   **Getting the Meaning of Words in Context.** Robert Service wrote the poem in the first person (using *I* and *me*) as though one of the men from the Gold Rush were telling his own story. So he uses the rough and colorful style of the Gold Rush men. That includes slang words, strong words, and even a few swear words that are not appropriate in polite conversation, except for expressing very strong feelings. Using the clues and the context, figure out the meaning of the italicized word(s) and underline the word or phrase closest to its meaning.

1. I wanted the gold and I *sought* it; (This is the past tense of the verb *seek*.)
   a. bought
   b. looked for
   c. loved
   d. tried out

2. I *hurled* my youth into a grave. (Try to imagine a grave and what he is saying about his lost youth.)
   a. began
   b. opened up
   c. threw
   d. yelled

3. Some say God was tired when he made it:
   Some say it's a fine land to *shun*; (Notice the line before this one.)
   a. go to see
   b. make your home
   c. offer to buy
   d. stay away from

4. You come to get rich (*damned* good reason) (This is usually a mild swear word that means "horrible," but here it is used as an intensifier.)
   a. funny
   b. never
   c. very
   d. wonderful

5. You hate it *like hell* for a season, (This is slang and also a mild swear word that is used here to express strong feeling.)
   a. a little bit
   b. for no reason
   c. not at all
   d. very much

6. It grips you like some kind of sinning; It twists you from *foe* to a friend; (The poet is talking about how the land changes you. Notice that the change implies going from one thing to its opposite.)
   a. enemy
   b. father
   c. soldier
   d. teacher

7. O God! how *I'm stuck on it* all. (Look at the context of this by reading line 34.)
   a. I don't do well with it.
   b. I don't understand it.
   c. I hate it
   d. I love it

Now read the poem silently for its meaning. Try to understand what kind of man is speaking in the poem and what he is feeling.

Have you ever wanted something very badly, worked and suffered for it, and then, after getting it, found out that it didn't make you happy? This is the experience described in the following poem by Canadian poet Robert Service (1874–1958). In 1896, gold was discovered in the Klondike area of the Yukon, a remote part of northern Canada, and the great "Gold Rush" was on. Thousands of people came from all walks of life with one dream: to get rich quick. Some did. Some became millionaires overnight only to lose everything in a card game the next day. Others died from the cold in a land where temperatures often drop to –50°C, or else were murdered or killed in accidents or fighting. The style of life was rough and hard. Robert Service lived in the Yukon during this period, working in a bank. He wrote his impressions of the Klondike Gold Rush in poems that became immensely popular and have remained so to this day. His style is rough and direct like the men he describes, but his poems are full of charm and humor and a deep love for the untamed wilderness of the Yukon.

Read

The Spell of the Yukon

I wanted the gold, and I sought it;
    I scrabbled° and mucked° like a slave.   *worked hard / got dirty*
Was it famine or scurvy°—I fought it;   *sickness from lack of vitamin C*
    I hurled my youth into a grave.
5   I wanted gold, and I got it—-
    Came out with a fortune last fall—
Yet somehow life's not what I thought it,
    And somehow the gold isn't all.
No! There's the land. (Have you seen it?)
10   It's the cussedest° land that I know,   *(slang) strangest*
From the big, dizzy mountains that screen it
    To the deep, deathlike valleys below.
Some say God was tired when He made it:
    Some say it's a fine land to shun;
15   Maybe; but there's some as would trade it
    For no land on earth—and I'm one.

You come to get rich (damned good reason);
    You feel like an exile° at first;   *someone sent away from home*
20   You hate it like hell for a season,
    And then you are worse than the worst.
It grips° you like some kinds of sinning;   *grabs, takes*
    It twists you from foe to a friend;
It seems it's been since the beginning;
25   It seems it will be to the end.

The summer—no sweeter was ever;
    The sunshiny woods all athrill;°   *full of excitement*
The grayling° aleap in the river,   *a type of fish good to eat and fun to catch*
30   The bighorn° asleep on the hill.   *wild sheep good for hunting*
The strong life that never knows harness;°   *limit*
    The wilds where the caribou° call;   *a type of large deer*
The freshness, the freedom, the farness—
    O God! how I'm stuck on it all.

35 The winter! the brightness that blinds you,
        The white land locked tight as a drum,
    The cold fear that follows and finds you,
        The silence that bludgeons you dumb.°   *bludgeons… beats you senseless*
    The snows that are older than history,
40   The woods where the weird shadows slant;
    The stillness, the moonlight, the mystery,
        I've bade° them good-bye—but I can't.   *said to*

    There's a land where the mountains are nameless,
45   And the rivers all run God knows where;
    There are lives that are erring°and aimless,°   *full of mistakes/without purpose*
        And deaths that just hang by a hair;
    There are hardships that nobody reckons;°   *thinks about*
        There are valleys unpeopled and still;
50 There's a land—oh it beckons and beckons,
        And I want to go back—and I will.

    They're making my money diminish;°   *grow smaller*
        I'm sick of the taste of champagne.
55 Thank God! when I'm skinned to a finish°   *without money*
        I'll pike to the Yukon again.
    I'll fight—and you bet it's no sham-fight';°   *fake fight*
        It's hell!—but I've been there before;
    And it's better than this by a damnsite°—   *(slang, mild swear word) a whole lot*
60   So me for the Yukon once more.

    There's gold, and it's haunting and haunting;°   *staying in my memory like a ghost*
        It's luring° me on as of old;°   *attracting/as…as it did before*
    Yet it isn't the gold that I'm wanting
65   So much as the finding the gold.
    It's the great, big, broad land 'way up yonder,
        It's the forests where silence has lease;
    It's the beauty that thrills me with wonder,
        It's the stillness that fills me with peace.

After You Read

3 With a partner or in a small group, read the poem again. Discuss any parts you did not understand. Then, answer the following questions.

1. What kind of man is supposed to be speaking in the poem? What can we infer about his education by the way he talks?

2. What happened to change his life "last fall"? What can we tell about the man's character from the line "They're making my money diminish"? Whom do you think the pronoun *they* refers to in this case?

3. How does this man describe the Yukon? What does he like about it? Do you think you would like it?

4. How did he expect to feel about his good fortune? How does he really feel now that he has it? What explanation can there be for this change?

5. What plans does the man have for his future? What do you think will happen to him?

4 **Paraphrasing Figurative Language.** Poetry often uses indirect language with figures and images that stand for certain ideas. Read the excerpts from the poem and then paraphrase (express the meaning in direct, simple words) what the poet is saying.

Example: "I'm sick of the taste of champagne." (line 54)
           I'm tired of the kind of life that goes with being rich.

1. "I hurled my youth into a grave." (line 4)

2. "It [the land] grips you like some kinds of sinning;/It twists you from foe to a friend;" (lines 22 to 23)

3. "There's a land where the mountains are nameless,/And the rivers all run God knows where;" (lines 44 to 45)

4. "[There are] deaths that just hang by a hair;" (line 47)

5. "Yet it isn't the gold that I'm wanting/So much as the finding the gold." (lines 64 to 65)

Talk It Over

In small groups, discuss the following questions.

1. Do you think the miner's reaction to his new-found wealth is typical for people who strive to reach a goal and accomplish it?

2. Have you ever been in a place that is real wilderness? Why do you think some people feel at home in a place like that? Do you prefer the wilderness to the city? Why?

3. Robert Service is the "Poet of the Yukon." If you go there, you will hear his words quoted everywhere. Have you heard of any other regions of the world that are associated with a particular poet? Or a writer? Or an artist?

4. In your opinion, what place in the world is the most beautiful? What is it like?

Chapter 10

Crime and Punishment

IN THIS CHAPTER

What is the difference between a folk hero and a criminal? We begin with the biography of a legendary outlaw from the American frontier of the 1800s, and we let you make your own judgment. Next is a fictional selection, a mystery story with a murder to be solved. The third selection is nonfiction: an essay examining the age-old question of Nature versus Nurture with regard to crime. Are criminals born or are they made into criminals by society?

| PART 1 | # Soapy Smith |

Before You Read

1   **Getting Meaning from Context.** Use the context to figure out the best definition for the words in italics.

1. Soapy Smith was the town's most *notorious* swindler.
    a. famous
    b. famous in a positive way
    c. evil
    d. famous in a negative way

2. Smith was born in Georgia but spent most of his *formative* years in Texas.
    a. early
    b. later
    c. difficult
    d. happy

3. Young Jeff earned a living as a runner for the hotel, a job in which he *rustled up* customers and thus discovered his natural gift for speech.
    a. attracted with persuasion
    b. scared away with insults
    c. entertained
    d. fought with

4. Smith spent several years drifting in the West where he *eventually* learned sleight-of-hand tricks and made a living in the mining camps.
    a. never
    b. always
    c. after awhile
    d. with no problem

5. He married Anna Nielsen, whom few people knew because he kept her *insulated* from his "public" life.
    a. informed
    b. inspired
    c. connected
    d. separated

2 **Skimming for Organization in Biography.** Biography is the life story of a real person, and therefore it is classified as *nonfiction* in libraries and bookstores. Here are the two common ways to organize a biography.

Organization 1
a. Begin with the person's birth.
b. Tell the events of the person's life.
c. Describe the person's death.

Organization 2
a. Begin with interesting facts about the person.
b. Tell the events of the person's life from birth to death.
c. Give a final comment or interesting detail about the person.

Skim the brief biography of Soapy Smith and tell which of the two formats is used. In your opinion, why did the author do it that way?

Read

Today many people complain about the prevalence of gangs and criminals, but in the 1800s in many parts of the United States this was a much bigger problem, and there were often no police to provide protection. Those were the days when the American frontier was moving more and more westward. Outlaws were common, but a few of them became famous, and some have been celebrated in song and legend. What do you think these outlaws were like? Heartless murderers? Brave heroes who helped the poor? Or simply *con men* (slang for swindlers), trying to get rich by tricking others? Read the biography of one of them in this selection. Since, as they say, "truth is stranger than fiction," you might be surprised by what you read.

Soapy Smith

Jefferson Randolph "Soapy" Smith probably ranks as Skagway's* best-known character from the gold-rush days. Certainly, he was its most noto-
5 rious con man. It is said that at the height of the gold rush, Smith and his gang virtually controlled the town, a reign that ended in a shoot-out with one of Skagway's leading citizens,
10 Frank Reid.

Smith was born in Georgia in 1860 to parents who were both members of prominent Southern families. Smith spent most of his formative years in Texas, where his family moved in
15 the 1870s. After his father, a lawyer, fell on hard times, young Jeff was forced to earn a living as a delivery boy and as a runner for a hotel, a job in which he rustled up customers and thus discovered his natural gift for speech.

*A town in southeastern Alaska near the famous passes that led to the Klondike gold fields.

20   When still in his teens, Smith hired on as a trail hand on cattle drives, and spent several years drifting about the West. He eventually learned sleight-of-hand tricks and made a living in the mining camps with gambling games such as the peas-under-the shell* game. He acquired his nickname "Soapy" from a game which involved hiding large bills in bars of soap.

25   Smith, who was generally opposed to violent methods, graduated to larger operations and set up in Denver where he formed a gang. In Denver, he acquired a wide reputation for his con games, as well as for his generosity to charities, churches, and those in desperate need. Also in Denver, he married a singer by the name of Anna Nielsen, whom he kept insulated from his "public" life and who eventually bore his children. About 1890, Smith set up operations, including a gambling hall, in Creede, Colorado, a wide-open

30   mining town, but eventually returned to Denver. After numerous run-ins with the law and local politicians, Soapy Smith quit Colorado and, in October 1897, arrived with his gang in Skagway, apparently with intentions of "taking over" the town.

35   Working out of an establishment called Jeff Smith's Parlor, an oyster parlor that also offered liquor and gambling, Smith and his gang soon were operating their con games, as well as taking part in some outright robbery, running a protection racket, and overseeing businesses like Smith's "Telegraph Office." This last business, which charged $5 to send a message anywhere in the world, might have been legitimate but for the fact that Skagway

40   had no telegraph lines.

    Despite his lawless ways, Smith was liked and respected by many for his charity, which included organizing a program to adopt stray dogs. The townspeople, however, had no use whatsoever for his gang. Eventually, several of Skagway's leading citizens formed a vigilante-style† "Committee of 101" to rid

45   the town of its criminal element. Among the committee's founders was 54-year-old Frank Reid, a former Indian fighter and surveyor who helped lay out the original town.

    The showdown between Soapy Smith and Frank Reid began when a young miner, J. D. Stewart, arrived in Skagway from the Klondike carrying

50    $2,700 in gold. Somehow, and apparently with the help of someone, Stewart and his gold parted ways. The Committee of 101, hearing Stewart's loud complaints, suspected Soapy Smith and his gang, and on July 8, 1898, called a meeting on the Skagway wharf to take action. Soapy Smith tried to force his way into the meeting, but found his path along the wharf blocked by Frank

55   Reid. After a brief struggle, the two exchanged gunfire and both fell to the deck. Smith died immediately of a bullet through the heart; Reid lingered 12 days longer.

    With the death of Soapy Smith, the law-abiding citizens of Skagway got rid of other members of the gang. Most of them were shipped south, and

60   many served time in prison. Smith and Reid were buried near each other in

---

**In this popular game, a small dry pea was placed under one of three walnut shells. The person running the game then moved the shells around quickly several times and invited the onlookers to bet money on which shell contained the pea. Since "the hand is quicker than the eye," the person running the game usually won the money. If tricks were used instead of just skill, the game became a "con game."

†A vigilante committee is a group formed by citizens to punish criminals when they feel the legal system is not doing enough.

Skagway cemetery, with Reid's tombstone bearing the words, "He gave his life for the Honor of Skagway." Soapy Smith's tombstone became a favorite among souvenir seekers, who believed a piece of the stone would bring them good luck.

Stan B. Cohen

After You Read

3 **Finding Examples to Support Main Ideas.** Like many well-known people, Soapy Smith seems to have been a mixture of good and bad. Fill in the chart with specific examples to show both sides of his character. Include traits, actions, and the opinions of others. An item for each side is given as an example. Then compare your charts in small groups.

The Character of Soapy Smith	
Good Side	**Bad Side**
1.	1.
2.	2.
3.	3.
4.	4.
5.	5.
6.	6.

4 **Scanning for Compound-Word Synonyms.** Many English words are compound words, combinations of two smaller words. Some have hyphens, such as *would-be*, and others, like *overlook*, do not. Scan the reading to find the compound-word synonyms for the words or phrases in italics.

1. Soapy Smith probably ranks as Skagway's *most famous* character from the gold-rush days. _____
2. He controlled the town until his reign ended in a(n) *exchange of gunfire* with Frank Reid. _____
3. About 1890 Soapy set up operations in Creede, Colorado, a *lawless and uncontrolled* mining town. _____
4. *The inhabitants of the town* had no use for his gang. _____
5. After numerous *encounters* with the law, Soapy quit Colorado. _____
6. He and his gang soon were running a protection racket and *supervising* businesses like Smith's "Telegraph Office." _____
7. *The deciding confrontation* between Soapy and Frank began when a young miner arrived. _____
8. With the death of Soapy, the citizens (*who generally obeyed the law*) of Skagway got rid of the gang. _____

Making Connections

From the library or on the Internet, find information to help you with one of the following tasks.

1. Read a biography of a well-known person and prepare a report in oral or written form to share with the class. Look especially to see if this person, like Soapy Smith, has a positive and a negative side, or if he or she seems to be almost completely good or completely bad. Explain your opinion with examples.
2. Give a brief description of a folk hero, such as Jesse James or Robin Hood, or some legendary figure from your culture. Tell who he (or she) was and why some people feared or hated him (or her). Also, describe the points of view of others who see this hero in a positive light.

Talk It Over

In small groups, discuss the following questions.

1. What was wrong with Smith's Telegraph Office? Do you think there are businesses like this nowadays?
2. What is a *con game*? A *protection racket*? What films have you seen about these activities? How do they portray the people involved?
3. Who was Frank Reid, and how did he die?
4. As long as someone does nothing illegal, he or she is a good person: true or false? Explain.
5. Who is famous in your culture for having broken the law or defied authority? Do you consider this person an outlaw or a folk hero? Why?

PART 2   # Eye Witness

Before You Read

1 **Identifying Narrative Elements.** You may recall that the three elements of a narrative (story) are setting, characters, and plot. (See page 156) The setting is New York sometime in the last 50 years. Think about the title, look at the illustration, and skim lines 1 to 50. Then answer these questions about the characters.

1. What does the title tell us about one of the main characters? What does he look like? What is his name? (You have to read carefully to find this out) Why is he important? Whom does he want to speak to?
2. Who is telling the narrative? Is it the omniscient narrator (someone who knows everything), or is it one of the characters in the story? Explain. What is the narrator's name? You have to read carefully to find this information.

3.   Who is Magruder?
4.   We are told at the beginning that the crime involved both a mugging (attacking someone with the intention to rob) and a murder. Who was the victim? What do we know about her?

2   **Scanning for Specific Terms.** Scan lines 1–66 of the story for the specific details that the author uses to make his characters seem real. The references are listed in the order of appearance in the story.

1.   The sight of the murder has caused a physical change in the face of the man who saw it. It has given him a __tic_____ over his left cheekbone.
2.   The narrator reacts to the eye witness' request to see the lieutenant and says, "None of us _____ will do, huh?"
3.   Magruder had been on the (police) force for a long time and was used to every type of person. But instead of saying *person*, the author uses police slang and says "every type of _____."
4.   Magruder uses slang to refer to the lieutenant. He asks, "You think maybe the _____ *would* like to see him personally?
5.   The narrator thinks at first that the witness is being stubborn. But when he looks in his eyes he doesn't see stubbornness. He sees _____.
6.   The narrator tries to scare the witness into talking to him. He uses a legal term and says that not talking about evidence can make a person an _____ *after the fact*.
7.   The author describes how the witness then thought about whether to talk with the detective or not. He uses a verb that means "considered, turned (something) over in his mind." The witness _____ for another moment and then said …

Read

While there is plenty of crime in real life, there is also a whole universe of imaginary crime present in fiction (stories that are not true). The murder mystery and the detective story are among the most widely read types of novels and short stories. The murder mystery presents a murder and a number of suspects (people who may or may not be the murderers). This type of story is also called a whodunnit (bad grammar for "who did it?") because part of the interest is to guess which suspect is the murderer. The detective story concentrates more on the reason for committing the crime and the process of solving it by the detectives or the police. The following short story was written by Ed McBain, a popular American writer who has written over 50 books and numerous short stories about crime. Many of his stories are based on true events that occurred years ago in the 87th precinct (police district) of New York. Read the story and follow the clues. Are you a good enough detective to discover who the murderer is?

Eye Witness

He had seen a murder, and the sight had sunken into the brown pits that were his eyes. It had tightened the thin line of his mouth and given him a tic over his left cheekbone.

He sat now with his hat in his hand, his fingers nervously exploring the narrow brim. He was a thin man with a moustache that completely dominated the confined planes of his face.

He was dressed neatly, his trousers carefully raised in a crease-protecting lift…. "That him?" I asked.

"That's him," Magruder said.

"And he saw the mugging?"

"He says he saw it. He won't talk to anyone but the lieutenant."

"None of us underlings will do, huh?"

Magruder shrugged. He'd been on the force for a long time now, and he was used to just about every type of taxpayer. I looked over to where the thin man sat on the bench against the wall.

"Well," I said, "let me see what I can get out of him."

Magruder cocked an eyebrow and asked, "You think maybe the Old Man would like to see him personally?"

"Maybe. If he's got something. If not, we'd be wasting his time. And especially in this case, I don't think…"

"Yeah," Magruder agreed.

I left Magruder and walked over to the little man. He looked up when I approached him, and then blinked.

"Mr. Struthers?"

"Yes," he said warily.

"I'm Detective Cappeli. My partner tells me you have some information about the…"

"You're not the lieutenant, are you?"

"No," I said, "but I'm working very closely with him on this case."

"I won't talk to anyone but the lieutenant," he said. His eyes met mine for an instant, and then turned away. He was not being stubborn, I decided. I hadn't seen stubbornness in his eyes. I'd seen fear.

"Why, Mr. Struthers?"

"Why what? Why won't I tell my story to anyone else? Because I won't, that's why."

"Mr. Struthers, withholding evidence is a serious crime. It makes you an accessory after the fact. We'd hate to have to…"

"I'm not withholding anything. Get the lieutenant, and I'll tell you everything I saw. That's all, get the lieutenant."

I waited for a moment before trying again. "Are you familiar with the case at all, sir?"

Struthers considered his answer. "Just what I read in the papers. And what I saw."

"You know that it was Lieutenant Anderson's wife who was mugged? That the mugger was after her purse and killed her without getting it?"

50 "Yes, I know that."

"Can you see then why we don't want to bring the lieutenant into this until it's absolutely necessary? So far, we've had ten people confessing to the crime, and eight people who claim to have seen the mugging and murder."

"I did see it," Struthers protested.

55 "I'm not saying you didn't, sir. But I'd like to be sure before I bring the lieutenant in on it."

"I just don't want any slip-ups," Struthers said. "I...I don't want him coming after me next."

"We'll offer you every possible protection, sir. The lieutenant, as you can 60 well imagine, has a strong personal interest in this case. He'll certainly see that no harm comes to you."

Struthers looked around him suspiciously. "Well, do we have to talk here?"

"No, sir, you can come into my office."

He deliberated for another moment, and then said, "All right." He stood 65 up abruptly, his fingers still roaming the hat brim. When we got to my office, I offered him a chair and a cigarette. He took the seat, but declined the smoke.

"Now then, what did you see?"

"I saw the mugger, the man who killed her." Struthers lowered his voice. "But he saw me, too. That's why I want to make absolutely certain that...that I 70 won't get into any trouble over this."

"You won't, sir. I can assure you. Where did you see the killing?"

"On Third and Elm. Right near the old paint factory. I was on my way home from the movies."

"What did you see?"

75 "Well, the woman, Mrs. Anderson—I didn't know it was her at the time, of course—was standing on a corner waiting for the bus. I was walking down toward her. I walk that way often, especially coming home from the show. It was a nice night and..."

"What happened?"

80 "Well, it was dark, and I was walking pretty quiet, I guess. I wear gummies—gum sole shoes."

"Go on."

"The mugger came out of the shadows and grabbed Mrs. Anderson around the throat, from behind her. She threw up her arm, and her purse 85 opened and everything inside fell on the sidewalk. Then he lifted his hand and brought it down, and she screamed, and he yelled, 'Quiet, you bitch!' He lifted his hand again and brought it down again, all the time yelling, 'Here, you bitch, here, here,' while he was stabbing her. He must have lifted the knife at least a dozen times."

90 "And you saw him? You saw his face?"

"Yes. She dropped to the ground, and he came running up the street toward me. I tried to get against the building, but I was too late. We stood face to face, and for a minute I thought he was going to kill me, too. But he gave a kind of moan and ran up the street."

95 "Why didn't you come to the police at once?"

"I...I guess I was scared. Mister, I still am. You've got to promise me I won't get into any trouble. I'm a married man, and I got two kids. I can't afford to..."

100 "Could you pick him out of a line-up? We've already rounded up a lot of men, some with records as muggers. Could you pick the killer?"

"Yes. But not if he can see me. If he sees me, it's all off. I won't go through with it if he can see me."

"He won't see you, sir. We'll put you behind a screen."

"So long as he doesn't see me. He knows what I look like, too, and I got a family. I won' identify him if he knows I'm the one doing it."

105 "You've got nothing to worry about." I clicked down Magruder's toggle on the intercom, and when he answered, I said, "Looks like we've got something here, Mac. Get the boys ready for a run-through, will you?"

"Right. I'll buzz you."

We sat around and waited for Magruder to buzz.

110 "I won't do it unless I'm behind a screen," Struthers said.

"You'll have a one-way mirror, sir."

We'd waited for about five minutes when the door opened. A voice lined with anguish and fatigue said, "Mac tells me you've got a witness."

I turned from the window, ready to say, "Yes, sir." And Struthers turned to
115 face the door at the same time.

His eyebrows lifted, and his eyes grew wide.

He stared at the figure in the doorway, and I watched both men as their eyes met and locked for an instant.

"No!" Struthers said suddenly. "I...I've changed my mind. I...I can't do it.
120 I have to go. I have to go."

He slammed his hat onto his head and ran out quickly, almost before I'd gotten to my feet.

"Now what the hell got into him all of a sudden?" I asked.

Lieutenant Anderson shrugged wearily. "I don't know," he said. "I don't
125 know."

After You Read

3 **Finding Descriptive Adverbs.** Good writers use good adverbs to describe the actions of their characters. Follow the clues in parentheses and choose one of the adverbs from the following list to complete the phrases taken from the story.

abruptly   nervously   quickly   warily
carefully   personally   suspiciously   wearily

1. He sat now with his hat in his hand, his fingers (with tension) _nervously_ exploring the narrow brim.
2. He was dressed neatly, his trousers (with care) _____ raised....
3. You think maybe the Old Man would like to see him (in person) _____?
4. "Yes," he said (with caution) _____.
5. Struthers looked around him (with doubt and mistrust) _____.
6. He stood up (in a sudden, rough manner) _____, his fingers still roaming the hat brim.
7. He slammed his hat onto his head and ran out (with a fast movement) _____....
8. Lieutenant Anderson shrugged (in a tired way) _____.

Focus on Testing

Judging Something True or False

Many reading-comprehension tests include a true/false section. The best strategy is to do all the obvious items first. Then look at the ones remaining. Are they difficult because they seem to be partly true and partly false? Remember that true and false are not equal. A statement is true only if every single part of it is completely true. A false statement may have many true parts, but it is false if it has even one small part that is false.

Exercise 1
Look quickly at the following true/false exercise. Write down the numbers of the items that are not immediately obvious. _____

What makes them tricky or difficult?

_____

Compare answers with your classmates.

Exercise 2
Write true or false in front of each statement. Correct the false statements to make them true.

_____ 1. Mr. Struthers was a thin, poorly dressed man with a moustache and a tic.

_____ 2. The name of the narrator is Detective Cappeli.

_____ 3. The victim who was murdered was the wife of Magruder.

_____ 4. The eye witness was important because no one else claimed to have seen the crime.

_____ 5. Mr. Struthers was afraid to talk because he didn't want the murderer to come after him.

_____ 6. The woman who was murdered was standing in a line in front of the movie theater.

_____ 7. The murderer killed the woman by stabbing her with a knife.

_____ 8. Mr. Struthers didn't come to the police at once because he felt sorry for the murderer.

_____ 9. Mr. Struthers said he had not seen the killer clearly enough to be able to identify him in a police line-up.

_____ 10. He did not want to take any risks because he had a wife and family.

_____ 11. Lieutenant Anderson never came to talk to Mr. Struthers because he was too busy.

_____ 12. At the end of this story, the identity of the murderer is revealed.

Solving the Murder. In a small group, make a list of the clues that point to the murderer. Do you all agree on who murdered Mrs. Anderson? How and when in the story did you know? Do you know the motive? Are there any clues early in the story? Are there any false clues? Was there really a mugging? Compare your ideas with those of other groups.

Talk It Over

With the class or in a small group, discuss the following questions.

1. Do you think this story was a murder mystery or a crime story? Or was it a combination? Explain.

2. There is an expression in English to refer to someone who is doing something wrong and not getting caught. People say, "that guy is getting away with murder!" Was there someone in this story who "got away with murder"? Who? Why? In general, what sort of people get away with murder, and what sort don't?

3. What detective stories or mysteries have you read or seen in the movies? Which ones do you like? Why?

4. When murder is such an unpleasant thing, why do you think that stories about it are so popular?

PART 3   # Born Bad?

Before You Read

1 **Surveying an Extended Nonfiction Reading.** A nonfiction piece discussing a controversial question with two distinct sides generally has one of the following three kinds of organization:

1. It first presents one side of the question, then the other, each in a complete fashion. It then discusses what is right and wrong with each side and comes to a conclusion in favor of one side.

2. It presents various different aspects of both sides of the question, a few at a time. It concludes that there is about an equal amount of truth on both sides.

3. It introduces the question and then presents evidence mostly in favor of one side, usually the side that is not popular. It mentions the other viewpoint briefly.

Before beginning the piece, survey it by skimming to decide which of the three types of organization it uses. The article is not divided into parts, so it is more difficult to get a general view. First, look at the title, photos, and chart for visual clues. Second, read the first paragraph and the first sentence of all the other paragraphs.
Which type of organization is used in this article: 1, 2, or 3?

2   **Finding the Main Point in Long, Complex Sentences.** "You can't see the forest for the trees." This is a common saying about the difficulty of finding the main point among many details. This is the problem with long sentences that have many clauses. Write down the connector words and then the main idea in each of the following sentences from the selection.

To find the main idea:

1. Cross out the connector words that introduce secondary clauses, along with the ideas following them.
2. See what is left and write it down.
3. If the idea seems incomplete, add a part—but not too much—in simple words to fill out the idea so it will make sense.

The first sentence is done as an example.
1. ~~Much as it may contradict the science of the past, which blamed crime on social influences such as poverty and bad parenting,~~ the outlaw may be onto something.

    Connectors: _Much as, which_

    Main idea: _The outlaw may be onto something._

2. But many researchers now believe that the reason one individual commits a crime and another person doesn't may have as much to do with neurological differences as it does with differences in upbringing or environment. (Remember that the word *but* can sometimes introduce the main idea of a sentence.)

    Connectors: _____

    Main idea: _____

3. After evaluating recent research on violence, a special panel gathered by the National Research Council (NRC) in Washington published a lengthy report last fall noting that "even if two individuals could be exposed to identical experiences, their potentials for violent behavior would differ because their nervous systems process information differently." (This sentence has a main idea within a main idea. Can you **find** both?)

    Connectors: _____

    Main idea: _____

    Main idea within main idea: _____

4. This fact suggests that certain hormones, particularly androgens, which characterize maleness, may help tip the balance from obeying to breaking the law.

    Connectors: _____

    Main idea: _____

5. While there's no such thing as a "crime gene," or indeed any single determinant that leads a person to break the law, each child is born with a particular temperament, or characteristic pattern of psychological response.

   Connectors: _____

   Main idea: _____

6. She found that lead poisoning, which is known to impair aspects of brain functioning, is the single best predictor of boys' disciplinary problems in school: such problems in turn are strongly associated with later adult crime.

   Connectors: _____

   Main idea: _____

7. After collaborating with Dr. Tomas Bouchard, Jr., on famous studies of more than 55 pairs of identical twins adopted separately at birth and reared apart, Dr. David Lykken, a psychologist at the University of Minnesota's Twin Research Center, says that "these traits correlate as strongly in twins who have been raised apart as in twins who were raised together."

   Connectors: _____

   Main idea: _____

Read

Born Bad?
New research points to a biological role in criminality.

The tattoo on the ex-con's beefy arm reads: BORN TO RAISE HELL. Much as it may defy the science of the past, which blamed crime on social influences such as poverty and bad parenting, the outlaw may be onto something. Though no one would deny that upbringing and environment play important
5   parts in the making of a criminal, scientists increasingly suspect that biology also plays a significant role.

Poverty and family problems, sex-role expectations, community standards—all may predispose individuals toward crime. But many researchers now believe that the reason one individual commits a crime and another per-
10   son doesn't may have as much to do with neurological differences as it does with differences in upbringing or environment. After all, says Dr. James Q. Wilson, a professor of management and public policy at UCLA, "it's hard to find any form of behavior that doesn't have some biological component."

After evaluating recent research on violence, a special panel gathered
15   by the National Research Council (NRC) in Washington published a lengthy report last fall noting that "even if two individuals could be exposed to identical experiences, their potentials for violent behavior would differ because their nervous systems process information differently."

First and most obvious among the clues that biology plays a role in criminal behavior is the simple fact that throughout history, crime has occurred in all cultures. One element in the universality of crime is the human capacity for aggression. Nobel prizewinning ethologist Konrad Lorenz, author of *On Aggression*, argued that just as people have an instinct for eating and drinking, nature evolved in them the impulse for aggression. Though Lorenz thought it was peculiar to people and rats, aggression has now been observed in every vertebrate species studied. In people, only a fine line separates aggression from violence—defined by researchers as behavior intended to inflict harm on others. "Criminals are, on the whole, angry people," says Harvard psychologist Richard Hemstein. "That's well substantiated."

Another simple fact pointing to a biological basis for criminality is that in all societies, about 90% of violent criminals are men—many of them young. The great majority of other crimes are also committed by men. Among animals too, the male is almost always more aggressive. This fact suggests that certain hormones, particularly androgens, which characterize maleness, may help tip the balance from obeying to breaking the law.

While there's no such thing as a "crime gene," or indeed any single determinant that leads a person to break the law, each child is born with a particular temperament, or characteristic pattern of psychological response. As Wilson notes, "One is shy, the other bold; one sleeps through the night, the other is always awake; one is curious and exploratory, the other passive. These observations are about differences that cannot be explained wholly or even largely by environment."

Linking an individual's temperament to criminality is, of course, a much more contentious matter. To search for the roots of violence, the members of the NRC panel asked several key questions. Why do some children show patterns of unusually aggressive behavior—hitting, kicking, biting peers or parents, or being cruel to animals—at an early age? Why do only a small

percentage of those children commit violent crimes as adults? The panel concluded: "Research strongly suggests that violence arises from *interactions*
among individuals' psychosocial development, their neurological and hor-
monal differences, and social processes." There is no basis, the researchers
added, for giving one of these elements more weight than another.

Nonetheless, two camps have emerged to debate whether criminality is
influenced more by nature (biology) or nurture (environment). And this is no
mere ivory tower[1] question. Public interest mounts with the statistics: Some
35 million offenses against people or households, 20% of them violent, are re-
ported in the U.S. every year.

Research that may help resolve this nature-nurture question focuses
mostly on three areas: biochemical imbalances, genetic factors and physical
damage such as head injury around the time of birth. Some studies suggest
a link between criminal behavior—particularly the violent sort—and birth-re-
lated trauma, premature birth or low birth weight. Similarly, a woman's use of
alcohol, cocaine, tobacco or other drugs during pregnancy also appears, in
some instances, to damage fetal development in a way that is related to later
criminality. On a more positive note, however, one recent study concluded that
when children who'd had a traumatic birth grew up in a stable family environment, they were no likelier than anyone else to develop into criminals.

Childhood injury to brain tissue may also figure in later criminal behavior.
Law professor Deborah Denno of Fordham University in New York City studied
a group of nearly 500 boys from birth to age 23. She found that lead poisoning, which is known to impair aspects of brain functioning, is the single best
predictor of boys' disciplinary problems in school; such problems in turn are
strongly associated with later adult crime. Denno had expected to find family
factors most strongly implicated in delinquency and criminal behavior and
was astonished by her results.

Both animal experiments and cases of human head injury and brain
damage have pinpointed areas of the brain where impairment or seizure can
trigger aggression. In monkeys, researchers can elicit "sham rage" by using
electrodes to stimulate the limbic system, a group of structures deep within
the brain that influence emotions. A rare condition called intermittent explo-
sive disorder is linked to periodic seizures in the same brain area.

Convincing evidence from the field of behavioral genetics implies that
certain biological predispositions to criminal behavior are inherited. Like test
pilots and mountain climbers, delinquents and criminals tend to be born with
relatively calm nervous systems that allow them to face risky situations with
minimal stress. Other personality traits, including aggressiveness and impulsivity, partly depend on genes.

After collaborating with Dr. Tomas Bouchard, Jr., on famous studies of
more than 55 pairs of identical twins adopted separately at birth and reared
apart, Dr. David Lykken, a psychologist at the University of Minnesota's Twin
Research Center, says that "these traits correlate as strongly in twins who have
been raised apart as in twins who were raised together." Moreover, the largest
twin study of criminality ever conducted, published in Denmark in 1987, found
that when a male identical twin[2] committed a crime, his twin was five times

---

[1]Place or situation removed from worldly or practical affairs.

[2]Twin developed from one fertilized ovum; twins look very much alike.

95   likelier than the average Danish man to commit a crime as well; when a fraternal twin[3] committed a crime, his twin was three times likelier than other Danish men to break the law.

One way or another, says Harvard psychologist Jerome Kagan, there's no question that people inherit different neurochemistries. He has categorized
100   babies by their patterns of excitability and identified four basic types. "Think of them as different breeds of puppies," he says, "just as Pekingese, for example, are naturally more irritable than beagles."

Dr. Kagan's research suggests that 35% to 40% of babies are born with a very relaxed approach to the world around them. Many of the babies he
105   studied react to stress with a low degree of excitability, as gauged by 185 physical indicators such as heartbeat, blood pressure and adrenaline secretion. By the time these children are between 20 and 30 months old, they can frequently be described as extroverted and relatively fearless. (Of the fraction who warrant the description *extremely* fearless, 80% are boys.)

110   According to Kagan, this personality type results from the unique combination of a baby's basic pattern of excitability with his physical response to his environment. But the baby's family also influences the type of adult he becomes. For example, if a relaxed baby who's not very excitable is raised by loving, attentive parents, he might grow up to be an intellectual risk taker—an
115   artist, a scientist or a politician. But in an unfavorable family environment, the same child might become, say, a bank robber.

Yet another area of research concerns biochemical imbalances. Even hypoglycemia (low blood sugar) has been linked to antisocial behavior. Mr. Matti Virkkunen, a psychiatrist at the University of Helsinki in Finland, has found that
120   the condition is more common among alcoholic, impulsive, violent offenders than among ordinary people.

The fact is that no single influence turns an individual into a criminal. Human traits—impulsivity or fearlessness—are by themselves neutral; they're as characteristic of leaders and artists as they are of criminals. Fyodor Dos-
125   toyevsky recognized this paradox in *Crime and Punishment*, as did Robert Louis Stevenson in *The Strange Case of Dr. Jekyll and Mr Hyde*.[4] The French sociologist Emile Durkheim even declared that he would not want to live in a society without crime.

Ominous statistics indicate that Durkheim's fears about life in an utterly
130   safe society are unlikely to be realized in the near future. The huge number of murders and muggings, rapes and robberies taking place in our society today ensure that scientists will expand their research on criminality and violence. "There's no magic bullet, no single approach that will end crime," says Harvard's Hemstein. "But each new advance in research raises the pos-
135   sibility of a constructive remedy."

Glenn Garelik

---

[3]Twin who developed from two fertilized ova; twins can look quite different from one another.

[4]Two nineteenth-century novels that present famous studies of people who have a good side to their character and an evil, criminal side at the same time.

After You Read

3   **Analyzing a Line of Argument.** Look back through the article and fill in the following chart with different points mentioned to support each side of the Nature-Nurture argument. Then finish the statement, telling what you infer as the main idea of the article.

Nature (genetics, biology)	Nurture (environment, influence)
1. Neurological differences as reason for committing crime	1. Poverty, bad parenting as social influences of crime
2. _____	2. _____
3. _____	3. _____
4. _____	4. _____

Main Idea:

The selection concludes that _____ is probably (as important as/ more important than/less important than) _____ in causing crime.

Talk It Over

In small groups, discuss the following questions.

1. What people have you heard of who seemed to be "born bad"?
2. In your opinion, what factors in the environment cause crime? Explain.
3. A person grows up to be a serial murderer. Therefore, his parents did something very wrong. True or false? Why?
4. Do you think that in times of war or terrible stress, almost anyone becomes a criminal? Explain.
5. What do you think of Emile Durkheim's idea about living in a society without crime mentioned in the last paragraph? Do you agree with him? Why or why not?

4   **Interpreting Charts.** Some people feel that one problem with crime in the U.S. is that the administration and maintenance of prisons has become a big business. For many small towns, having a prison nearby is a source of jobs. Police officers, detectives, prison guards, lawyers, and court psychologists make a good living when there are lots of criminals. In the 1980s new laws came in that made the simple possession of certain drugs a serious crime, punishable by imprisonment. By the end of the year 2000, one in every 137 people in America was behind bars! It used to be different. In 1973, only one in every 1,042 people in America was behind bars. This change did not happen because the rate of violent crime went up. In fact, it was just the opposite. The rate of violent crime went down considerably since the early 1970s.*

Look at the two charts and answer the questions after each one.

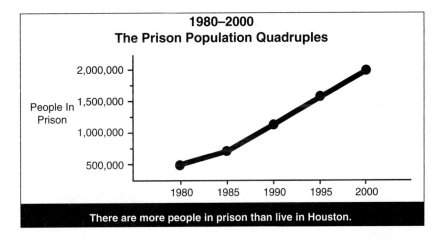

1.   What change has occurred in the U.S. prison population recently?
2.   How long did it take to change this way?
3.   What effects do you think this has had on the American people? Do you think this is a good change or a bad one? Explain.

---

*The statistics and the two charts are taken from *Rolling Stone*, Dec. 7, 2000.

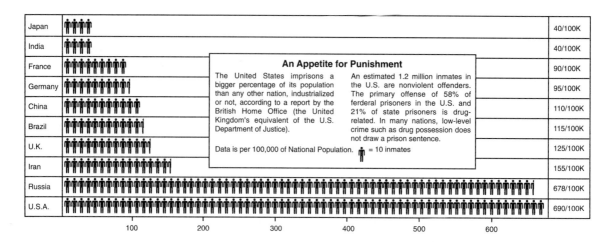

Japan		40/100K
India		40/100K
France		90/100K
Germany		95/100K
China		110/100K
Brazil		115/100K
U.K.		125/100K
Iran		155/100K
Russia		678/100K
U.S.A.		690/100K

An Appetite for Punishment

The United States imprisons a bigger percentage of its population than any other nation, industrialized or not, according to a report by the British Home Office (the United Kingdom's equivalent of the U.S. Department of Justice).

An estimated 1.2 million inmates in the U.S. are nonviolent offenders. The primary offense of 58% of ferderal prisoners in the U.S. and 21% of state prisoners is drug-related. In many nations, low-level crime such as drug possession does not draw a prison sentence.

Data is per 100,000 of National Population.   = 10 inmates

1. What are the main differences betwcen this chart and the previous one?
2. What countries have a much smaller percentage of their population in prison, as compared to that of the U.S.A.? What countries have a larger percentage?
3. What country has a percentage that is almost the same?
4. What reason is suggested on the chart for the high percentage of Americans in prison?
5. What, if anything, could be done about this situation?

What Do You Think?

Using the Death Penalty

"An eye for an eye, a tooth for a tooth." This Biblical statement from the Old Testament is indicative of one type of thinking about crime and punishment. If someone takes another person's life, the life of that someone should also be taken. This practice is called "capital punishment" in English. It means that the state has the right to kill the killer.

Do you agree with this type of punishment? Do you think that the threat of capital punishment stops people form committing murder? Do you think killers should be kept in prison for life instead of being executed? Why or why not? What are the various types of punishments for different crimes in your country?

Video Activities: Victim Support Groups

Before You Watch.   Discuss these questions in small groups.

1.   What do you think a support group is? Who is in it? What is the purpose of the group?

2.   What murderer cases have you heard about? What was the punishment? Do you think it was fair?

3.   In most countries, convicted criminals have the right to appeal their conviction. What do you think *appeal* means?

Watch.   Answer the following questions.

1.   The video is about a support group for _____.
     a.   families of murderers   b.   murder victims
     c.   families of murder victims   d.   murderers

2.   Who are the "monsters" referred to in the video?

     _____

3.   According to Susan Field, how is murder different from a natural death for the victim's family?
     a.   The grief period is longer.   b.   They feel angrier.
     c.   There is a lot of publicity.
     d.   They have had no time to prepare for it.
     e.   They have to deal with the judicial system.

4.   According to Jim Roche, what should the United States Supreme Court do to help the families of murder victims?
     a.   Put more murderers in prison.   b.   Change the appeal process.
     c.   Stop all appeals.   d.   Get rid of the death penalty.

5.   According to Kate Elke, execution is state law and it should be _____.
     a.   changed   b.   abolished   c.   enforced

Watch Again.   Compare answers in small groups.

1.   Write these names in the correct row.

     Ron Russe   Susan Fisher   Linda Ricio   Virgina Allen
     Pamela Allen   Sammy Smith   Kate Elke   Jim Roche

Murder Victim   _____ _____
Murderer   _____
Relative of Murder Victim   _____ _____ _____
Government Official   _____ _____

After You Watch.   Find an article about a criminal trial. Write a summary about the trial. Your summary should answer these questions:

1.   What was the crime?

2.   Who were the victims?

3.   What was the punishment?

Chapter 11

The Physical World

IN THIS CHAPTER

The first selection includes two views of the earth given by members of the first nations to inhabit North America. The second selection is from a textbook that describes some mysteries from the animal kingdom that scientists are just now beginning to understand through ingenious experiments. The chapter finishes with a timed reading on one of the most serious problems threatening the future of our planet.

| PART 1 | # Touch the Earth |

Before You Read

1 **Imagining the Historical Context.** This response was given at the end of the nine-teenth century. Try to visualize (see in your "mind's eye") what the country that is now the United States looked like back then. Skim the short excerpt and answer these questions.

1. Who is giving this response and to whom?
2. What is being asked for?
3. What differences in appearance and dress were there between the two sides?
4. What differences in education and lifestyle were there between the two sides?

2 **Scanning for Facts and Terms.** Read through the selection quickly to find out the information requested.

1. Name of the Indian nation the chief belonged to: the ___Blackfeet___
2. Word beginning with *t* that means "agreements": _____
3. Name of the river in the region: the _____ River
4. Two-word phrase referring to God: the _____ _____

Read

Touch the Earth: A Chief's Response

A chief of one of the principal bands of the northern Blackfeet, upon being asked by U.S. delegates for his signature to one of the first land treaties in his region of the Milk River, near the northern border of Montana and the Northwest Territories, responds with a rejection of the money values of the
5 white man.

Our land is more valuable than your money. It will last forever. It will not even perish by the flames of fire. As long as the sun shines and the waters flow, this land will be here to give life to men and animals. We cannot sell the lives of men and animals; therefore we cannot sell this land. It was put here for us by
10 the Great Spirit and we cannot sell it because it does not belong to us. You can count your money and burn it within the nod of a buffalo's head, but only the Great Spirit can count the grains of sand and the blades of grass of these plains. As a present to you, we will give you anything we have that you can take with you; but the land, never.

From Touch the Earth: A Self-Portrait of Indian Existence, by T.C. McLuhan.

After You Read

3 **Identifying the Arguments.** Working with a partner or a small group, answer the following questions.

1. What reasons does the Chief give to the delegates for rejecting their offer?
2. How does he explain to them the length of time that the land will be there, giving life to its inhabitants?
3. How does he explain to them why it is impossible for him to sell the land?
4. What counter offer does he make?
5. Viewing this from today's point of view, what do you think of the Chief's reasoning? Was he right or wrong? Why?

4 **Inferring the Values of Another Culture.** Working with a small group, see what values you can infer from the response given by the Chief. What things are important to him and his culture and what things aren't? Why? How do you feel these values compare to those of the dominant values in North America today?

Before You Read

5   **Reading Poetic Prose.** The following short excerpt is not a poem, but it is written in a poetic style because it uses images. More important than showing us ideas, this kind of writing tries to communicate to us the beauty and emotion that the author feels. In this case, Black Elk, a Native chief from the 1800s, expresses his ideas and feelings about the main symbol of his culture: the circle. As you read, try to see the images in your imagination and share in the emotions. Skim the selection, and answer these questions.

1. What reference can you find to the sad changes that occurred in the lives of Native people during Black Elk's lifetime?
2. What references does he make to the pride and happiness of his people in earlier times?
3. With what animals does he identify his people at the end? How does he make this comparison?

6   **Scanning for Background Facts.** Scan the first paragraph for facts about the background of Black Elk, the author of the following excerpt.

1. Name of the Indian nation the chief belonged to: the _____Sioux_____
2. Name of the river in the region where he was born: the _____ River
4. Name of the famous battle in which he participated: the Battle of _____
    _____ _____.
5. Name of the queen of England for whom he danced: Queen _____.
6. Years in which he dictated his autobiography: 19_____ to 19_____.
7. State in the United States where he spent his last days on a reservation: _____ _____.

Read

Touch the Earth: The Meaning of the Circle

Hehaka Sapa, or Black Elk, belonged to the Oglala division of the Teton Dakota, one of the most powerful branches of the Siouan family (Sioux nation). He was born in "the Moon of the Popping Trees [December] on the little Powder River in the winter when the Four Crows were killed" in 1863. Related to the
5   great Chief Crazy Horse, he had known Sitting Bull and Red Cloud and was well acquainted with the early days of his people when they had roamed the Plains: he was also present at the battle of Little Big Horn. Later on in life he traveled with Buffalo Bill to Italy, France and England, where he danced for Queen Victoria. Black Elk possessed unique spiritual power recognized by
10 everyone and had been instructed in his youth in the sacred traditions of his people by the great priests. His father had been a medicine man; several of his brothers also. He had spent his last days on the Pine Ridge Reservation in South Dakota. The following passage is taken from his autobiography, which he dictated in 1930–31 to Flaming Rainbow. The configuration of the circle,
15 referred to here by Black Elk, had a fundamental place in Indian life.

You have noticed that everything an Indian does is in a circle, and that is because the Power of the World always works in circles, and everything tries to
be round. In the old days when we were a strong and happy people, all our
power came to us from the sacred hoop of the nation and so long as the hoop
was unbroken the people flourished. The flowering tree was the living center
of the hoop, and the circle of the four quarters nourished it. The east gave
peace and light, the south gave warmth, the west gave rain, and the north
with its cold and mighty wind gave strength and endurance. This knowledge
came to us from the outer world with our religion. Everything the Power of the
World does is done in a circle. The Sky is round and I have heard that the
earth is round like a ball and so are all the stars. The Wind, in its greatest
power, whirls. Birds make their nests in circles, for theirs is the same religion
as ours. The sun comes forth and goes down again in a circle. The moon does
the same, and both are round.

Even the seasons form a great circle in their changing, and always come
back again to where they were. The life of a man is a circle from childhood to
childhood and so it is in everything where power moves. Our tipis were round
like the nests of birds and these were always set in a circle, the nation's hoop,
a nest of many nests where the Great Spirit meant for us to hatch our children.

From *Touch the Earth: A Self-Portrait of Indian Existence*, by T.C. McLuhan.

After You Read

7   **Using More Exact or Colorful Synonyms.** Find the more exact or colorful synonym in the reading to replace the following words in parentheses. The phrases are listed in order of their appearance.

1. one of the most powerful (parts) _____branches_____ of the Siouan family (Sioux nation).
2. and was well (familiar) _____ with the early days of his people…
3. when they had (wandered) _____ the Plains…
4. The (shape) _____ of the circle…
5. had (an important) _____ place in Indian life.
6. and so long as the hoop was unbroken the people (did well) _____.
7. and the circle of the four quarters (gave strength to) _____ it.
8. and the north with its cold and mighty wind gave strength and (the ability to keep on going) _____ .
9. The Wind, in its greatest power, (goes round and round) _____ .

8   **Discussing the Symbolism of the Circle.** With a partner or in a small group, discuss the following questions.

1. What was said to be in the middle of the great circle, or hoop, of the Indian nation when it was strong? What was given to it from each of the four directions? Where did its knowledge come from?
2. What images from Nature does Black Elk use to show the importance of the circle?
3. How does he show that time also moves in a circle, both in the natural world and in human life?

Talk It Over

Discuss the following questions in small groups.

1. Black Elk is said to have possessed "unique spiritual power recognized by everyone." From reading that, what kind of person do you think he was? What people today are considered by many to have spiritual powers? How do they show this?
2. Most of the Native peoples of the Americas have been known to be democratic. They generally have elected chiefs, rather than hereditary rulers. For their councils and discussions they sit in a circle. How does this emphasize the idea of equality? What symbols and types of seating exist in other cultures that show a preference for hierarchy (the arrangement of people, with some more important than others)?
3. In Canada and the United States, many Native people feel that their culture is becoming commercialized and "appropriated" by the dominant European culture, and they don't like this. It is in fashion to be Indian and many movies, books, and works of art are produced by people who are not Indian. What do you think of this? What movies, books, or art have you seen with Native themes?

4. Who are the Native people in your culture? What names do they use? How are they doing culturally and economically?

Making Connections

From the library or on the Internet, find information on one of the following topics to present to the class: the Lakota Sioux and their land claims, Mt. Rushmore, the Chief Crazy Horse Monument and why it is controversial, Buffalo Bill, Sitting Bull, the Battle of Little Big Horn.

| PART 2 | **Migration and Homing** |

Before You Read

1 **Scanning for Important Details.** One way of gaining knowledge about the world is through tradition and spiritual study. Another way is through science. In the last century, with its technique of carefully designed experiments, science has solved mysteries that have puzzled human beings for centuries, such as what causes lightning, or why we become ill.

Have you ever heard of *Lassie*, the old-time Hollywood movie star? She was a good-looking actress, a four-footed one. Lassie was a dog, a collie, to be exact. Her movies were based on an old-fashioned story that was said to be true about a Yorkshire terrier in Scotland who had been taken hundreds of miles away and later "found" her way home. This is called *homing* and it has mystified people since ancient times.

The following excerpt from the college biology textbook *Life on Earth* gives some explanations for this. As you can see from the title, it deals with homing and also with another mystery of nature: migration. How and why do birds travel thousands of miles across open oceans and find their way to one particular island? Skim lines 1–39 and answer these questions.

1. What type of fish is used to show an amazing ability to find its way back to the place of its birth?

    _____

2. What tropical bird species is used to show its migration ability across the Atlantic ocean?

    _____

3. What bird species makes the record annual journey in the Western Hemisphere?

    _____

2   **Getting Meaning from Context.** Underline the correct synonym or meaning for each word from the selection. Use the line number to locate the context, if necessary.

1. astonishing (line 1)
   a. <u>amazing</u>
   b. interesting
   c. misunderstood
   d. upsetting

2. to spawn (line 5) (Read carefully the sentence before and the one after.)
   a. to eat
   b. to get sick
   c. to grow old
   d. to have babies

3. almost invariably (line 6)
   a. always
   b. sometimes
   c. never
   d. practically always

4. tributary (line 10)
   a. combination of two rivers
   b. smaller branch of a river
   c. scientific test
   d. government rule

5. guideposts (line 13) (Break this one into two parts.)
   a. fish
   b. signs
   c. food
   d. plants

6. breed (line 26) (Read carefully the sentence before and the one after.)
   a. fly
   b. swim
   c. get ill
   d. have babies

7. isolated (line 28) (Read carefully and use logic.)
   a. crowded
   b. dry
   c. separated
   d. tropical

8. celestial clues (line 43) (If you have trouble with this one, read several sentences farther.)
    a. from the sky
    b. from the ground
    c. from the water
    d. from the wind

9. overcast (line 46)
    a. bright
    b. blue
    c. covered with clouds
    d. filled with stars

10. oriented (line 52)
    a. stopped flying
    b. went to sleep
    c. started to sing
    d. lined up

Read

3 As you read the following selection, try to answer the questions, How did scientists design special experiments to discover the answers to two ancient mysteries?

Migration and Homing

The annals of natural history contain many astonishing examples of the ability of animals to find their way home after making distant journeys. Salmon, for example, are born in freshwater streams and soon afterward journey down to the sea. Several years later, after they have attained maturity, they swim back
5   upstream to spawn and, in many cases, to die. The particular stream that serves as the journey's end is almost invariably the same one in which they were born. It is chosen out of dozens or hundreds of equally suitable streams. The expression "almost invariably" is used advisedly in this case. In one investigation by Canadian biologists, 469,326 young sockeye salmon were
10   marked in a tributary of the Fraser River. Several years later almost 11,000 were recovered after they had completed a return journey to the very same stream, but not a single one was ever recovered from other streams nearby. What underwater guideposts can these fish possibly follow? It has been discovered by A. D. Hasler and his associates at the University of Wisconsin that
15   the salmon, like many other fish, have an acute sense of smell and are able to remember slight differences in the chemical composition of water. The most reasonable theory to explain salmon homing is that each individual remembers the distinctive "fragrance" of its native stream. As it moves upstream it makes the correct choice each time a new tributary is encountered, until fi-
20   nally it arrives home.

Long-distance migration is especially common in birds, because many species must make annual journeys between their nesting grounds and prime

feeding areas far away. Each year over 100,000 sooty terns, an attractive tropical sea bird, travel from the waters off the west coast of Africa all the way
across the Atlantic to Bush Key, a tiny island near the tip of Florida. Here they
build their nests and breed. Once the young can fly, all journey back over the
Atlantic. Why do the sooty terns migrate at all? Like many other sea birds, they
find protection from cats, foxes, and other predators on isolated islands. It is
evidently safer for them to make an entire transoceanic voyage to reach one
such haven than it would be to try to nest on the nearby African shores. A
somewhat different reason lies behind the north-south migration of birds in the
temperate zones. Each spring a legion of migratory forms, from robins, thrush-
es, and warblers to geese and ducks, makes its way north into the greening
countryside, where large quantities of food are becoming freshly available.
Working rapidly, they are able to rear one or more broods of young. As winter
approaches and the food supply declines, all head south again. Some
species proceed all the way to Central and South America. The record annual journey in the Western Hemisphere is made by the golden plover, one
group of which travels from northern Canada to southern South America. A
second group of the same species migrates from Alaska to Hawaii and the
Marquesas Islands. Human beings could never make such journeys unaided
by maps and navigational instruments. How do the birds do it? A large part
of the answer lies in their ability to use celestial clues. At migration time, caged
starlings become unusually restless. If permitted to see the sun, they begin
to fly toward the side of the cage that lies in the direction of their normal migration route. However, when the sky is overcast and the sun is obscured from
view, their movements persist, but they are nondirectional. Other migratory
birds fly at night and can evidently use the position of the stars to guide them.
This surprising fact has been established by several biologists, including
S. T. Emien of Cornell University, who allowed a type of bird called indigo
buntings to attempt flights under the artificial night sky of a planetarium. The
birds oriented "correctly" with reference to the planetarium sky even when the
positions of its constellations did not correspond with the position of the true

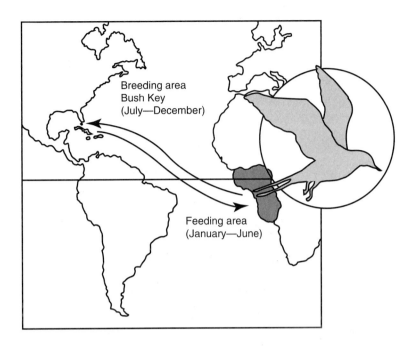

Breeding area
Bush Key
(July—December)

Feeding area
(January—June)

constellations outside. Thus other outside influences were eliminated, and it
could be concluded that the birds were able to orient to what they believed
to be the position of the stars.

Even more impressive than the guidance of migratory movements by celestial clues is the phenomenon of homing. If you were blindfolded, taken to
some completely unfamiliar place and handed a magnetic compass, you
could head north, south, or in any direction you arbitrarily chose—but you
could not head home. Simple compass reading is also the essential ability
demonstrated by migrating birds. But it is not enough in itself to explain how
homing pigeons are able to return to their own lofts from as far as 600 miles
away in a single day. Nor is it enough to account for such feats as that of one
particular Manx shearwater (a kind of sea bird), which, after being carried in
an airplane from England to Boston, flew back across the Atlantic and arrived
at its nest in England twelve days later. For a bird to travel home over unfamiliar terrain requires true navigation—that is, the ability to reckon its position
on the surface of the earth with reference to the position of the distant goal.
One of the currently most attractive hypotheses is that the birds somehow
sense the earth's magnetic field, which varies systematically from point to
point over the earth's surface. Evidence supporting this idea has come from
experiments by William T. Keeton of Cornell University, who attached tiny magnets to the necks of homing pigeons in order to cancel the effects of the
earth's magnetic field. Birds thus encumbered lost their homing ability, but
birds burdened with nonmagnetic metal bars placed at the same position on
the neck managed to travel home correctly. These birds were used as "controls" in the experiments.

From Life on Earth

After You Read

4   **Explaining the Mysteries.** What are the answers to the mysteries of homing and migration? Fill in the blanks of the following sentences.

1. After a salmon has spent years in the sea, it find its way back to the exact stream where it was born by _____

2. The birds called sooty terns leave Africa and fly all the way across the Atlantic to nest in Florida because _____.

3. Many birds migrate thousands of miles every year and find their way by
    _____.

4. The best hypothesis to explain the homing ability of certain birds is that they
    _____.

Talk It Over

In small groups, discuss the following questions.

1. What other animals, besides birds and fish, seem to have special abilities and instincts that we human beings lack? Which animals have very keen senses of hearing or of smell? Do you think some animals are actually intelligent in a way similar to human beings? Why or why not?

2. The experiments on homing discussed at the very end of the article used certain birds called "control" birds. Can you explain what they are and why "controls" like these are necessary to make the experiment scientific?

3. What do you think of the use of animals for scientific experiments? Under what circumstances is it justifiable to kill animals or cause them pain in order to gain more knowledge? Or do you feel that it is never justified? Explain.

4. Do you feel that animals in general have special instincts that we human beings lack? Can animals be our friends? Could a wild animal ever be brought in to live in a house with a family? What kind of animal do you think makes the best pet? Explain.

Focus on Testing

Doing the Easy Ones First

Tests include some items that are designed to be easy, some to be moderately difficult, and others to be hard. Usually students do the items in the order given. Sometimes they get stuck on one item and do not finish the test during the time limit. A good strategy is to quickly do the easy items first, skipping the ones that seem hard. Then go back and do the difficult ones.

Skim the following exercise to find the easy items that you can do right away. Which ones are they? Compare the item numbers you wrote with the ones selected by your classmates. Did you all choose the same ones? Now look at the remaining ones. What makes them harder?

Practice picking out hard items quickly and leaving them for later. Use this technique for exercises and tests in the future, and you will learn to "beat the clock."

Take a minute or two to look over your outline of the selection "Migration and Homing." Then test your understanding of the article by selecting the correct answers to complete the following statements.

1. After becoming mature, salmon swim back to spawn _____ .
   a.   in the sea.
   b.   in the same stream in which they were born
   c.   in any one of hundreds of tributaries

2. Salmon are able to find their way back because of their good sense of _____.
   a.   sight
   b.   taste
   c.   smell

3. Each year sooty terns fly from Africa to an island near Florida to nest, probably because _____ .
   a.   there is no food for birds on the nearby African shores
   b.   they are safe there from animals that would eat them
   c.   their wing muscles become developed from the flight

4. Caged starlings fly in the direction of their migration route on sunny days but make only nondirectional movements when there is no sun. This experiment suggests that the starlings _____ .
   a.   navigate by an inborn compass
   b.   fly only when it is warm
   c.   use celestial clues for migration

5. Other experiments indicate that indigo buntings and certain other birds that fly at night navigate by _____ .
   a.   the position of the stars
   b.   the shape of the land
   c   their sense of hearing

6. At present, one of the best hypotheses to explain the homing of birds over areas they do not know is that they use _____ .
   a.   their keen sense of smell
   b.   the movement of wind currents
   c.   the magnetic field of the earth

PART 3

Down the Drain

Before You Read

1   In small groups, choose three cities that you know about and rank the following dangers in order of importance to each country: air pollution, water pollution, earthquakes, wind storms, flooding. For example, the list for New York City might be the following:

1.   (most dangerous) air pollution
2.   flooding
3.   wind storms
4.   water pollution
5.   earthquakes

Read

2   **Timed Reading.** The following magazine article discusses one of the biggest environmental problems in the world today. Use it as a means to practice reading fast under a time constraint. First skim the quiz at the end to see what kinds of questions you will be asked. Then read the article quickly and check your comprehension by taking the quiz at the end. Be sure to do the easy ones first, as suggested in the Focus on Testing on page 205, and then go back for the harder ones. Use a watch to time yourself. Fill in the following blanks.

Time begun: hour: _____ minutes: _____

Time finished: hour: _____ minutes: _____

Down the Drain

The Coming World Water Crisis

A roadside village between New Delhi and Agra, India, is obscured by clouds of dust and smoke from passing trucks and scooters. Between an open-air restaurant and a tire-changing shop is a stagnant pond, its banks bare of veg-
5   etation. Bright green algae the color of artificial turf floats on the surface, which is periodically disturbed by splashing children and thirsty cows.

There's nothing unique about this contaminated water supply; the scene is repeated hundred of thousands of times throughout the world. Our belea-guered planet is in the midst of an acute fresh water crisis that is likely to in-
10   tensify in the coming years, exacerbated by global warming, industrial pollution, high-tech agriculture, misplaced development priorities and the steady pressure of exploding populations.

Fresh water is the most finite of finite resources, constituting just 2.5 per-cent of the planet's total moisture (with two-thirds of that supply entombed in
15   glaciers). A mere 0.008 percent of the earth's water is part of the hydrologic cycle, meaning it falls as precipitation. Of that tiny percentage, two thirds evaporates or is used by plants. The rest, so-called runoff, is what's left to fill our rivers, streams and aquifers. In water-scarce California, more than 80 per-

cent of that limited resource goes to agriculture, energy production, recreation
and the need to ensure adequate water flow. Cities get less than 10 percent of
that total. As California goes, so goes the rest of the world. Agriculture con-
sumes 65 percent of all the water that people take out of rivers and streams or
pump from underground, according to a 1996 article in *Science* magazine.
Twenty-two percent goes to industry. A mere 7 percent is left over for towns
and cities.

It takes 291,000 gallons of water to supply a single person with a modest, low-meat diet for a year. To grow just one ton of grain, farmers need to
use 1,000 tons of water. In her book *Last Oasis: Facing Water Scarcity*, San-
dra Postel, director of the Global Water Policy Project, predicts that providing
drinking water for the 2.4 billion people expected to be added to the world's
population in the next 30 years would take resources equivalent to 20 Nile or
97 Colorado rivers. "It is not at all clear where that water could come from on
a sustainable basis," she says.

Because of our chronic misuse of water, shortages loom around the
world. Based on a subsistence level of 1,700 cubic meters of water per person per year, the World Bank estimates that 31 countries have scarce water
resources, mostly in Africa and the Middle East. The U.N. Food and Agriculture Organization predicts "a worsening in food security" in Sub-Saharan
Africa, because irrigated farmland is disappearing and grain imports are
growing. By 2021, Postel estimates 1.1 billion Africans, or three-quarters of
the continent's population, will be living in water-stressed countries.

Unsanitary water is responsible for as much as 80 percent of all disease
in the developing world and around 10 million deaths a year according to Alan
Dupont of Australia's Strategic Defense Studies Center. Writing in a recent
issue of the *Straits Times*, a Singapore newspaper, he asks, "Will future wars
be fought over increasingly scarce fresh water resources?" It's becoming a
common question. Former U.N. Secretary General Boutros Boutros-Ghali has

predicted that the next war in the Middle East will be "over the waters of the Nile, not politics."

50   The world's cities are projected to gain more than 2 billion people (the population of India and China combined) by 2025, and it's unknown whether the water resources exist to serve them. "We can see examples of cities collapsing in the developing countries because the water is no longer useable," says Malin Falkenmark, a professor at the Swedish Natural Science Research

55   Council and co-winner of the 1998 Volvo Environmental Prize with Canadian scientist David Schindler.

Speaking with Falkenmark at a press conference in Belgium, Schindler said that the acceleration of global warming is worsening the water crisis by, among other things, melting glaciers and releasing pollutants that were stored

60   in the ice during the '60s and '70s. The two scientists warn that unless food exports to dry developing countries increase six-fold, industrial and agricultural water pollution is cut to a minimum, and conflicts between upstream and downstream water users can be resolved (as in the case of people living on the lower Yellow River in China, who are deprived of water 200 days a year

65   because of intense upstream industrial use), the world will face a series of increasingly bloody confrontations over water.

It won't simply be water rights they're fighting over. Rivers, lakes and ponds are important ecosystems, which are losing biological diversity because of relentless human intervention. Today, our rivers are becoming bio-

70   logical deserts, thanks to overfishing, direct and runoff pollution, and an ongoing policy of "taming" our wild waterways with endless dams. Dams, especially the giant, pharaonic projects that are proliferating in the developing world, have come under intense scrutiny, but that hasn't kept them from being built. China today has more than 20,000 large dams, half of the world's count,

75   and is building the stupefying Three Gorges Dam, which will displace 1.5 million people and create a 372-mile reservoir.

Are there any hopeful signs? Most American rivers and streams are cleaner than they were 30 years ago (though the reverse is true in many developing countries.) Massachusetts' sewage-ridden Nashua River, for instance ran red

80   with paper mill dye in the '60s; the highest form of life it supported was sludge worms. But through the work of groups like Adopt-A-Stream, and Save Our Streams, rivers like Colorado's San Juan and Florida's Kissimmee, now teem with life because their natural flow has been restored, saving them from near-death at the hands of the Army Corps of Engineers.

85   Internationally some countries have agreed to work together to better share their water resources. The U.N. General Assembly started observing a World Water Day (March 22) in l993, and one of its objectives is building an international movement for universal clean water.

Ultimately, the world will have to learn to live within its natural limits. Just

90   as we will have to cope with a declining supply of oil in the face of increasing world demand, so too will we have to learn how to cope with this vastly more precious and equally finite resource.

Peter Tonge, *In These Times* magazine Independent News & Views

After You Read

3   Circle the letter of the correct answers to each of the following questions about the article.

1.   Which of the following does not contribute to the shortage of fresh water?
    a.   global warming
    b.   industrial pollution
    c.   high-tech agriculture
    d.   declining populations

2.   What percentage of the world's water falls as rain or other types of precipitation?
    a.   2.5
    b.   0.008
    c.   80
    d.   65

3.   According to a scientific source, how much of the water taken from rivers, streams and the ground goes to agriculture?
    a.   10%
    b.   65%
    c.   22%
    d.   7%

4.   According to that same source, how much of the water goes to towns and cities?
    a.   10%
    b.   65%
    c.   22%
    d.   7%

5.   How much water does it take to supply one person with a modest, low-meat diet for one year?
    a.   291,000 gallons
    b.   1,000 tons
    c.   2.4 billion pounds
    d.   the equivalent of 20 Nile rivers

6.   In what area of the world does the U.N. Food and Agriculture Organization predict "a worsening in food security"?
    a.   the state of Colorado in the U.S.
    b.   Eastern Europe
    c.   Sub-Saharan Africa
    d.   the South of Australia

7. What percent of all disease is due to unsanitary water, according to Alan Dupont?
   a. 31%
   b. 1.1%
   c. 10%
   d. 80%

8. How many people are predicted to be added to the world's cities by the year 2025?
   a. 10 million
   b. 2 billion
   c. 6 billion
   d. 2025

9. Besides overfishing and pollution, what is contributing to the great loss in biological diversity in the world's important ecosystems?
   a. the building of bridges
   b. the increase in swimming pools
   c. the use of air conditioning
   d. the construction of dams

10. What hopeful sign can be mentioned with regard to the world's water supply?
    a. The Nashua River in Massachusetts ran red with paper mill dye, and the highest form of life it supported was sludge worms in the 1960s.
    b. There are many conflicts between people living upstream on the Yellow River and those living downsteam who are deprived of water 200 days a year.
    c. Many rivers in the United States are much cleaner than they were 30 years ago, showing that pollution problems can be solved with money and effort.
    d. Some scientists see examples in the world today of cities collapsing because the water is no longer useable.

4 **Discussing the Timed Reading.** In a small group, correct the test and talk about the process of reading with a time limit. Compare your time with that of your classmates. How accurate were your answers? Are there any ways of working better under pressure? What advice can you give to others? Is there anything you can do to improve your time or your accuracy?

What Do You Think?

Littering

Wherever you go today, from New York City to Bombay, to the ancient tourist sites of Greece and Egypt, to the beaches of the Mediterranean and Rio, you find litter. Garbage, plastic bags, and bottles are thrown everywhere without regard. In some places in the United States, there is a $500 fine for throwing litter on the

ground. Do you think this is a good idea? Why or why not? In other areas, organizations or businesses "adopt a highway." A group, such as a Boy Scout troop, will adopt a portion of the highway and make sure that section stays clean. Do you think this is a good idea? Why or why not? Would it work in your country? Do you have any other ideas as to how the world can clean up its litter?

Video Activities: Air Pollution

Before You Watch.   Answer the following questions in small groups.

1. Smog is a kind of _____ pollution.
    a. air   b. water   c. noise
2. What causes smog?
    a. cars and factories   b. bad weather   c. construction
3. What problems does smog cause?

Watch.   Answer the following questions.

1. The Environmental Protection Agency's new rules will _____ air pollution.
    a. decrease   b. eliminate   c. cause
2. How does the oil industry feel about the new rules? Why?
3. The new rules will make diesel fuel _____.
    a. cleaner and cheaper
    b. less expensive but more dangerous
    c. safer but more expensive

Watch Again.

1. The EPA's new rules will decrease sulphur emissions by _____.
    a. 90%   b. 7%   c. 97%
2. The EPA is particularly worried about emissions from which two kinds of vehicles?
    a. cars   b. trucks
    c. motorcycle   d. buses
    e. motorhomes
3. According to an official from the oil industry the new rules will create new national standards that the industry cannot _____ for a _____ that fuel distributions systems cannot _____ at _____ American consumers cannot _____.
4. What diseases does air pollution cause?
    a. cancer   b. tuberculosis   c. malaria   d. asthma
5. When do the new rules start to go into effect?
6. How long will old vehicles be on the roads?

After You Watch.   Find an article about pollution. Write a summary of the article. Your summary should answer these questions.

1. What kind of pollution is it?
2. What is causing the pollution?
3. What problems is the pollution causing?
4. What is being done about the pollution?

Chapter 12

Together on a Small Planet

IN THIS CHAPTER

Here you will read selections from four literary genres—essays, poetry, a speech, and a short story—using skills you practiced in previous chapters. These are presented without prereading exercises so you have the chance to choose from the methods you have learned for each reading. The selections were written by authors from different cultures who share their unique viewpoints and feelings about human existence and values.

PART 1   # Books

Read

In an age of films and TV, with multiscreen cinemas, videotape recorders, and cable systems extending visual communication, many people predict that books will soon become obsolete. In the following short essay, the world-renowned Argentine poet and short story writer Jorge Luis Borges (1899–1986) gives his opinion on this topic.

Books

I believe books will never disappear. It is impossible for it to happen. Of all mankind's diverse tools, undoubtedly the most astonishing are his books. All the others are extensions of the body. The telephone is an extension of his voice; the telescope and microscope extensions of his sight; the sword and the plow are extensions of his arms. In *Caesar and Cleopatra*, when Bernard Shaw refers to the Library of Alexandria, he says it is mankind's memory. I would add it is also mankind's imagination. Humanity's vigils have generated infinite pages of infinite books. Mankind owes all that we are to the written word. Why? What is our past but a succession of dreams? What difference is there between dreaming and remembering? Between remembering dreams and recalling the past? Books are the great memory of the centuries. Consequently their function is irreplaceable. If books were to disappear, history would disappear. So would men.

After You Read

1 **Recalling Information.** Select the phrase that best completes the statement about Borges' ideas on books according to the essay.

1. Books are humanity's most astonishing _____ .
   a. possibility
   b. tool
   c. dream

2. A book is an extension of the human _____ .
   a. body
   b. voice
   c. imagination

3. If books were to disappear, human history would also disappear because people would _____ .
   a. feel too sad to live
   b. no longer remember the past
   c. keep on dreaming of the future

2 **Discussing the Reading.** In small groups, discuss the following questions.

1. In your opinion, what is the main idea of this essay? Do you agree with it or not? Why?

2. Which would you prefer: to read a particular book or to see a film based on it? Why?

3. What is one of the best books you have read? In what language was it written? By whom? To what kind of person would you recommend it?

| PART 2 |

Three Days to See

Read

Imagine that you are both blind and deaf. You see nothing. You hear no sound. How could you connect to reality? What would your life be like? Helen Keller (1880–1968), an American born in Alabama, lost her sight and hearing from illness at the age of 19 months, yet she became a world-renowned writer and lecturer who graduated *cum laude* from Harvard University and received the Presidential Medal of Freedom in 1963. She tells the chronicle of her journey out of darkness in her most popular book, *The Story of My Life* (1902). She was helped by the famous inventor Alexander Graham Bell and a wonderful teacher named Annie Sullivan. This teacher patiently used the sense of touch to make contact with her young student, who at first behaved like a wild animal, and later to subdue, stimulate, and support the awakening of the brilliant intelligence that speaks to us in the following essay. This amazing story was later made into the play and film *The Miracle Worker*. The writings of Helen Keller serve as an inspiration not only for people with disabilities but for all people the world over.

Three Days to See

All of us have read thrilling stories in which the hero has only a limited and specified time to live. Sometimes it was as long as a year; sometimes as short as 24 hours. But always we were interested in discovering just how the doomed man chose to spend his last days or his last hours. I speak, of
5   course, of free men who have a choice, not condemned criminals whose sphere of activities is strictly limited.

Such stories set us thinking, wondering what we should do under similar circumstances. What events, what experiences, what associations, should we crowd into those last hours as mortal beings? What happiness should we find
10   in reviewing the past, what regrets?

Sometimes I have thought it would be an excellent rule to live each day as if we should die tomorrow. Such an attitude would emphasize sharply the values of life. We should live each day with a gentleness, a vigor, a keenness of appreciation which are often lost when time stretches before us in the con-
15   stant panorama of more days and months and years to come. There are those, of course, who would adopt the epicurean motto of "Eat, drink, and be merry," but most people would be chastened by the certainty of impending death.

In stories, the doomed hero is usually saved at the last minute by some stroke of fortune, but almost always his sense of values is changed. He be-
20   comes more appreciative of the meaning of life and its permanent spiritual values. It has often been noted that those who live, or have lived, in the shadow of death bring a mellow sweetness to everything they do.

Most of us, however, take life for granted. We know that one day we must die, but usually we picture that day as far in the future. When we are in buoy-
25   ant health, death is all but unimaginable. We seldom think of it. The days

stretch out in an endless vista. So we go about our petty tasks, hardly aware of our listless attitude toward life.

30   The same lethargy, I am afraid, characterizes the use of all our faculties and senses. Only the deaf appreciate hearing, only

35   the blind realize the manifold blessings that lie in sight. Particularly does this observation apply to those who have lost sight and hearing in adult life. But those who have never suffered impair-

40   ment of sight or hearing seldom make the fullest use of these blessed faculties. Their eyes and ears take in all sights and sounds hazily, without concentration and

45   with little appreciation. It is the same old story of not being grateful for what we have until we lose it, of not being conscious of health until we are ill.

I have often thought it would be a blessing if each human being were

50   stricken blind and deaf for a few days at some time during his early adult life. Darkness would make him more appreciative of sight; silence would teach him the joys of sound.

Now and then I have tested my seeing friends to discover what they see. Recently I was visited by a very good friend who had just returned from a long

55   walk in the woods, and I asked her what she had observed. "Nothing in particular," she replied. I might have been incredulous had I not been accustomed to such responses, for long ago I became convinced that the seeing see little.

How was it possible, I asked myself, to walk for an hour through the

60   woods and see nothing worthy of note? I who cannot see find hundreds of things to interest me through mere touch. I feel the delicate symmetry of a leaf. I pass my hands lovingly about the smooth skin of a silver birch, or the rough shaggy bark of a pine. In spring I touch the branches of trees hopefully in search of a bud, the first sign of awakening Nature after her winter's sleep. I

65   feel the delightful, velvety texture of a flower, and discover its remarkable convolutions, and something of the miracle of Nature is revealed to me. Occasionally, if I am fortunate, I place my hand gently on a small tree and feel the happy quiver of a bird in full song. I am delighted to have the cool waters of a brook rush through my open fingers.

70   To me a lush carpet of pine needles or spongy grass is more welcome than the most luxurious Persian rug. To me the pageant of seasons is a thrilling and unending drama, the action of which streams through my fingertips.

At times my heart cries out with longing to see all these things. If I can get so much pleasure from mere touch, how much more beauty must be re-

75   vealed by sight. Yet those who have eyes apparently see little. The panorama

of color and action which fills the world is taken for granted. It is human, perhaps, to appreciate little that which we have and to long for that which we have not, but it is a great pity that in the world of light the gift of sight is used only as a mere convenience rather than as a means of adding fullness to life.

After You Read

1   **Recalling Information.** Fill in the blanks of the following summary of Helen Keller's ideas with key words from the essay.

Summary

Helen Keller at times thought that it would be an excellent rule to live each day as if we should __die__ tomorrow. In adventure stories, a doomed hero is usually saved from death at the last minute, but almost always his sense of _____ has been changed. Most people who have never suffered impairment of their eyes or ears take in all sights and sounds with very little _____. Only the _____ seem to truly appreciate hearing and only the _____ really appreciate sight. Once a friend of Helen's returned from a walk in the woods and said that she had observed _____. Helen, however, always found hundreds of things to _____ her in the woods through touch. By feeling leaves, flowers, and trees, she felt that the miracle of _____ was revealed to her. In her opinion, the panorama of color and action that fills the world is taken for _____ by most people.

2   **Separating Fact from Opinion.** Put F in front of the statements taken from the essay that are facts, and O in front of those that are opinions.

_____ 1.   All of us have read thrilling stories in which the hero has only a limited and specified time to live.

_____ 2.   Such stories set us thinking, wondering what we should do under similar circumstances.

_____ 3.   Most of us, however, take life for granted.

_____ 4.   Only the deaf appreciate hearing, only the blind realize the manifold blessings that lie in sight.

_____ 5.   I have often thought it would be a blessing if each human being were stricken blind and deaf for a few days at some time during his early adult life.

_____ 6.   I who cannot see find hundreds of things to interest me through mere touch.

_____ 7. To me a lush carpet of pine needles or spongy grass is more welcome than the most luxurious Persian rug.

_____ 8. If I can get so much pleasure from mere touch, how much more beauty must be revealed by sight.

Talk It Over

In small groups, discuss the following questions.

1. According to Keller, what advantage did her "disabilities" or "handicaps" give her?
2. How are people with disabilities treated in your culture? What kind of education or assistance do they receive? Is there discrimination against them? Should there be?
3. In your opinion, what can we learn from Keller?

PART 3

Good Friends...Dogs, Sons and Others

Read

Willie Morris is a Southern journalist, author, and editor. He is the winner of several literary awards, and in 1981 he was the writer-in-residence at the University of Mississippi. In the following excerpt from his essay "Good Friends...Dogs, Sons and Others," Morris writes about the value of a small group of friends from varied backgrounds.

Good Friends...Dogs, Sons and Others

We are all terribly alone in this life, I fear. This is part of our mortality, and there is not really much we can do about it. The awful armor of our isolation is pierced only by those fragile loyalties which we pray will abide—children, or a lover, or friends. All of these ask for tenderness and care.

5   I am not just talking here about male friendships and female ones, but also about friendships of a nonsexual nature between men and women. One of the dividends of the women's movement of this generation, perhaps, has been the enhanced freedom of American women to choose affectionate relationships with men whom they trust outside the bedroom. Some of my own closest friends are women; I can count four whom I believe I would go to the

10   brink for. Two are married to men I admire, one is a widow, one is divorced, and they are as important to me as anything in my existence, including my male friends, who are also only a few. I suspect a person can only have a handful of steadfast friends, if that. Be wary of those who claim to count their friendships by the dozens, unless they are politicians up for reelection.

15   Parenthetically, I must also go so far as to confess that one of my best
friends is a big black dog of acute warmth and intelligence. He and I are huckleberry friends who ride the river together. By my personal measure, another
of my finest friends is my twenty-year-old son. We have lived through too many
moments as a twosome to be forgetful of them. Among genuine friendships,
20   never discount the possibility of good dogs and good sons.

At the core of friendship, I feel, is fidelity. We all make fools of ourselves
now and again, and do things which cause us guilt—or worse, shame—and
there are our times of ineluctable grief and sorrow. A trusting friend can call
us back to earth and remind us of the universal failures and sufferings. Laugh-
25   ter is no less an ingredient of friendship than loyalty, or charity, or forgiveness.
Conversely, in the lexicon of human cruelty, I rank the betrayal of a friend—
even a friend from an earlier part of one's life—as dastardly almost as child
abuse or manslaughter. I am reminded of the New York editor and writer who
recently published a memoir belittling old friends, ferreting out their faults in
30   retrospect as finely as a sculptor chiseling at a bust, all in the spirit of his own
aggrandizement. Gratuitous betrayal often exacts its own special price.

I am reminded too of a worthier example, one that remains with me as
vividly as the moment I first heard of it as a boy, so that it has become a kind
of symbol for me. In his rookie season with the Brooklyn Dodgers, Jackie
35   Robinson, the first black man to play Major League baseball, faced venom
wherever he traveled—fastballs at his head, spikings on the bases, brutal ep-
ithets from the opposing dugouts and from the crowds. During one game on
a hot day in St. Louis, the taunts and racial slurs seemed to reach a crescen-
do. In the midst of all this, the Dodger who was Jackie Robinson's particular
40   friend, a Southern white named Peewee Reese, called time out. He walked
from his position at shortstop toward Robinson at second base, put his arm

around Robinson's shoulder and stood there with him for a long time. The gesture spoke more eloquently than the words: This man is my friend.

Even across the divide of death, friendship remains, an echo forever in the heart. The writer James Jones has been gone for more than three years, yet so alive was he for me that I have never quite admitted he is dead. He and his family lived down the road from me on eastern Long Island, and he struggled against death in his last months to finish his fictional trilogy of World War II. He was a connoisseur of cigars, a believer in the written word, and an enemy of meanness and pretense. He was courageous without ever talking much about courage; he appreciated mirth and he understood sorrow. I'm not sure why we were closer than brothers, for he was older than I and more inured of the siftings and winnowings of this world. Yet we were. Two years ago, as I began a book which means much to me—struggling with the very first sentences with a radio somewhere in the background—the song that came on was the theme to the movie of Jim's big novel, *From Here to Eternity*. "Keep the faith," he might have said.

When I see an honored friend again after years of separation, it is like reassuming the words of an old conversation which had been halted momentarily by time. Surely, as one gets older, friendship becomes more precious to us, for it affirms the contours of our existence. It is a reservoir of shared experience, of having lived through many things in our brief and mutual moment on earth. To paraphrase another writer from Mississippi, it is a prop, a pillar, to help us not merely endure, but prevail.

After You Read

1 **Recalling Information.** Write T (for True) or F (for False) in front of the statements about Morris's essay. Correct the false ones to make them true.

_____ 1. One good result of the women's movement is that now American women can have real, nonsexual friendships with men.

_____ 2. A person should have dozens of steadfast friends.

_____ 3. Two of his best friends are his twenty-year-old son and a big black dog.

_____ 4. Laughter is an important part of a friendship.

_____ 5. The New York editor who wrote an article about the faults of his old friends did nothing wrong.

_____ 6. Sometimes a personal gesture of friendship speaks louder than words.

_____ 7. Death is the only real end of friendship.

_____ 8. Friendship becomes more precious as a person gets older.

2   **Outlining One View of Friendship.** This essay presents one man's view of what it means to be a friend. Work with a partner to make a list of the key ideas of the essay, along with one or more illustrations or examples of each idea. Afterwards, share your outlines with another group or the class.

Talk It Over

In small groups, discuss the following questions.
1.   In your opinion, what is the main idea of this essay?
2.   What can you infer about the author's character from what he has written?
3.   What do you feel are the important qualities of a friend?
4.   Do you think a person should have many friends or just a few? Why?
5.   How do friendships differ around the world?

PART 4   # Poetry

Read

Any object, feeling, or thought can be the subject of a poem, but poets everywhere tend to speak mostly about the traditional themes of love, friendship, life, death, and the meaning of human existence. The following poems are by poets from different cultures and historical eras: Yevgeny Yevtushenko, Russian, twentieth century; Ono no Komachi, Japanese, ninth century (Heian period); Paavo Haavikko, Finnish, twentieth century; Maya Angelou, American, twentieth century; Omar Khayyam, Persian, twelfth century. Most poetry is written to convey feelings more than ideas. Poets generally employ unusual language in an original way to force us to see ordinary aspects of human experience in a new light. Read each poem several times, preferably aloud, to discover what feeling the poet is trying to convey.

People

No people are uninteresting.
Their fate is like the chronicle of planets.

Nothing in them is not particular
and planet is dissimilar from planet.

5   And if a man lived in obscurity
making his friends in that obscurity
obscurity is not uninteresting.

To each his world is private
and in that world one excellent minute.

10   And in that world one tragic minute.
These are private.

In any man who dies there dies with him
his first snow and kiss and fight.
It goes with him.

15   There are left books and bridges
and painted canvas and machinery.

Whose fate is to survive.
But what has gone is also not nothing.

By the rule of the game something has gone.
20   Not people die but worlds die in them.

Whom we knew as faulty, the earth's creatures.
Of whom, essentially, what did we know?

Brother of a brother? Friend of friends?
Lover of lover?

25   We who knew our fathers
In everything, in nothing.

They perish. They cannot be brought back.
The secret worlds are not regenerated.

And every time again and again
30   I make my lament against destruction.

—Yevgeny Yevtushenko

Poem

That which fades away
Without revealing its altered color
Is in the world of love
The single flower which blossoms
5 In the fickle heart of man.

—Ono no Komachi

Poem

You marry the moon
and the sea and the moon and the woman:
    earless all.

You'll listen to their voices, you'll talk to them
5 and they say
    It's a game.

—Paavo Haavikko

Caged Bird

A free bird leaps
on the back of the wind
and floats downstream
till the current ends
5 and dips his wing
in the orange sun rays
and dares to claim the sky.

But a bird that stalks
down his narrow cage
10 can seldom see through
his bars of rage
his wings are clipped and
his feet are tied
so he opens his throat to sing.

15 The caged bird sings
with a fearful trill
of things unknown
but longed for still
and his tune is heard
20 on the distant hill
for the caged bird
sings of freedom.

The free bird thinks of another breeze
and the trade winds soft through the sighing trees
25 and the fat worms waiting on a dawn-bright lawn
and he names the sky his own.

But a caged bird stands on the grave of dreams
his shadow shouts in a nightmare scream
his wings are clipped and his feet are tied
30 so he opens his throat to sing.

The caged bird sings
with a fearful trill
of things unknown
but longed for still

35 and his tune is heard
on the distant hill
for the caged bird
sings of freedom.

—Maya Angelou

The Rubaiyat of Omar Khayyam[1] (Selections)

VIII
Come, fill the Cup, and in the fire of Spring
Your winter garment of Repentance fling.
The Bird of Time has but a little way
To flutter—and the Bird is on the wing.

XII
5   A Book of Verses underneath the Bough,
A Jug of Wine, a Loaf of Bread and thou[2]
Beside me singing in the Wilderness—
Oh, Wilderness were Paradise enow![3]

XIII
Some for the Glories of This World and some
10   Sigh for the Prophet's Paradise[4] to come,
Ah, take the Cash, and let the Credit go
Nor heed[5] the rumble of the distant Drum!

[1]Translated into English verse by Edward Fitzgerald, fifth edition
[2]You
[3]Enough
[4]Heaven
[5]And don't listen to

After You Read

1   **Recalling Information.** Circle the letter of the best response, according to the poems you just read.

"People"

1.   To Yevtushenko the people who are interesting are _____ .
   a.   those who live in obscurity
   b.   those who study the planets
   c.   all people

2. After a person's death, some of the things that are left are _____ .
   a.   painted canvas and machinery
   b.   his first snow and kiss and fight
   c.   a private world

3. When a person dies, what dies?
   a.   a book
   b.   a world
   c.   nothing

"Poem," Ono No Komachi

4. Love is compared to _____ .
    a. the sea
    b. a flower
    c. rain
5. Love is seen as something _____ .
    a. momentary
    b. permanent
    c. unchanging

"Poem," Paavo Haavikko

6. The moon, women, and the sea are shown as things that cannot _____ .
    a. feel
    b. see
    c. hear
7. Love is shown as _____ .
    a. serious
    b. playful
    c. meaningless

"Caged Bird"

8. The main theme of the poem is _____ .
    a. the beauty of birds
    b. the fear of the unknown
    c. the importance of freedom
9. The poem is written with _____ .
    a. rhyme
    b. rhythm
    c. both rhyme and rhythm

"The Rubaiyat of Omar Khayyam"

10. The poet tells us that the most important thing in life is _____ .
    a. to gain Paradise after death
    b. to enjoy the present moment
    c. to earn a lot of money

2 **Finding the Themes.** Here are some themes which are traditional in poetry. With a partner or in a small group, look at the themes and answer the questions. Remember that the word of the theme does not need to be stated in the poem, only the idea.

> beauty
> death
> freedom
> happiness
> human nature
> love
> suffering
> truth

1. Which of these appear in poems in this selection?
2. How many appear in more than one of the poems?
3. What do the poems tell us about these themes?

Talk It Over

In small groups, discuss the following questions.

1. Which of the poems did you like best for its sound? Why?
2. Which of the poems did you like best for its meaning? Explain.
3. Why do you think that people compose poems? Why do people enjoy reading or listening to poems?
4. Think of a short poem or part of a poem that you like from your culture. Write down a simple translation or description of it here to share with your group.

PART 5 # Inaugural Address

Read

> John Fitzgerald Kennedy was the thirty-fifth president of the United States. He was the first Roman Catholic to be elected to the office and the youngest president in United States history. A popular and eloquent speaker, Kennedy, in his inaugural address in January, 1961, urged his fellow citizens to become committed to a new vision of peace, freedom, and prosperity with these words: "Ask not what your country can do for you—ask what you can do for your country." Unfortunately, Kennedy didn't have much time to see his dreams for a new society become reality; he was assassinated in Dallas, Texas, on November 22, 1963. The following is an excerpt from his famous inaugural address.

Inaugural Address

...Let both sides,* for the first time, formulate serious and precise proposals for the inspection and control of arms—and bring the absolute power to destroy other nations under absolute control of all nations.

Let both sides seek to invoke the wonders of science instead of its ter-
5 rors. Together let us explore the stars, conquer the deserts, and encourage the arts and commerce.

Let both sides unite to heed in all corners of the earth the command of Isaiah—to "undo the heavy burdens... [and] let the oppressed go free" And if a beachhead of cooperation may push back the angels of suspicion, let both
10 sides join in creating a new endeavor: not a balance of power, but a new world of law, where the strong are just and the weak secure and the peace pre-served.

All this will not be finished in the first 100 days. Nor will it be finished in the first 1,000 days, nor in the life of this administration, nor even perhaps in
15 our own lifetime on this planet. But let us begin.

In your hands, my fellow citizens, more than mine, will rest the final suc-cess or failure of our course. Since this country was founded, each genera-tion of Americans has been summoned to give testimony to its national loyalty. The graves of young Americans who answered the call to service surround
20 the globe.

Now the trumpet summons us again—not as a call to bear arms, though arms we need—not as a call to battle, though embattled we are but as a call to bear the burden of a long twilight struggle year in and year out, "rejoicing in hope, patient in tribulation"—a struggle against the common enemies of man:
25 tyranny, poverty, disease, and war itself. Can we forge against these enemies a grand and global alliance, north and south, east and west, that can assure a more fruitful life for all mankind? Will you join in that historic effort?

---

*Kennedy was referring to the tension that existed then between the Communist nations and the non-Communist nations.

30

In the long history of the world, only a few generations have been granted the role of defending freedom in its hour of maximum danger. I do not
shrink from this responsibility—I welcome it. I do not believe that any of us
would exchange places with any other people or any other generation. The
energy, the faith, the devotion which we bring to this endeavor will light our
country and all who serve it—and the glow from that fire can truly light the
world.

35

And so, my fellow Americans: Ask not what your country can do for you—
ask what you can do for your country.

My fellow citizens of the world: Ask not what America will do for you but
what together we can do for the freedom of man.

40

Finally, whether you are citizens of America or citizens of the world, ask of
us here the same high standards of strength and sacrifice which we ask of
you. With a good conscience our only sure reward, with history the final judge
of our deeds, let us go forth to lead the land we love, asking His blessing and
His help, but knowing that here on earth God's work must truly be our own.

After You Read

1 **Recalling Information.** Write T (for True) in front of those statements that express
ideas from Kennedy's speech and F (for False) in front of those that do not. Correct the
false statements to make them true.

_____ 1.   Both sides should try to identify and discuss the problems that divide
them.

_____ 2.   Each side should try to gain complete control for itself of the inspection and control of arms.

_____ 3.   The two sides together should unite in their efforts to explore space and
improve commerce and the arts.

_____ 4.   These goals should be accomplished in the first 1,000 days of
Kennedy's administration as president.

_____ 5.   The common enemies of human beings are poverty, disease, commu-
nism, and socialism.

_____ 6.   Most people realize that the present moment is one of great challenge
and are glad to be alive at this time.

_____ 7.   Americans should ask how their country can help them.

_____ 8.   People from other countries should ask how America can help them.

Talk It Over

In small groups, discuss the following questions.

1. Which of the goals mentioned in Kennedy's speech have been accomplished?
2. Do you think all the goals he mentioned are possible to achieve? Why or why not? Which one do you consider the most important for today's world?
3. Why do you think that Kennedy's ideas were very popular with the young people of his time?
4. In 1961, Kennedy created the U.S. Peace Corps, an organization that sends Americans to countries in the developing world to work for two-year periods. In your opinion, is this a good idea or not? Explain.
5. Think about an inaugural address of a head of another country. How was it similar to the one by President Kennedy? How was it different?

PART 6

Susana and the Shepherd

Read

This is the longest reading in the book. You may choose to read it straight through and then go back and reread it and do the exercises. Or, you may choose to read it in three sections. The exercise after the reading provides a comprehension exercise on each section, followed by questions called Focus on Development that can be used for group discussion. These questions trace the changes that occur in the main character, Juan Varra, a young man who comes from Spain to work in California.

Margaret Craven was born in Helena, Montana, and received her college degree from Stanford University. She is a former journalist and has written many short stories about life in the western United States and in Canada as well as the novel *I Heard the Owl Call My Name*. This short story discusses the loneliness and dreams of a young Basque shepherd in his early days in America.

Susana and the Shepherd

Section 1

All the passengers on the big transcontinental plane were interested in the young Basque who occupied the rear seat. He was a good-looking lad with his dark eyes and his proud, inscrutable face, tagged on the jacket with a check badge like a piece of luggage because he couldn't speak an English

5   word.

"He's a sheepherder from the Spanish Pyrenees," the stewardess replied to an inquiry. "The California Range Association is flying over many of them. Usually three or four come together. He's the first to come alone."

10

Several of the passengers tried to be friendly, but the young Basque only stared at them, too bewildered and confused to smile, and finally a sure blonde, who had traveled in Spain, said she'd draw him out. She'd toss a little Spanish at him. She'd just go over and sit on the arm of his chair and give him the good old American *bienvenida*.

15

So she did it, and the young Basque fixed upon her a pair of scornful, suspicious eyes and ignored her.

"You know what I think?" said the defeated blonde to the stewardess. "I think his mother warned him to have nothing to do with American women. They'd eat him alive." And she was wrong; it was his grandmother who had warned him.

20

"Oh, he's a strange one," the stewardess told the navigator. "They're all silent, but this one wouldn't even talk if he knew how. I hope somebody meets him in San Francisco. I have strict orders not to turn him loose unless he's met."

25

The navigator was wiser. "He's from some small village, probably," he said. "Never seen a big city. Never been in a plane. If he's afraid, it's the kind of fear only the brave know. Otherwise he wouldn't be crossing an ocean and a continent to herd sheep for a stranger in a land he doesn't know. Let him alone. He's a kid with a dream."

30

And after that, across the plains and the mountains, the boy sat undisturbed, holding his dream, and his was the old dream many Basque boys have held in their hearts. The land was not big or rich enough to support all. By custom, a family's land was left to the eldest son. The younger sons, therefore, must emigrate; their only hope of keeping the land they loved was to leave it—and come back rich.

35

It was possible. From his own village in the Valle de Arce in the province of Navarra, several had done it. Felipe Lacabe had done it. He had herded sheep for six years in a place called Nevada. In all that time he had learned no more than fifty English words, and been to town twice, and spent not one coin on drink, smokes, and girls. He had come back with twelve thousand dollars—a fabulous fortune—and he had bought himself a band of fine sheep and married the prettiest girl in Uriz.

40

Many had come back, and more had not. Whenever American tourists came to the remote villages of the Pyrenees some Basque father, prodded by his wife, said slowly, "If you have been to California, is it possible you know our son, Bonifacio?" or Fermin. Or Esteban. But they never did.

45

He, Juan Varra, was going to be one of the lucky ones. He had made up his mind. The American consul at Bilbao before whom he had appeared for his sheepherder's examination had praised him. The doctor who had given him his physical had spoken of his strength. And while he had waited the long months for the completion of his papers, the priest had strengthened him.

50

No Basque had ever been remembered for his words, the priest had said. Only for deeds and for courage. And if the ignorant thought he had a mist in his head like the mists of the mountains he loved, what of it? The thing to do was to be strong.

55

Yet when it was almost time to land, the boy found it hard to be strong. He reminded himself that an unknown *americano* had paid seven hundred and eleven dollars and ten cents for his passage, sight unseen, and why?

Because he knew—as who does not—that for two thousand years the Basques have been famous for their skill with sheep.

60   He thought hard on *abuelita*, his grandmother. How confidently she had smiled at him as she had prepared his favorite omelet for his last supper at home. With no teeth, she looked like a little old baby, and he vowed now that with his first wages he would send her enough money to buy a set of shiny white store teeth, so she could walk through the village, head high and smiling.

65   Also he thought of his little brother, who had begged to come along, who must emigrate, too, when he was older. He must set him an example. He must not fail.

Then the plane landed. The passengers began to file out slowly. He followed them. Surely El Cid, the bravest knight in all Christendom, never went

70   forth to battle more staunchly than Juan Varra left that plane, the little stewardess at his heels, praying fervently somebody would meet him and ready to grab his jacket tails if no one did.

He was the first to pass the gate, and as he stepped through he saw the most beautiful sight possible to any Basque far from home. He saw another

75   Basque. He saw a browned face, no longer young, which was smiling and showing some splendid gold teeth. And the voice was speaking his own di-
alect and it said, "Welcome, Juan Varra, and are the girls still as pretty in Navarra?" And this was Ancelito, thirty years from home and as much of a Basque as ever.

80   Ancelito collected his luggage and led him to the pickup truck. When they had left the confusion of the city, and were driving through the great wide green Sacramento Valley, Ancelito dropped pleasantries and began to speak so slowly and seriously in Spanish that the boy knew he must remember every word.

85   Now in early May the *alfilaria* was already dry. The corkscrew spirals on the wild grass that can work their way into the sheep's hides had already formed. It was vital, therefore, that the sheep be moved at once from the low range. Separated into bands, sheared, and branded, they had been driven to a central campsite, the trailer houses of the herders accompanying them. At

90   the campsite, freight cars waited. The rich *americano* who owned the sheep had rented a whole train, and this very moment he was supervising the load-
ing of the sheep bands into the cars. Tonight the train would carry the sheep across the great mountains into Nevada, where the long summer drive would begin at dawn.

95   Usually, said Ancelito, a youngster from the homeland was kept on the valley ranch for several weeks to accustom him to the strange American ways. But now they were desperate for herders. Last year they had lost two older men from heart attacks. The camp tender had found them at eight thousand feet, stiff in their blankets. It would be necessary for Juan Varra to go with them

100   to Nevada and to start out at dawn with a band of two thousand sheep. Every other day a camp tender would bring him supplies and tell him where to find water. He would have a burro, of course, and a dog which Ancelito, himself, had trained.

"There is nothing to fear," Ancelito told him gravely. "The dog will know

105   what you do not."

The boy said with dignity, "I have no fear."

Ancelito questioned him carefully, and in response the boy told him, shyly and briefly, a little of his dream. After four hours' driving, they came at last to the campsite.

In the trailer house Juan Varra ate a quick meal while Ancelito checked the clothes and the bedding he'd need. Then it was time to go, and they walked together through the dark to the train.

"You will go in the caboose," said Ancelito. "You will sleep better and tomorrow you will need that sleep. I will go by truck with the others, and I will see you at daybreak."

Once, at night in his bunk, the boy woke and felt the train moving under him and the cold air on his cheek, and he could hear the hard pull of the engine, and knew they were crossing the mountains. When he woke again, it was to the smell of coffee and the touch of a trainman's hand on his shoulder. He put on his shoes and his jacket and drank two cups of coffee. When he left the caboose, he stepped out into the clear dawn and such a sight as he had never seen.

Already the sheep were being spilled out onto the sage, each band at a time, its loaded burro, herder, and dog waiting to drive it away.

Because he was new, his band was the last. Then it, too, was spilled into the sage, and his burro and dog and a sheep tender drove the band away from the tracks as Ancelito motioned him to wait.

The train moved on, the boy waiting by the truck while Ancelito talked earnestly to the *americano* who owned the sheep, and though they spoke English and the boy could not understand a word, he knew the *americano* was worried.

"Andy, I'm scared to death to send him out. Can he do it?"

"Yes. He's used to hardship. He is not an American boy. He does not put his manhood in a car that can go ninety miles an hour. It is in himself."

"I know. He'll have the inbred willingness to endure."

"He has something else. He has a dream."

"All right. Let him go."

Then Ancelito gave the boy his directions and told him where he would find water. The owner shook his hand.

Juan ran into the sage and took the crook from the tender and he gave the old signal to the dog with a lift of his hand and he was off and on his own. He did not permit himself to look back for some moments. When he did so, it was as if the truck, the men, and the other bands of sheep had never existed, so quickly had the land taken them. And it was unlike any land he had ever seen, and vaster than any he had ever imagined.

The sage and the green buckbrush stretched as endlessly as eternity, broken only by a few small yellow sunflowers and a very occasional pine. No friendly villages. No small white houses with cheerful red-tiled roofs. Nothing but mountains which did not stand up proudly as mountains should, but lay rolling beneath his old high shoes.

He could scarcely bear to look at the sheep, so great was his disappointment. How ugly they were with their strange snub-nosed faces. The factory-made crook was awkward to his hand, and so long that he was sure he would never be able to trip a ewe neatly by the hind leg. Even the motley-colored Australian shepherd was unlike any dog he had known.

But the burro was the same. It trudged along with the sheep, carrying his supplies, topped by his big square bedroll. And the sheep baaed like sheep. The lambs frolicked like the lambs at home. And the dog let the sheep scatter only so far, rounding in the strays, circling watchfully.

160 He counted the black sheep—the markers—carefully. There were twenty-one. He counted the bellwethers. At the nooning-up he would unpack the burro, check his supplies and repack in his own precise way. He would make a fire and set a pot of beans to simmer, and cook himself a meal of ham and eggs. And this night when the coyotes yapped and the dog answered them,
165 prowling the bed grounds, thoughts of home would creep to his little tent and he would begin the long battle against loneliness. And he swore now, by all the lady saints and the gentlemen saints in the entire heaven, that he would fight it each night until he won.

Section 2

170 It took him six weeks. He had no calendar and no watch, and he needed neither. Each day followed the familiar pattern. He was up before daylight, building his fire beneath the heavy U-shaped iron, brewing his coffee. When the burro was packed, the daily trek began, the sheep scattering over a mile, the boy following, his beat-up .30.30 in a sling on his back, the dog circling, alert
175 to every sound of his voice, every movement of his hands.

Each nooning-up Juan cooked his meal while the sheep lay in the sage, chewing their cud. And every other day the sheep tender came bumping through the buck brush in his four-wheel-drive truck, bringing fresh meat and food, even water if necessary, and an eight-pound round loaf of white Basque
180 bread which he had baked in a long pit. The sheep tender was a Basque also, but he had been too long alone. He had lost his dream. He could not talk easily to anyone, and when he spoke, it was always of some café called Estrellita or Española in some valley town where he could fill himself up on red wine, poured from a goatskin, and eat prodigiously.

185 Sometimes on the rainy nights when the coyotes cried like women, the boy was so homesick for his land and his people that it was an agony within him, and he rose shaken and white. He dreamed one night of his *abuelita*, smiling and showing her toothless gums, and when he awoke, his cheeks were wet, and though never for an instant did he admit it was from anything
190 but rain leaking in the tent, after that he felt better.

Gradually the sheep did not seem quite so snub-nosed and ugly. They became the familiar sheep. He knew them, and a few too well—especially the cantankerous ewe with the twin lambs which he called "*La Bruja*," the witch. He grew fond of his burro, and he loved the dog as deeply as a man can love
195 a friend.

Then the six weeks were over, and with his band he took the old trail toward the higher mountains, the little burro leading the way because it knew it well. They reached the river, followed and forded it into the great national forest, traveling twenty miles in three days into the juniper range.

200 They were in the juniper forest a week, working their way up to the ponderosa and the sugar pine, and here the boy's loneliness left him. Often he saw deer browsing at dawn and dusk; a doe keeping herself carefully between him and her fawn. Once, in the early evening when the sheep had settled for the night, he came on a mother bear, scolding, slapping, and cuffing

205 her two cubs to hurry them out of his way. Even the birds were a delight, the mountain bluebirds and jays, and sapsuckers and the black and yellow orioles. Here he was no longer a boy far from home. He was a Basque herder at his best, responsible and resourceful, like a soldier at some lonely outpost.

210 The tender's truck could not follow them now. The *americano* who owned the sheep had established two cabins at seventy-five hundred feet from which several tenders took supplies to the various sheep bands by pack mule. And when Juan saw Ancelito riding through the trees leading a mule he laughed aloud, startled by the sound of his own voice.

The mule was a walking grocery, its pack bags heavy with flour sacks,
215 each fat with supplies.

Then for the first time Juan Varra was afraid. He was so afraid he wanted to bolt like *La Bruja*, the witch ewe. On the mule bringing up the rear was a girl.

Ancelito dismounted.... Had it gone well?... Yes.... Had he been lonely?...
220 No—perhaps a very little at first. And as he spoke not once did the boy glance at the girl.

It was only Susana, said Ancelito; and she was his daughter, come to the cabins for a few days, as he had promised her. She was quite harmless. As women go, she was no trouble. She would get the noon meal while they un-
225 packed the supplies.

And she did. While the boy and Ancelito unpacked the supplies and discussed the best sites for the bed grounds and the danger of bears, Juan could hear the girl moving at the fire.

When the meal was ready and they sat down for slabs of jack cheese,
230 ham and eggs, fresh bread and coffee, he was forced to look at her. Her feet were as big as a boy's. Her legs were encased in thick blue cotton pants like a boy's. Her top half was submerged in a shirt like a boy's. Her hair was drawn tight to the back of her head, and hung in a thick brush, suitable only for a horse's tail. Furthermore, she did not look up at him from under her lashes and

235 touch him with the briefest of cool, sweet glances to tell him she saw every single thing about him and found it good. She looked straight at him, and boldly, as one boy takes the measure of another.

He did not direct to her one word. When the meal was over and Ancelito and his daughter were mounted and leaving, he cast an "*adios*" into the air,
240 which she could take to include her if she wished.

"Is he alive?" Susana asked her father, when the mules had started. "Is he stupid?"

"No. He is silent. He is Basque. I am Basque."

"When you came to this country, you were not like that."
245 "I was exactly like that. He is afraid of you. But do not worry. I have told him you are harmless."

"Father, you didn't."

"But certainly. It would do you no good to make eyes at this one. He has a dream. He will save his money. He will go back to his village a *millonario*
250 and will marry the most beautiful girl in all Navarra. Now, if you were as wise as your mother—"

"Papacito," said Susana slowly, "are the girls so pretty in Navarra?" And Ancelito smiled at her and said, "Beyond description." The voices carried back to the boy in the high clear air, and though they were in English, he did
255 not miss the scorn in the girl's voice. That night among the supplies he found that Ancelito had left him a beginner's Spanish-English reader.

Love may need no words, but resentment can use several. The next day Juan Varra opened the first crack in the dark tomb in which he was determined to bury himself for six years. He began to learn to read English.
260 Two days later, when the grocery mule came through the trees, the boy put on his most proud and silent Basque face, lest the girl think he was glad to see her. But it was not Ancelito and Susana who followed the mule. It was the dull camp tender who had lost his dreams.

Juan did not admit his disappointment. He had no time to think of girls.
265 The bears were troublesome. One old killer bear followed the sheep band, killing a ewe each night, and the boy tracked him and shot him. In all, he killed four bears.

In July the rams were brought in, and in August all the sheep band were driven to a mountain valley where the ewes were culled, the lambs separat-
270 ed into the fats and the feeders. On the way back to the high range with his re-assembled band, Juan passed his first campers, and they were friendly. A little boy chased the lambs and couldn't catch them. The father gave him cigarettes, and the wife smiled at him and made him a present of a kitten.

After that, the cat followed along with the sheep, and though Juan told
275 himself he kept her only to keep the chipmunks from his food, he carried her under his jacket in the thunderstorms, and let her sleep at the foot of his bedroll.

Then, in October, the long drive was done. The sheep were carried by two- and three-decker trucks from the mountains to the low delta to browse
280 on the corn stubble; the burro was left behind, the cook wagon carried supplies. Just before Christmas the bands were driven to the home ranch to wait for the lambing, and it was here, in a neat white house, that Ancelito, the foreman, lived with Susana. The boy did not ask for her.

"Am I rich yet?" he asked Ancelito anxiously.

285 "In this country you are poor as a thin mouse," said Ancelito. "But at home already you can buy the finest house in the village."

It was Ancelito who helped him send money to his *abuelita* for the store teeth and presents for the family. It was Ancelito who brought from town the clothes he needed. After that, he spent nothing, and each month the *ameri-*
290 *cano* who owned the sheep deposited his wages in a savings account in his name. When, at Christmas, the other herders left the trailer houses and drove to town for a fine binge, he did not go. And when he was working with the sheep near the white house and saw something soft and obviously feminine fluttering on the clothesline in the rear, he looked the other way, so tight was
295 the dream still within him.

Right after Christmas the drop band was collected in a big open field and lambing began. Four hundred lambs were born each night, the boy working out in the cold, helping the young ewes that were having touble with their first-born, turning the lambs. One morning the *americano* was helping put each
300 ewe and her new lamb into a portable *chiquero*, or pen, so she would claim her lamb, and he watched the boy work.

"He is wonderful," he said. "He will save twenty-five percent more lambs.... Andy, we must keep this one."

"I have thought of it," said Ancelito.
305 The last night of the lambing, through no fault of his own, the boy lost two little lambs, and this, to a Basque herder, is not cause for sadness, but for heartbreak. Ancelito took him to the white house for food and comfort, and there in the warm kitchen waited Susana.

Gone were the boy's shoes, the pants, and the horse's tail. She was as
310 shy as a forest creature and as sweet as any young girl in Navarra on her saint's day. She was the daughter of a Basque and she, too, could be silent. She placed the coffee pot before them without a word, and plates of ham and eggs. Then she left them, turning at the door.

"I am so sorry, Juan," and for an instant her glance touched his cheek
315 and was gone.

He did not see her again, because this was the busy time. Lamb tails to be docked. New sheep bands to be formed. The ewes to be sheared and branded, and the winter was gone, and May here again, and the sheep drive to the campsite to go by train to Nevada. And the first year was over, and the
320 cycle began again.

Now repetition had replaced newness, making the second year even lonelier than the first. In the buckbrush, loneliness became an entity, pressing constantly upon him. The boy talked aloud sometimes to the cat and the burro. The dog, of course, was his abiding friend.
325 Rarely the camp tender brought him letters from home. Those from his *abuelita* and his little brother were the same. They loved him; they missed him. But the letter from his eldest brother, who was head of the family, held a new tone. How fortunate Juan was to be in that land where everyone was rich and all was easy. How hard it was to be the one who was left behind. Oh, he must
330 not stay away too long. If he worked harder and was given a raise—if he saved all beyond the barest necessities, perhaps five years would be enough or even four.

In the juniper forest one June day he heard a strange little whimpering, crying sound, and came on a lone fawn. He longed to make a pet of it, to keep

305 it with him, as the herders did sometimes. But he could not bear to take it from its mother, to teach it to be unafraid of man, to notch its ear so that when some hunter shot it he would know that once it had had too good a friend in man. It reminded him of the girl.

310 Then again he had driven the sheep band into the ponderosa and sugar pines of the high ranges, and he was home in the mountains.

When the grocery mule came through the trees, Ancelito was with it, but not Susana. This time the boy asked for her.

"And how is your daughter?" he asked formally, and Ancelito said she was well. She was going to school this summer. She was educating her head.

315 "It is that she does not wish a husband?" the boy asked slowly, and Ancelito said that, like all girls, she hoped to find one. But in this country it was the custom for many girls to help their husband get started. Suppose Susana should marry a man who wished to own a sheep band of his own. What a fine thing if she could help him. Did Juan know that the sheepman chosen as the 320 year's best in all California was the son of a Basque whose father had come first as a herder? No doubt his wife had helped him, as his mother had helped his father. It was one of the strange American ways.

Section 3
Several times this year the forest ranger came by at nooning-up and shared 325 his meal. And once a party of mountaineers coming out from a climb passed by and hailed him. He had picked up enough English to say a few words now, but he was alone so much that the sound of a voice always startled him and filled him with uneasiness, because it broke the quiet monotony in which he lived.

330 Then at last it was fall and he and the sheep were back on the delta, working their way toward the home ranch.

"How rich am I now?" he asked Ancelito, who took out his pencil for a bit of figuring and replied gravely, "In this country you have a modest savings, but in Navarra you are a man of some means. All your relatives are trying to 335 borrow money."

When the sheep band neared the home ranch, the boy watched eagerly for Susana to come home for the holidays from the school she attended, forty miles distant. And one afternoon just before Christmas, while he was working in the big field where the drop band was to be collected for the lambing, he 340 saw her arrive, and the sight filled him with horror.

There was a loud and sudden roar, and into the ranch road from the highway bounced a small, open, ancient and rattletrap car, Susana at the wheel, her legs in jeans, her hair streaming behind her in a horse-tail.

"She goes back and forth to school this way," said Ancelito calmly.

345 "Scares the sheep. It is amazing what an *americano* will do to educate her head and get ready to help her husband."

It was cold during this year's lambing, and again Juan worked each night in the big open field with the ewes, and late one night twin lambs lost their mother, arriving in this world so weak that in the morning he and Ancelito car-350 ried them to the house and bedded them in the warmth of the kitchen stove.

When the boy had finished working with the lambs and stood up, ready to return to the field, he saw that Susana was watching him quietly, sweet and feminine as she had been when she had prepared breakfast the year before.

"You had a good year, Juan?" she asked in Spanish.

355
"Sí."

"You were lonely?"

"A Basque is never lonely."

"See, *papacito*, he is afraid of me."

"I am afraid of no one."

360
"He is afraid of me. He is like the others. He learns nothing. He gives nothing. All he sees in this country is money. All he wants is to grab. He is stupid, *papacito*. He is more stupid than the sheep."

The boy followed Ancelito back to the field.

"She likes you," said Ancelito complacently. "if she did not like you, she

365
would not be so *furiosa*."

One day from the fields Juan saw the little rattletrap car take off down the road, and he knew Susana had gone back to school. He put her resolutely from his mind, and the months slipped by until the sheep bands were driven to the campsite and the second year was done.

370
The third year was as like the second as the second had been like the first. The loneliness and the constant movement of the sheep. The noonings-up and the bedding-down, and the watchful eye that never forgot to count the bellwethers and the black sheep. The coyotes yapping in the night, and the bears coming in the night, and the cat, the dog, and the burro. Only the details

375
differed, and the girl's scornful words, and the thought of the girl was constantly in his mind.

In October, two days before the sheep bands were to leave the mountains, an early blizzard caught them; the snow falling so fast and heavily that they could not be driven out in time. The boy built a fire of green wood, so

380
much smoke would rise to guide the camp tender, and Ancelito saw it and came with horses and men to trample and pack the snow so the sheep could move.

"Am I rich now?" Juan asked, sitting beside Ancelito in the truck on their way down to the delta.

385
"You are not quite a *millonario*," said Ancelito. "You have a little more than five thousand dollars. In your village it would be a very large sum," and he spoke sadly.

"My work has not been good?" asked the boy. "The *americano* is not satisfied?"

390
"He is much pleased. This morning when the sheep were safe from the blizzard, I called Susana to tell him. She says there are many letters for you. When a Basque family takes thus to the pen, the news must be bad."

They rode in silence, not to the corn stubble this time, but to the white house, and when they went into the kitchen, Susana handed his letters to the

395
boy, her eyes big and worried.

They left him to read them alone, and when they returned to the kitchen, he was sitting quietly, the letters spread on the table before him, his face stricken. He did not look up.

"My *abuelita* is dead," he said, and when Ancelito tried to comfort him,

400
he made no response, and when Susana set hot coffee before him, he did not thank her. He was silent as only a Basque can be silent.

"Shall I tell you what is wrong?" asked Ancelito. "Shall I tell you how I know?"

The boy did not answer.

405 "When I came to this country," said Ancelito, "I spent ten years alone with the sheep. I had a dream also. I thought only of my people and the day I would return to them. When I did so, I could not stand it. I had forgotten such poverty. Things were bad in my village. Everyone was poor and I was rich, and between us was a wall of jealousy I could not tear down or climb over."

410 The boy did not look up.

"Have you not seen the wall in these letters? Is not your elder brother already resentful? Does he not complain bitterly of your good fortune?" The boy was silent.

"I bought my parents the finest house in the village! I paid sixty Ameri-415 can dollars for it. I gave them money to care for them, and I came back here where I shall never be rich. It is a friendly country. This is what matters."

"*Papacito*, it is useless!" cried Susana. "He is so stupid! Can you believe it? He does not know we love him of truth. He does not know you feel to him as a man to his own son. Let him save and go back. Let him be rich and miser-420 able. Let him marry the most beautiful girl in all of Navarra. What do I care?" And she sat down at the table and began to cry as only a Basque girl can cry—loud and furiously.

Then the boy looked up. "Is it possible to bring my little brother to this country?" he asked slowly.

425 "It would take time, but it is possible. He could live with us. He could go to school. Susana could teach him to speak English."

"Is it possible Susana could teach me also? Could she teach me to tell her in English that in the mountains when I am alone with the sheep I do not think of any girl in Navarra? I think of her."

430 "This she would do gladly."

"Then if I have lost my dream, I can replace it with another. And if I do not return, it is nothing. I am a Basque," said the boy proudly, "and a Basque cannot lose his homeland, because he takes it with him always."

After You Read

1   **Recalling Information.** Choose the phrase that best answers each question about the story.

1.   What was the attitude of the other passengers on the plane toward Juan Varra?
    a.   They were afraid of him because he seemed so proud and silent.
    b.   They were friendly and interested in him and wanted to draw him out.
    c.   They disliked him and looked down on him for being poor and ignorant.

2.   Why did so many Basque boys leave their homeland?
    a.   They longed for travel and adventure.
    b.   They wanted to keep the land they loved.
    c.   They needed money for drinks, smokes, and girls.

3.   According to tradition, what were Basques especially known for?
    a.   Their excellence in speaking
    b.   Their courage and actions
    c.   Their physical strength

4.   The two people Juan missed and thought about the most were his *abuelita* and _____ .
    a.   the village priest
    b.   El Cid
    c.   his little brother

5.   Who was Ancelito?
    a.   A Basque who had left home long ago
    b.   A rich *americano* who owned sheep
    c.   A camp tender who brought supplies

6.   Why did Juan have to start work right away?
    a.   Two of the herders had died recently.
    b.   It was the custom to start boys immediately.
    c.   The law did not permit rest periods.

7.   At first, what did Juan think of the sheep that were given to him?
    a.   They were the most beautiful he had ever seen.
    b.   They were just like the sheep back in Spain.
    c.   They were ugly and different from those he knew.

Section 1 Focus on Development

What is the boy, Juan Varra, like? What is important to him? What is his dream? What fears does he have?

8. Who was Juan's best friend during his time in the mountains?
    a. La Bruja
    b. the dog
    c. his burro

9. When was Juan really afraid for the first time?
    a. When he lost some sheep
    b. When he tracked the killer bear
    c. When he saw the girl

10. Why did Juan begin to learn English?
    a. He had fallen in love with Susana.
    b. He felt resentful toward Susana.
    c. He wanted to talk with Susana's father.

11. What was the important gift that Juan received from one of the campers?
    a. a dictionary
    b. a gun
    c. a cat

12. What was the new tone that Juan noticed in the letters from his oldest brother?
    a. admiration
    b. envy
    c. friendship

13. According to Ancelito, why had Susana gone away to school?
    a. To learn a profession and become famous
    b. To educate herself to help her future husband
    c. To see more of the world and learn about customs

Section 2 Focus on Development

How has Juan changed? What differences are there in the letters from his family? What differences are there in his attitude toward his new environment?

14. What made Ancelito think that Susana liked Juan?
    a. She got very angry with him.
    b. She asked about him often.
    c. She dropped her eyes when she said his name.

15. What was the bad news that Juan received by letter?
    a. His relatives wanted to borrow money.
    b. Susana was going to get married.
    c. His grandmother had died.

16. At the end, what did Juan discover about his dream?
    a. It was silly and worthless.
    b. He could put another in its place.
    c. He would never lose it.

Section 3 Focus on Development

What changes occur in Juan's feelings toward his past, his present, and his future? Why do these changes occur?

3   **Expressing an Opinion.** Write down your opinion of the story's ending, answering the following question: Did Juan Varra make the right decision or not? Why? After you have finished, in small groups read your answers aloud and comment on them. Then share your group's comments with the rest of the class.

Talk It Over

In small groups, discuss the following questions.

1. What big problem does the main character, Juan Varra, have at first when he arrives in California? How does he overcome it? How long does it take him?

2. How does Juan change during the story? What people and experiences cause this change?

3. In your opinion, which of the characters in the story are realistic? Explain.

4. Have you ever known anyone who left his or her native country to work or study for a long period of time? Did that person return or not? Why? Do you think it would be possible for most people to live happily in a foreign country for the rest of their lives? Why or why not?

What Do You Think?

Reading

Although products of the technological age—TV, videos, CD-ROMs, Internet, computer games—have taken many people away from reading books, the book industry is still thriving. What kinds of books do you prefer?

- ■ Which types do you think are most popular nowadays?
- ■ Have you seen or used e-books?
- ■ Would you like all your textbooks to be in that format? Why or why not?
- ■ What other forms will books take in the future?

Video Activities: An Endangered Species

Before You Watch.   Answer the following questions in small groups.

1. What is a kangaroo and where are they found?
2. How do kangaroos move?
    a. They run.   b. They fly.   c. They swim.   d. They jump.
3. Have you ever seen a kangaroo in a tree?

Watch.   Answer these questions in small groups.

1. What kind of animal is this video about?
2. How is this animal different from a normal kangaroo?
3. What helps this animal climb trees?
    a. large teeth   b. muscular tail
    c. strong legs   d. curved claws
4. Where is this animal found?
5. Scientists believe that there are _____ tree kangaroos left.
    a. many   b. no   c. few
6. What are the two threats to this animal's survival?
    a. other kangaroos   b. loss of habitat
    c. hunting by people   d. disease

Watch Again.

1. What adjectives describe tree kangaroos?
    a. dangerous   b. shy   c. friendly
    d. happy   e. reclusive
2. Dr. Betts studies how these animals _____, _____, and _____.
    a. eat   b. reproduce   c. live   d. behave
3. People hunt tree kangaroos for their _____.
    a. meat   b. skins   c. claws   d. tails
4. How many new species of tree kangaroos have been found in the past
    decade? _____

After You Watch.   Find an article about an endangered species. Scan to answer
these questions.

1. Where does the animal live?
2. How many are left in the wild?
3. Why are they endangered?
4. What is being done to save them?

Literary Credits

Page 2 From *Living in the USA* by Alison R. Lanier, revised by Charles William Gay, 5th Ed., reprinted with permission of Intercultural Press, Inc., Yarmouth, ME. Copyright © 1986; **Page 11** "My Country" by Pierre Berton. Reproduced by permission; **Page 21** "How to Read Faster" by Bill Cosby. Reprinted with permission of International Paper; **Page 26** Reprinted with permission from "Twain, Mark" in *Encyclopaedia Britannica, 14th edition*, © 1972 by Encyclopaedia Britannica, Inc.; **Page 31** "How to Take Tests: Scoring What You're Worth" from *You Can Succeed* by Eric Jensen. Copyright © 1979 by Barrons Educational Series, Inc. Reprinted by permission; **Page 40** "Who's Taking Care of the Children?" by Miki Knezevic. Reprinted by permission; **Page 44** From *Time Almanac 2000* © 1999 by Family Education Company. All rights reserved worldwide. Reprinted by permission; **Page 45** From "70 Brides for 7 Foreigners" by S. Kuzina from *World Press Review*, July 1993, p. 47. Reprinted by permission; **Page 55** "Eat Like A Peasant, *Feel* Like a King" by Andrew Revkin. Reprinted with permission from the March 1986 *American Health*. Copyright © 1986 by RD Publications, Inc.; **Page 62** From "Going Global in Battle Against Smoking" by Sue Ellen Christian, *Chicago Tribune*, August 11, 2000. Reprinted with permission of Knight-Ridder/Tribune Information Services; **Page 66** Excerpt from *Rethinking Tourism and Ecotravel* by Deborah McLaren (West Hartford, Conn.: Kumarian Press, Inc., 1998) 82-84. Reprinted by permission; **Page 71** From *Time Almanac 2000* © 1999 by Family Education Company. All rights reserved worldwide. Reprinted by permission; **Page 76** From "Wired World Leaves Millions Out of the Loop" by Brian Knowlton as appeared in *International Herald Tribune*, October 8, 1999. Reprinted by permission. **Page 82** Excerpts from "Tracks to the Future" by Peter Boisseau from *enRoute Magazine*, August 2000. Reprinted by permission of Peter Boisseau, an award-winning freelance writer in Toronto; **Page 91** "Executive Takes Chance on Pizza, Transforms Spain," by Stephen Wade, as appeared in *Wisconsin State Journal*, May 29, 1994. Reprinted by permission of Associated Press; **Page 99** "The Luncheon" by W. Somerset Maugham from *Cosmopolitans* by W. Somerset Maugham. Reprinted by permission of The Royal Literary Fund and A.P. Watt Ltd.; **Page 109** "Confucius" from *The 100: A Ranking of the Most Influential Persons In History* by Michael E. Hart. All rights reserved. Reprinted by permission of Citadel Press/Kensington Publishing Corp. Copyright © 1978, 1992 by Michael H. Hart. Reprinted by permission of Simon & Schuster UK; **Page 120** From "Courage Begins With One Voice" by Kerry Kennedy Cuomo, *Parade Magazine*, September 24, 2000. Reprinted with permission from Parade, copyright © 2000. From *Speak Truth To Power* by Kerry Kennedy Cuomo, 2000, Crown Publishing, New York; **Page 131** "Guggenheim Museum U.S.A." from *Individual Creations* by Flavio Conti, Rizzoli Editore, SpA. Reprinted with permission; **Page 139** Excerpt from "If You Invent the Story, You're The First To See How It Ends" by Roxana Robinson, *New York Times*, July 17, 2000. Reprinted by permission of the author; **Page 143** From "We Can't Just Sit Back and Hope" by Dotson Rader. Copyright © March 27, 1994 by Dotson Rader. Originally published in *Parade Magazine*. Reprinted with permission of author; **Page 146** From "Are Men More Creative Than Women?" by Margaret Mead from *Margaret Mead: Some Personal Views*. Copyright © 1979 by Mary Catherine Bateson and Rhoda Metraux. Reprinted by permission of Walker and Company, 435 Hudson Street, New York NY 10014, 1-800-289-2553. All Rights Reserved; **Page 150** John Friedl and Michael B. Whiteford, *The Human Portrait:*

Photo Credits